SAFETY AND DISASTER MANAGEMENT EDUCATION IN SCHOOLS

SAFETY AND DISASTER MANAGEMENT EDUCATION IN SCHOOLS

Arul Jothi

M.Sc., M.Ed.

Principal, Arcot Sri Mahalakshmi Women's Teacher Training Institute, Villapakkam, Vellore Dist.-632521 T.N.

Dr. D.L. Balaji

B.Com., M.A., M.Phil., D.Lit.

Correspondent, Arcot Sri Mahalakshmi Educational Institutions, Villapakkam, Vellore Dist.-632521 T.N.

Dr. Jagdish Prasad Sharma

Reader, Teachers Training College, Patna

CENTRUM PRESS

NEW DELHI-110002 (INDIA)

CENTRUM PRESS
H.O.: 4360/4, Ansari Road, Daryaganj,
New Delhi-110 002 (India)
Ph.: 23278000, 23261597
B.O.: No. 1015, Ist Main Road, BSK IIIrd Stage
IIIrd Phase, IIIrd Block,
Bangalore - 560 085 (India)
Tel.: 080-41723429
Visit us at: www.centrumpress.com

Safety and Disaster Management Education in Schools

First Edition, 2009

PRINTED IN INDIA

Printed at Balaji Offset, Delhi

Contents

Preface

Natural disasters have been visiting every part of the globe at one time or the other. The world is becoming increasingly vulnerable to natural disasters. From earthquakes to floods and famines, mankind is even more threatened by the forces of nature. Disasters can strike at any time, at any place. Nearly three million people worldwide may have been killed in past 20 years due to natural disasters such as landslides, earthquakes, floods, snow avalanches, cyclones etc.

India, a country with diverse hypsographic and climatological conditions, 70 per cent of the cultivable land is prone to drought, 60 per cent of the land area is prone to Earthquake, 12 per cent to Floods, 8 per cent to Cyclones, 85 per cent of the land area is vulnerable to number of natural hazards and 22 States are categorized as multi hazards States. Tens of thousands of people are affected by these natural disasters. We have seen in the recent past that country suffered impact of earthquake even where the seismicity was low as per the seismic zoning map, as in the case of Maharashtra and droughts have occurred in the areas with highest rainfall i.e. Cherrapunji in the North East. In spite of the best efforts by the Governments, external assistance and available technologies and media, the 1999 Super Cyclone of Orissa and 2001 Earthquake of Gujarat have inflicted untold misery. The socio-economic backwardness of the majority of our population, coupled with lack of skills or for mitigating preparing for and responding to disasters increases their vulnerability, negatively affecting their ability to respond and recover from periodic and intense disasters. The lesson learnt clearly bring out the fact that no State, no Government can meet the challenges alone. The Governments' effort have to be strengthened by communities themselves getting involved in the emergency response system and being aware of the do's and don'ts to be prepared for any eventuality.

In ancient India, disaster management finds mention in Kautily's Arthashastra as a primary duty of the State. Disaster Management as a post disaster activity has been well established in India especially since independence. The novelty of the new approach lies in taking well-planned and timely proactive measures to prevent disasters, to prepare people to cope with disasters and to motivate them to safeguard their own lives, livelihoods and habitat. Prevention is better than cure, is an old saying which is very apt in the context of disaster management. Every year colossal amount of resources are used by our Government as well as Aid agencies in relief and rehabilitation measures. It is now becoming increasingly evident and mitigation and investment in disaster preparedness can save thousand of lives, vital economic assets, livelihoods and reduce the cost of overall disaster relief.

Government of India, Ministry of Human Resource Development in its Tenth Five Year Plan emphasized the need for integrating disaster management in the existing education system in India. In addition, the government of India launched a set of nation-wide *disaster risk mitigation* initiatives that addresses larger aspects of development in order to safeguard the developmental gains.

The book deals with the concept and theoretical framework essential for prevention, relief, mitigation, preparedness and rehabilitation. These have been supplemented with framework to avoid or lessen the impact of man-made or natural disasters. The impact of disasters can be lessened through advance planning, developing warning system as well as prompt implementation.

— *Dr. Jagdish Prasad Sharma*

UNIT-I

Disaster Types

Introduction

This chapter provides an overview of disaster management definitions and principles useful to military and civil defence planners in conducting humanitarian and disaster relief operations.

The Role of Military and Civil Defence Assets (MCDA) in Disaster Relief and Humanitarian Assistance

MCDA—A National Treasure: Within the resources of most nations, MCDA represents unique technological and logistical capabilities that can be mobilized on short notice in a self-contained, self sufficient and highly mobile fashion, to support lifesaving relief efforts on behalf of Affected States. Nearly all nations have at one time or another used their military assets and capabilities for national disaster relief. A number of nations have also done so in international relief operations lead by the UN, regional organizations, or bilaterally. UN Member States have recognized that natural or manmade disasters can pose as lethal a threat as that of war, to the stability of any society.

Unfortunately, there are no diplomatic initiatives great enough to thwart earthquakes or negotiate an accidental nuclear power plant radiation release. Disasters do not recognize national borders and require international cooperation to prepare for and respond to their associated challenges and horrors.

All Nations are Vulnerable: Any nation can fall victim to catastrophic disaster and may be in need of international assistance and the resources found within the international MCDA community. The organized methodology by which MCDA can be deployed is its greatest asset in attending to the challenges and uncertainties associated with disaster response.

Self-reliance: Access to MCDA resources can protect and/or restore critical lifelines and services lost during sudden onset disasters. Governments who earmark national MCDA solely for defence, yet are willing to receive international humanitarian and disaster relief assistance, violate the principle of self reliance. International disaster relief assistance should be offered to nations whose resources-whether private or public-have been mobilized to respond to an emergency. International MCDA, along with other international relief providers, can leverage the Affected State's internal response capabilities by offering specifically targeted resources and services. The Affected State will most likely reciprocate by providing disaster relief support back to the international community once it has recovered sufficiently. It behooves all nations to prepare themselves to respond to disasters using their own resources first, before requesting IDRA. This is the essence of self reliance.

UN-DHA Objective: The objective of the UN DHA Project 213/3 on "The Use of Military and Civil Defence Assets in Disaster Relief," is to create an environment where MCDA resources can be effectively, efficiently and responsibly coordinated to relieve the shortfalls of an Affected State in crisis following a sudden onset disaster. This manual describes how this can be done.

Foundation Definitions and Principles

Disaster: A disaster is a serious disruption of the functioning of a society, causing widespread human, material, or environmental losses which exceed the ability of the affected society (or community) to cope using only its own resources. Disasters are often classified according to their speed of onset (slow or sudden), or according to their cause (natural, man-made or complex).

Disasters may take many forms, and occur as a result of one or more wide range of events, both natural and man induced. The duration of these events may range from a few seconds to many years. The severity of the effects of a disaster may vary according to the degree to which man has created an environment susceptible to damage, that is, an environment in which life and property are at risk.

Hazards: A hazard is a rare or extreme event in the natural or human-made environments that adversely affects human life, property or activity to the extent of causing a disaster.

The list of hazard types are very long. Many occur infrequently or impact a very small population. Other hazards, such as severe snowstorms, often occur in areas that are accustomed to dealing with them and seldom become disasters. However, from the perspective of a disaster victim it is not particularly useful to distinguish between minor and major disasters. Where natural hazards become disasters, they become potential focal points for International Disaster Relief Assistance (IDRA). A detailed listing of hazards can be found in Annex A. Examples include:

- Sudden onset hazards—(geological and climatic hazards) earthquakes, tsunamis, floods, tropical storms, volcanic eruptions, landslides.
- Slow onset hazards —(environmental hazards) drought, famine, environmental degradation, desertification, deforestation, pest infestation.
- Industrial/technological—system failures/accidents, spillages, explosions, fires.
- Wars and civil strife—armed aggression, insurgency, terrorism, and other actions leading to displaced persons and refugees.
- Epidemics—water and/or food-born diseases, person-to-person diseases (contact and respiratory spread), vector-born diseases and complications from wounds.

Natural Phenomena: Natural phenomena are extreme climatological, hydrological, or geological processes that do not pose any threat to persons or property. A massive earthquake in an unpopulated area, for example, is a natural phenomena, not a hazard. So is the annual flood along the Nile, an essential element to the well being of its neighboring inhabitants.

Emergency: Another term closely related to disaster is emergency. An emergency might be regarded as a particular type (or sub-set) of a disaster. "Emergency" suggests an intense time period and level of urgency. An emergency is bound by a specific period in which lives and essential property are immediately at risk. A disaster can encompass a more general period in which there is a clear and marked deterioration in the coping abilities of a group or community. Unusual initiatives by groups, communities and external intervention are also evident during this period.

Disasters and Emergencies are Fundamental Reflections of Normal Life: They are consequences of the way societies structure themselves, economically and socially; the way societies and states interact; and the way relationships between decision-makers are sustained. It is essential to make a distinction between hazards and disasters (to include emergencies), and to recognize that the effect of the former upon the latter is essentially a measure of society's vulnerability.

Vulnerability: The term vulnerability stems from the fact that certain communities or groups have settled in areas susceptible to losses resulting from the impact of a particular phenomenon, hazards or disasters.

The following diagram illustrates this combination of opposing forces. Vulnerability is seen as the progression of three stages:

1. *Underlying Causes:* a deep-rooted set of factors within a society that together form and maintain vulnerability.
2. *Dynamic Pressures:* a translating process that channels the effects of a negative cause into unsafe conditions; this process may be due to a lack of basic services or provisions or may result from a series of macro-forces.
3. *Unsafe Conditions:* the vulnerable context where people and property are exposed to the risk of disaster; the

fragile physical environment is one element; other factors include an unstable economy and low income levels.

Population Displacements: This term is associated with crisis-induced mass migration in which large numbers of people are forced to leave their homes to seek alternative means of survival. Such mass movements normally result from the effects of conflict, severe food shortages or collapse of economic support systems.

Human-made Emergencies: Disasters or emergency situations where the principal, direct cause(s) are identifiable human actions, deliberate or otherwise. Apart from "technological" and "ecological" disasters, this mainly involves situations in which civilian populations suffer causalities, losses of property, basic services and means of livelihood as a result of war or civil strife. Human-made disasters/emergencies can be of the rapid or slow onset types, and in the case of internal conflict, can lead to "complex emergencies" as well.

Complex Emergencies: These emergencies are a form of human-made emergencies in which the cause of the emergency as well as the assistance to the afflicted are bound by intense levels of political considerations. This sort of emergency is normally associated with problems of displaced people during times of civil conflict or populations trapped within their own communities, isolated from a government or private support structures as well as access to international relief. People fleeing with the intent of not returning to their native countries are considered refugees and may be affected by complex emergencies.

Seven Causal Factors of Disasters

Common causal factors play a large role in determining the severity and magnitude of a disaster. The following causal factors are general in nature, and not ranked. They may be more or less applicable to any given society and contributes to determining the vulnerability of a society to disasters.

Poverty: The single most important factor that increases the vulnerability of a people to disaster is poverty. An impoverished people who lack education, usually lack the economic and political clout to cope with the hazards of their surroundings.

Ungoverned Population Growth: Ungoverned population growth can lead to settlements in hazardous areas susceptibility to disease, competition for scare resources, and civil strife. Disaster losses are significantly reduced when the people of any given society are organized with effective laws and controls to protect the population from potentially hazardous areas, access to public utilities, medical care, education, and economic resources. Vulnerability to disaster increases when a nation's capacity to govern does not consider the impact and trends in population growth in potentially hazardous areas. Even in the most benign climates rapid urbanization can create slowly evolving timebombs which could lead to disaster vulnerability.

Rapid Urbanization and Migration: Rapid population growth and migration are related to the major phenomenon of rapid urbanization. It is characterized by the rural poor or civilians in an area of conflict moving to metropolitan areas in search of economic opportunities and security. These massive numbers of urban poor increasingly find fewer options for availability of safe and desirable places to build their houses. Here again, competition for scarce resources, an inevitable consequence of rapid urbanization, can lead to man-made disasters. Many landslides or flooding disasters are closely linked to rapid and unchecked urbanization forcing low-income families to settle on the slopes of steep hillsides or ravines, or along the banks of flood-prone rivers. Many earthquake victims in urban areas have been impoverished families where the physical location vice the structure of their houses were hazardous, as evidenced by landslides onto the house or out from under it.

Transitions in Cultural Practices: Many of the inevitable changes that occur in all societies lead to an increase in societies' vulnerability to disasters. Obviously, all societies are in a continual state of transition and change. These transitions are often extremely disruptive and uneven, leaving gaps in social coping mechanisms and technology. These transitions include nomadic populations that become sedentary, rural people who move to urban areas, and both rural and urban people who move from one economic level to another. More broadly, these examples are typical of a shift from non-industrialized to industrializing societies.

One example of the impact of these transitions is the introduction of new construction materials and building designs in a society that is accustomed to traditional designs and materials. This often results in new materials being used incorrectly. In disaster prone areas, inadequate use of new construction techniques contribute to houses unable to withstand earthquakes or wind storms.

Compounding the problem is the formation of post disaster communities of survivors who find themselves without social support systems or networks to assist in relief and recovery. Traditional coping mechanisms may not exist in new settlements and the population becomes increasingly dependent on outside intervention for assistance.

Conflicting cultural practices can also lead to civil conflict, and strife. Examples include events leading to violence triggered by religious intolerance.

Environmental Degradation: Many disasters are either caused or exacerbated by environmental degradation. Deforestation leads to rapid rain runoff, which contributes to flooding. The destruction of mangrove swamps decreases the coastlines ability to resist tropical winds and storm surges. The creation of drought conditions-and the relative severity and length of time the drought lasts-is mainly a natural phenomena. Man-made contributions to drought conditions include: poor cropping patterns, overgrazing, the stripping of topsoil, poor conservation techniques, depletion of both the surface and subsurface water supply, and, to an extent, unchecked urbanization.

Lack of Awareness and Information: Disasters can also occur when people who are vulnerable, have not been educated on how to get out of harm's way or take protective measures at the inset of a disaster event. This ignorance may not necessarily be a function of poverty, but a lack of awareness of what measures can be taken to build safe structures on safe building sites. People may be unaware of safe evacuation routes and procedures. Others may be unaware on where to turn for assistance in times of acute distress. Nevertheless, this point should not be taken as a justification for ignoring the coping mechanisms of the majority of people affected by disasters. In most disaster-prone societies, there is a wealth of understanding about disaster threats and responses. This understanding should be incorporated into external assistance initiatives and planning.

War and Civil Strife: War and civil strife are regarded as hazards or extreme events that produce disasters. War and civil strife often cause the displacement of the population. The causal factors of war and civil strife include competition for scarce resources, religious or ethnic intolerance, and ideological differences. Many of these are also byproducts of the preceding six causal factors of disasters.

Compound and Complex Disasters

Socio/political Forces: Throughout many parts of the world one type of hazard can trigger a domino effect of disasters. For example, a drought may lead to a famine, which in turn leads to civil conflict resulting in a mass displacement of the population. Another example includes flooding which may force people to seek refuge across international borders upsetting the balance of needs and resources and weakening the ability of the government to receive the added population growth. This in turn may lead to civil strife and disorder.

Such compound hazards and disasters need not occur sequentially; they can occur simultaneously. Thus, people may become caught between contending forces in a civil war and also suffer from a major drought with limited means to grow food or to receive outside assistance.

In a growing number of countries, complex disasters are also becoming more evident. Essentially a complex disaster is a form of human-made emergency in which the cause of the emergency as well as the assistance to victims are bound by intense levels of political considerations. The single most prevalent political condition of a complex emergency is civil conflict, resulting in a collapse of political authority. In such cases, at least one of three situations arise:

- The government's ability to assist their disaster-afflicted becomes severely constrained.
- The government becomes extremely suspicious of or uninterested in afflicted people who have fled from non-government to government held areas.
- The government or opposition groups actually create or compound a disaster through actions that generate refugees and the mass displacement of people.

In fact, many affected people live in areas outside of government control. These are often the people in the most need and yet, the most difficult to reach.

The disaster becomes "complex" because either the collapse or diffusion of political control makes assistance highly problematic. Solutions ultimately depend upon agreements with all parties involved in the conflict to permit assistance to be provided to recognized civilian noncombatants. These solutions may include agreements that are seen essentially as compromising fundamental aspects of sovereignty in exchange for humanitarian assistance. UN sponsored safe havens on corridors of tranquillity are examples.

Displaced Persons and Refugees

One of the most serious consequences of compound and complex emergencies is the creation of populations of displaced persons. The term "displaced person" applies in several contexts. These include people who are:

- forced to leave their homes as a result of drought, famine, or other disaster, usually in search of food, water and shelter.
- non-combatant individuals and families forced to leave their homes because of the direct or indirect consequences of conflict but who remain inside their country.
- forcibly resettled by their government if the resettlement is ethnically, tribal or racially motivated.

- expelled from a country, forced out for economic or political reasons especially as an ethnic or national group.

Consequences and Effects: The variety of possible situations generating displaced people makes generalizations difficult, but the following maybe experienced in varying degrees:

- loss of means of livelihood.
- communities becoming separated from services previously provided.
- loss of normal sources of food.
- lack of shelter and household necessities.
- lack of fuel for cooking.
- lack of potable water.
- communicable diseases and over-crowding.
- additional burdens for women, especially as heads of households.
- large numbers of unaccompanied children separated from family.
- loss of land and tenure.
- possible communication and logistics problems.
- insecurity due to tensions and military activities.

Not to be forgotten is the population that remains at home and, even though they are not "trapped in combat areas," they maybe in places that are hard to reach because of political, logistical and/or security reasons. This population group may end up suffering from many of the some problems as those who are displaced due to isolation from a national support structure or access to international humanitarian relief assistance.

Code of Behavior

The International Federation of Red Cross and Red Crescent Societies (IFRC) has recommended a code of behavior for military and civil defence personnel in international disaster relief assistance in times of peace. The code is important to military planners as they work with international and non-governmental organizations who base their mandates on what they consider the three basic principles behind all humanitarian actions. These principles are humanity, impartiality and neutrality. Conformity to this code of behavior in providing humanitarian relief should reduce potential friction that might occur between military and civil defence relief personnel and those in the international community that subscribe to these principles. The code has been included in Annex J.

Scope and Need

Considering how much damage can result from something as innocuous as a faulty sprinkler system, it may be understandable that many law firm disaster planners previously gave their first attention to common threats, and then never got around to considering large-scale disasters. Firm planners could pat themselves on the back if they maintained proper fire safeguards, kept the firm properly insured, arranged for regular backups of key data files, and the like. Some firms were convinced as a result of 9/11 that such a patchwork of miscellaneous point solutions was inadequate. For other firms, Hurricane Katrina should drive that point home. While we can't expect disaster plans to protect our firms from all possible risks, we should expand our planning perspective to include more catastrophic scenarios.

One approach would review each practice area within the firm separately and ask: How long can we afford to be "out of business"? Plans should then be created to address the need of each practice area in accord with its particular assessment of risks. Different practice areas will produce different scenarios. Following are a few suggestions to consider when enlarging the scope of disaster plans to accommodate widespread disruptions.

Comprehensive Disasters are Different

Planning for a widespread major disaster must go far beyond planning for more localized threats. Not only are the individual losses to be contemplated more severe, but the sheer magnitude of possible destruction makes reliance on "normal" backup solutions unwise.

Katrina's key demonstration of the latter concern was the wiping out of cell phone communication towers across a wide area. Cell phones were supposed to be the backup for landline phones. Many emergency plans failed because they assumed ongoing communication capabilities. In some extreme disaster scenarios, electronic communication may simply be impossible, so team instructions should explicitly cover the case of a total communications blackout.

The usual math for recovery facilities can similarly become inapplicable in a comprehensive disaster. Having some available backup office space in a community may be sufficient to cover the needs of a few firms concurrently. But if practically every firm in a whole area suddenly needs backup facilities, the latter will be overwhelmed, even if they themselves were not put out of commission. Again, Katrina provided a future textbook case: all the nursing homes in New Orleans counted on the same few bus companies to evacuate their patients, with tragic results. The same peak-load problem applies to local backup suppliers, staffing agencies, etc.

Mirror-location Strategies

Geographically dispersed firms clearly have an advantage when it comes to many sorts of backup measures. A firm with multiple offices can in principle have backup data from each office automatically streamed to other firm location(s) for ready backup, as a supplement to high-security commercial offline backups. Similarly, firm branches could be arranged into a "buddy system" whereby evacuees from one community would know in advance that they had a place to go for emergency housing assistance as well as business recovery. Consortia of small firms could, of course, pursue analogous arrangements, though historically they have not.

Accounting system and IT specialists are accustomed to think of off-site backups and even online mirror sites, but the CIO should extend this concept to all sorts of vital information. Certainly it should apply to word processing documents and electronically imaged case files, but the concept could be applied more pervasively to include CRM (client relations) and HR (firm personnel information). When lawyers sync their contact and calendar information from PDAs to their own office PC, it would similarly make sense for the updated file to be shipped off automatically (again securely) to their "buddy" location.

It must be added that security passwords known only to one or more individuals in a single office location are themselves a vulnerability. The firm's CIO should work out a secure multi-site strategy for ensuring that secured information does not become altogether irretrievable in a truly worst-case scenario.

Plan Accountability and Currency

The usual complaint with regard to disaster plans is that they get put in a binder and shelved. While inattention to important-but-not-urgent matters is commonplace, an aggravating factor in some firms may be that a threat-oriented plan is not properly aligned with people's main jobs. After all, how many primary job descriptions at a law firm deal with floods, earthquakes or terrorism? An approach more conducive to keeping disaster planning on the front burner is to align responsibilities along functional lines such as the following:

- The HR Director has responsibility for all aspects of protecting all the people who work for or at the firm (including on-site contractors, visitors, etc.).
- The CIO has responsibility for all aspects of protecting and recovering the firm's information assets and communication capabilities.
- The CFO has responsibility for protecting and recovering the firm's financial assets.
- The Facilities Manager has responsibility for protecting and recovering the firm's offices, office equipment, and other physical assets.
- The Managing Partner has responsibility for ensuring the recoverability of matters in progress, for protecting the interests of clients (including pro bono clients), and for contributing the firm's support to recovery of the overall legal system.
- Disaster planning specialist consultants (for physical safety, IT backup-recovery, etc.) work with all the above individuals but report directly to the Executive Director.

- The Executive Director has overall responsibility for disaster planning; s/he coordinates efforts to limit plan overlaps and oversights, and ensures that all components of the plan are coherent.

Integrating Disaster and Security Planning

Disasters are not limited to natural events: disgruntled employees, unhappy clients and deranged strangers have also wreaked havoc on law firms. So it's important that your disaster plan is complemented by good routine security operations. When employees depart, obtain all keys, computer disks and other proprietary or confidential documents that may have been taken home or offsite. Employee agreements should acknowledge that certain (carefully specified) information is confidential and proprietary, and always remains the property of the firm.

Make sure clients are happy with your services by seeking to develop loyalty amongst and with them. Create a comprehensive system of communication with them, so that you know who they are, what they need and want from their relationship with you and whether they believe you've addressed their wants. Effective communication is the cornerstone of loyalty, and loyalty begets assistance beyond the call of duty in time of need.

Conclusion

The sidebar suggests some topics to consider when expanding your disaster plan. Detailing a disaster plan and practicing its emergency procedures have always been challenging, however, and doing so for an expanded plan will be even more difficult — so it's time to get started.

Businesses of all types need to understand the importance of disaster recovery solutions. Even call centers are at risk for down time and if a system for recovery is not in place, it could be the end of the business. Unforeseen events happen, whether man made or natural and when they do, the entire business operation can be disrupted. For every minute a call center's computer and phone systems are down, they are not only losing a lot of money but also potential patients/customers.

Simply put, every call center should have a disaster recovery plan, which is a detailed plan on how the different disaster recovery solutions would be implemented in case of trouble. Disasters can be the result of sabotage, break-in, cyber attack, utility outages, earthquake, flood, tornado, hurricane, fire, and even terrorism. These are serious problems, which can bring an entire company down.

One of the reasons disaster recovery solutions are so vital has to do with the amount of money being lost when systems and components are down. To a call center, an answering service company or any company for that matter, a disaster could permanently cripple operations. For instance, studies show for companies that have experienced a major loss of documents and records maintained on a computer system hit with a disaster, only 43% of those companies ever reopened for business.

Interestingly, the companies that realized the value of disaster recovery solutions prior to the terrorism attack on the New York Trade Centers, those businesses were completely functional within less than one week. Any business needs to have a number of plans in place and knowing the plan needed associated with disaster recovery solutions is by far one of the most critical. Today, both inshore and offshore call centers are implementing plans that include more seating space to handle overload such as:

- *Site Level Disaster Recovery Solutions*-This means additional seating within a facility was increased by 50% should disaster strike
- *State Level Disaster Solutions*-More seats were reserved within the same city or state of the call center
- *National Level Solutions*-Again, additional seats were reserved in a different city or stat

Coming up with all the necessary disaster recovery solutions is complex, which is why companies hire professionals in the field to devise appropriate recovery plans. Not only do these plans focus on computer and phone systems, they also look at insurance coverage, businesses processes, backup and recovery for customer support, administration, documentation, information, essential equipment, and the premises. Protecting the call center is a primary focus and understanding different disaster recovery solutions so a plan can be developed is the key to success.

Natural

Natural disaster is the effect of a natural hazard (e.g. flood, volcanic eruption, earthquake, or landslide) that affects the environment. Human interaction, changes by the lack of heat or appropriate use of sun light such as photosynthesis. Photosynthesis, leads to financial, environmental or human losses. The resulting loss depends on the capacity of the population to support or resist the disaster, and their resilience. This understanding is concentrated in the formulation: "disasters occur when hazards meet vulnerability." A natural hazard will oooopoohence never result in a natural disaster in areas without vulnerability, e.g. strong earthquakes in uninhabited areas. The term *natural* has consequently been disputed because the events simply are not hazards or disasters without human involvement.

Natural Hazards

A natural hazard is a threat of an event that will have a negative effect on people or the environment. Many natural hazards are related, e.g. earthquakes can result in tsunamis, drought can lead directly to famine and disease. A concrete example of the division between hazard and disaster is that the 1906 San Francisco earthquake was a disaster, whereas earthquakes are a hazard. Hazards are consequently relating to a future occurrence and disasters to past or current occurrences ....

Earthquakes

An earthquake (also known as a tremor or temblor) is the result of a sudden release of energy in the Earth's crust that creates seismic waves. Earthquakes are recorded with a seismometer, also known as a seismograph. The moment magnitude of an earthquake is conventionally reported, or the related and mostly obsolete Richter magnitude, with magnitude 3 or lower earthquakes being mostly imperceptible and magnitude 7 causing serious damage over large areas. Intensity of shaking is measured on the modified Mercalli scale.

At the Earth's surface, earthquakes manifest themselves by shaking and sometimes displacing the ground. When a large earthquake epicenter is located offshore, the seabed sometimes suffers sufficient displacement to cause a tsunami. The shaking in earthquakes can also trigger landslides and occasionally volcanic activity.

In its most generic sense, the word *earthquake* is used to describe any seismic event—whether a natural phenomenon or an event caused by humans—that generates seismic waves. Earthquakes are caused mostly by rupture of geological faults, but also by volcanic activity, landslides, mine blasts, and nuclear experiments. An earthquake's point of initial rupture is called its focus or hypocenter. The term epicenter refers to the point at ground level directly above the hypocenter.

Tectonic earthquakes will occur anywhere within the earth where there is sufficient stored elastic strain energy to drive fracture propagation along a fault plane. In the case of transform or convergent type plate boundaries, which form the largest fault surfaces on earth, they will move past each other smoothly and aseismically only if there are no irregularities or asperities along the boundary that increase the frictional resistance. Most boundaries do have such asperities and this leads to a form of stick-slip behaviour. Once the boundary has locked, continued relative motion between the plates leads to increasing stress and therefore, stored strain energy in the volume around the fault surface. This continues until the stress has risen sufficiently to break through the asperity, suddenly allowing sliding over the locked portion of the fault, releasing the stored energy. This energy is released as a combination of radiated elastic strain seismic waves, frictional heating of the fault surface, and cracking of the rock, thus causing an earthquake. This process of gradual build-up of strain and stress punctuated by occasional sudden earthquake failure is referred to as the Elastic-rebound theory. It is estimated that only 10 percent or less of an earthquake's total energy is radiated as seismic energy. Most of the earthquake's energy is used to power the earthquake fracture growth or is converted into heat generated by friction. Therefore, earthquakes lower the Earth's available elastic potential energy and raise its temperature, though these changes are negligible compared to the conductive and convective flow of heat out from the Earth's deep interior. Earthquake fault types.

There are three main types of fault that may cause an earthquake: normal, reverse (thrust) and strike-slip. Normal and reverse faulting are examples of dip-slip, where the displacement along the fault is in the direction of dip and movement on them involves a vertical component. Normal faults occur mainly in areas where the crust is being extended such as a divergent boundary. Reverse faults occur in areas where the crust is being shortened such as at a convergent boundary. Strike-slip faults are steep structures where the two sides of the fault slip horizontally past each other ; transform boundaries are a particular type of strike-slip fault. Many earthquakes are caused by movement on faults that have components of both dip-slip and strike-slip; this is known as oblique slip.

Earthquakes Away from Plate Boundaries

Where plate boundaries occur within continental lithosphere, deformation is spread out a over a much larger area than the plate boundary itself. In the case of the San Andreas fault continental transform, many earthquakes occur away from the plate boundary and are related to strains developed within the broader zone of deformation caused by major irregularities in the fault trace (e.g. the "Big bend" region). The Northridge earthquake was associated with movement on a blind thrust within such a zone. Another example is the strongly oblique convergent plate boundary between the Arabian and Eurasian plates where it runs through the northwestern part of the Zagros mountains. The deformation associated with this plate boundary is partitioned into nearly pure thrust sense movements perpendicular to the boundary over a wide zone to the southwest and nearly pure strike-slip motion along the

Main Recent Fault close to the actual plate boundary itself. This is demonstrated by earthquake focal mechanisms.

All tectonic plates have internal stress fields caused by their interactions with neighbouring plates and sedimentary loading or unloading (e.g. deglaciation). These stresses may be sufficient to cause failure along existing fault planes, giving rise to intraplate earthquakes.

Shallow-focus and Deep-focus Earthquakes: The majority of tectonic earthquakes originate at the ring of fire in depths not exceeding tens of kilometers. Earthquakes occurring at a depth of less than 70 km are classified as 'shallow-focus' earthquakes, while those with a focal-depth between 70 and 300 km are commonly termed 'mid-focus' or 'intermediate-depth' earthquakes. In subduction zones, where older and colder oceanic crust descends beneath another tectonic plate, deep-focus earthquakes may occur at much greater depths (ranging from 300 up to 700 kilometers). These seismically active areas of subduction are known as Wadati-Benioff zones. Deep-focus earthquakes occur at a depth at which the subducted lithosphere should no longer be brittle, due to the high temperature and pressure. A possible mechanism for the generation of deep-focus earthquakes is faulting caused by olivine undergoing a phase transition into a spinel structure.

Earthquakes and Volcanic Activity: Earthquakes also often occur in volcanic regions and are caused there, both by tectonic faults and by the movement of magma in volcanoes. Such earthquakes can serve as an early warning of volcanic eruptions, like during the Mount St. Helens eruption of 1980.

Earthquake Clusters: Most earthquakes form part of a sequence, related to each other in terms of location and time.

Aftershocks: An aftershock is an earthquake that occurs after a previous earthquake, the mainshock. An aftershock is in the same region of the main shock but always of a smaller magnitude. If an aftershock is larger than the main shock, the aftershock is redesignated as the main shock and the original main shock is redesignated as a foreshock. Aftershocks are formed as the crust around the displaced fault plane adjusts to the effects of the main shock.

Earthquake Swarms: Earthquake swarms are sequences of earthquakes striking in a specific area within a short period of time. They are different from earthquakes followed by a series of aftershocks by the fact that no single earthquake in the sequence is obviously the main shock, therefore none have notable higher magnitudes than the other. An example of an earthquake swarm is the 2004 activity at Yellowstone National Park.

Earthquake Storms: Sometimes a series of earthquakes occur in a sort of earthquake storm, where the earthquakes strike a fault in clusters, each triggered by the shaking or stress redistribution of the previous earthquakes. Similar to aftershocks but on adjacent segments of fault, these storms occur over the course of years, and with some of the later earthquakes as damaging as the early ones. Such a pattern was observed in the sequence of about a dozen earthquakes that struck the North Anatolian Fault in Turkey in the 20th century and has been inferred for older anomalous clusters of large earthquakes in the Middle East.

Drought

A drought is an extended period of months or years when a region notes a deficiency in its water supply. Generally, this occurs when a region receives consistently below average precipitation. It can have a substantial impact on the ecosystem and agriculture of the affected region. Although droughts can persist for several years, even a short, intense drought can cause significant damage and harm the local economy. This global phenomenon has a widespread impact on agriculture. The United Nations estimates that an area of fertile soil the size of Ukraine is lost every year because of drought, deforestation, and climate instability. Lengthy periods of drought have long been a key trigger for mass migration and played a key role in a number of ongoing migrations and other humanitarian crises in the Horn of Africa and the Sahel.

Drought is a normal, recurring feature of the climate in most parts of the world. It is among the earliest documented climatic events, present in the Epic of Gilgamesh and tied to the biblical story of Joseph's arrival in and the later Exodus from Ancient Egypt. Hunter-gatherer migrations in 9,500BC Chile have been linked to the phenomenon, as has the exodus of early man out of Africa and into the rest of the world around 135,000 years ago. Modern peoples can effectively mitigate much of the impact of drought through irrigation and crop rotation.

Failure to develop adequate drought mitigation strategies carries a grave human cost in the modern era, exacerbated by ever-increasing population densities. Recurring droughts leading to desertification in the Horn of Africa have created grave ecological catastrophes, prompting massive food shortages, still recurring. To the north-west of the Horn, the Darfur conflict in neighboring Sudan, also affecting Chad, was fueled by decades of drought; combination of drought, desertification and overpopulation are among the causes of the Darfur conflict, because the Arab Baggara nomads searching for water have to take their livestock further south, to land mainly occupied by non-Arab farming peoples.

According to a UN climate report, the Himalayan glaciers that are the sources of Asia's biggest rivers-Ganges, Indus, Brahmaputra, Yangtze, Mekong, Salween and Yellow-could disappear by 2035 due to global warming. Approximately 2.4 billion people live in the drainage basin of the Himalayan rivers. India, China, Pakistan, Bangladesh, Nepal and Myanmar could experience floods followed by droughts in coming decades. Drought in India affecting the Ganges is of particular concern, as it provides drinking water and agricultural irrigation for more than 500 million people. The west coast of North America, which gets much of its water from glaciers in mountain ranges such as the Rocky Mountains and Sierra Nevada, also would be affected.

In 2005, parts of the Amazon basin experienced the worst drought in 100 years. A 23 July 2006 article reported Woods Hole Research Center results showing that the forest in its present form could survive only three years of drought. Scientists at the Brazilian National Institute of Amazonian Research argue in the article that this drought response, coupled with the effects of deforestation on regional climate, are pushing the rainforest towards a "tipping point" where it would irreversibly start to die. It concludes that the rainforest is on the brink of being turned into savanna or desert, with catastrophic consequences for the world's climate. According to the WWF, the combination of climate change and deforestation increases the drying effect of dead trees that fuels forest fires.

By far the largest part of Australia is desert or semi-arid lands commonly known as the outback. A 2005 study by Australian and American researchers investigated the desertification of the interior, and suggested that one explanation was related to human settlers who arrived about 50,000 years ago. Regular burning by these settlers could have prevented monsoons from reaching interior Australia.

In June 2008 it became known that an expert panel had warned of long term, maybe irreversible, severe ecological damage for the whole Murray-Darling basin if it does not receive sufficient water by October. Australia could experience more severe droughts and they could become more frequent in the future, a government-commissioned report said on July 6, 2008. The Australian of the year 2007, environmentalist Tim Flannery, predicted that unless it made drastic changes, Perth in Western Australia could become the world's first ghost metropolis, an abandoned city with no more water to sustain its population.

Causes

Generally, rainfall is related to the amount of water vapor in the atmosphere, combined with the upward forcing of the air mass containing that water vapor. If either of these are reduced,the result is a drought. This can be triggered by an above average prevalence of high pressure systems, winds carrying continental, rather than oceanic air masses (ie. reduced water content), and ridges of high pressure areas form with behaviors which prevent or restrict the developing of thunderstorm activity or rainfall over one certain region. Oceanic and atmospheric weather cycles such as the El Niño-Southern Oscillation (ENSO) make drought a regular recurring feature of the Americas along the Pacific coast and Australia. Guns, Germs, and Steel author Jared Diamond sees the stark impact of the multi-year ENSO cycles on Australian weather patterns as a key reason that Australian aborigines remained a hunter-gatherer society rather than adopting agriculture.

Human activity can directly trigger exacerbating factors such as overfarming, excessive irrigation, Deforestation, and erosion adversely impact the ability of the land to capture and hold water. While these tend to be relatively isolated in their scope, activities resulting in global climate change are expected to trigger droughts with a substantial impact on agriculture throughout the world, and especially in developing nations. Overall, global warming will result in increased world rainfall. Along with drought in some areas, flooding and erosion will increase in others. Paradoxically, some proposed solutions to global warming that focus on more active techniques, solar radiation management through the use of a space sunshade for one, may also carry with them increased chances of drought.

Consequences

Periods of drought can have significant environmental, agricultural, health, economic and social consequences. The effect varies according to vulnerability. For example, subsistence farmers are more likely to migrate during drought because they do not have alternative food sources. Areas with populations that depend on subsistence farming as a major food source are more vulnerable to drought-triggered famine. Drought is rarely if ever the sole cause of famine; socio-political factors such as extreme widespread poverty play a major role. Drought can also reduce water quality, because lower water flows reduce dilution of pollutants and increase contamination of remaining water sources. A few common consequences of drought include:

- Diminished crop growth or yield productions and carrying capacity for livestock;
- Dust bowls, themselves a sign of erosion, which further erode the landscape;
- Dust storms, when drought hits an area suffering from desertification and erosion;

- Famine due to lack of water for irrigation;
- Habitat damage, affecting both terrestrial and aquatic wildlife.
- Malnutrition, dehydration and related diseases;
- Mass migration, resulting in internal displacement and international refugees;
- Reduced electricity production due to insufficient available coolant for power stations; and reduced water flow through hydroelectric dams.
- Shortages of water for industrial users;
- Snakes migration and increases in snakebites;
- Social unrest;
- War over natural resources, including water and food;
- Wildfires, such as Australian bushfires, are more common during times of drought;

Types of Drought

As a drought persists, the conditions surrounding it gradually worsen and its impact on the local population gradually increases. People tend to define droughts in three main ways:

1. Meteorological drought is brought about when there is a prolonged period with less than average precipitation. Meteorological drought usually precedes the other kinds of drought.
2. Agricultural droughts are droughts that affect crop production or the ecology of the range. This condition can also arise independently from any change in precipitation levels when soil conditions and erosion triggered by poorly planned agricultural endeavors cause a shortfall in water available to the crops. However, in a traditional drought, it is caused by an extended period of below average precipitation.
3. Hydrological drought is brought about when the water reserves available in sources such as aquifers, lakes and reservoirs fall below the statistical average. Hydrological drought tends to show up more slowly

because it involves stored water that is used but not replenished. Like an agricultural drought, this can be triggered by more than just a loss of rainfall. For instance, Kazakhstan was recently awarded a large amount of money by the World Bank to restore water that had been diverted to other nations from the Aral Sea under Soviet rule. Similar circumstances also place their largest lake, Balkhash, at risk of completely drying out.

Floods

This guide lists simple things you and your family can do to stay safe and protect your property from floods.

Before flooding occurs.

- All your family members should know the safe route to nearest shelter/ raised pucca house.
- if your area is flood-prone, consider alternative building materials. Mud walls are more likely to be damaged during floods. You may consider making houses where the walls are made of local bricks upto the highest known flood level with cement pointing.
- Have an emergency kit on hand which includes a:
  1. A portable radio, torch and spare batteries;
  2. Stocks of fresh water, dry food (chura, mudi, gur, biscuits), kerosene, candle and matchboxes;
  3. Waterproof or polythene bags for clothing and valuables, an umbrella and bamboo stick (to protect from snake), salt and sugar.
  4. A first aid kit, manual and strong ropes for tying things

When you hear a flood warning or if flooding appears likely:

- Tune to your local radio/TV for warnings and advice.
  1. Keep vigil on flood warning given by local authorities
  2. Don't give any importance to rumours and don't panic
  3. Keep dry food, drinking water and clothes ready

- Prepare to take bullock carts, other agricultural equipments, and domestic animals to safer places or to higher locations.
- Plan which indoor items you will raise or empty if water threatens to enter your house
- Check your emergency kit

During Floods:

- Drink boiled water.
- Keep your food covered, don't take heavy meals.
- Use raw tea, rice-water, tender coconut-water, etc. during diarrhoea; contact your ANM/AWW for ORS and treatment.
- Do not let children remain on empty stomach.
- Use bleaching powder and lime to disinfect the surrounding.
- Help the officials/volunteers distributing relief materials.

If you need to evacuate:

- Firstly pack warm clothing, essential medication, valuables, personal papers, etc. in waterproof bags, to be taken with your emergency kit.
- Take the emergency kit
- Inform the local volunteers (if available), the address of the place you are evacuating to.
- Raise furniture, clothing and valuables onto beds, tables and to the top of the roof (electrical items highest).
- Turn off power.
- Whether you leave or stay, put sandbags in the toilet bowl and over all laundry / bathroom drain-holes to prevent sewage back-flow.
- Lock your home and take recommended/known evacuation routes for your area.
- Do not get into water of unknown depth and current.

If you stay or on your return:

- Stay tuned to local radio for updated advice.

- Do not allow children to play in, or near, flood waters.
- Avoid entering floodwaters. If you must, wear proper protection for your feet and check depth and current with a stick. Stay away from drains, culverts and water over knee-deep.
- Do not use electrical appliances, which have been in floodwater until checked for safety.
- Do not eat food, which has been in floodwaters.
- Boil tap water (in cities) until supplies have been declared safe. In case of rural areas, store tubewell water in plastic jars or use halogen tablets before drinking.
- Be careful of snakes, snakebites are common during floods.

Cyclones

Washington, April 21 : Scientists at Harvard University, US, have found that tropical cyclones readily inject ice far into the stratosphere, possibly feeding global warming.

The finding provides more evidence of the intertwining of severe weather and global warming by demonstrating a mechanism by which storms could drive climate change.

Many scientists now believe that global warming, in turn, is likely to increase the severity of tropical cyclones.

"Since water vapor is an important greenhouse gas, an increase of water vapor in the stratosphere would warm the Earth's surface," said David M. Romps, a research associate in Harvard's Department of Earth and Planetary Science.

"Our finding that tropical cyclones are responsible for many of the clouds in the stratosphere opens up the possibility that these storms could affect global climate, in addition to the oft-mentioned possibility of climate change affecting the frequency and intensity of tropical cyclones," he added.

Romps and co-author Zhiming Kuang, assistant professor of climate science in Harvard's Faculty of Arts and Sciences, were intrigued by earlier data suggesting that the amount of water vapor in the stratosphere has grown by roughly 50 percent over the past 50 years.

Scientists are currently unsure why this increase has occurred.

The Harvard researchers sought to examine the possibility that tropical cyclones might have contributed by sending a large fraction of their clouds into the stratosphere.

Using infrared satellite data gathered from 1983 to 2006, Romps and Kuang analyzed towering cloud tops associated with thousands of tropical cyclones, many of them near the Philippines, Mexico, and Central America.

Their analysis demonstrated that in a cyclone, narrow plumes of miles-tall storm clouds can rise so explosively through the atmosphere that they often push into the stratosphere.

Romps and Kuang found that tropical cyclones are twice as likely as other storms to punch into the normally cloud-free stratosphere, and four times as likely to inject ice deep into the stratosphere.

According to the researchers, if very deep clouds, such as those in a tropical cyclone that can rise through the atmosphere at speeds of up to 40 miles per hour, can punch through the tropopause, they can deposit their ice in the warmer overlying stratosphere, where it then evaporates.

"This suggests that tropical cyclones could play an important role in setting the humidity of the stratosphere," said Romps and Kuang.

Landslides

Landslide may be defined as a process involving downward and outward movement of a part of slope forming material along a definite plane i.e. plane of failure. It is caused due to shear failure along this plane.

Landslides are ubiquitous and occur in all climates on most hilly terrains, and in lakes and oceans. Some rocks are more landslide resistant than others, but regolith is likely to be landslide prone.

When landslides endanger humans and their installation, they are known as hazards; when they cause property damage and loss of life, they are disasters.

Main Causes of Landslides

Geological causes :

- Weak or sensitive materials
- Sheared, jointed, or fissured materials
- Adversely oriented discontinuity (bedding, schistosity, fault, unconformity, contact, and so forth)
- Contrast in permeability and/or stiffness of materials

Morphological causes:

- Tectonic or volcanic uplift
- Fluvial, wave, or glacial erosion of slope toe or lateral margins
- Subterranean erosion (solution, piping)
- Deposition loading slope or its crest
- Vegetation removal (by fire, drought)
- Thawing
- Freeze-and-thaw weathering
- Shrink-and-swell weathering

Anthropogenic causes:

- Excavation of slope or its toe
- Loading of slope or its crest
- Drawdown (of reservoirs)
- Deforestation
- Irrigation
- Mining
- Artificial vibration
- Water leakage from utilities

The factors that cause most of the damaging landslides around the world are generally combination of these.

Causes of failure are a combination of unstable structure and trigger event.

Major Triggers of Landslides

Water: Slope saturation by water is a primary cause of landslides. This effect can occur in the form of intense rainfall, snowmelt, changes in ground-water levels, and water-level changes along coastlines, earth dams, and the banks of lakes, reservoirs, canals, and rivers.

Toe Removal: Artificial toe removal by quarrying or mining, excavation for building site, or road widening.

Head Loading: Adding material above neutral line of a slide increases it driving force. Natural head loading causes slope instability on many active volcanoes.

Strength Reduction: Weathering ultimately weakens all slope materials; slow creep causes restructuring of clays stressed within slopes; slow processes eventually reach critical points. Cyclic and temporarily increased stresses may cause soil restructuring or rock fracturing.

Earthquakes

Vibration: Artificial vibrations, as from heavy road traffic.

Landslide Issues

- Natural calamities including earthquakes, landslides, avalanches, floods, cyclones, draughts and volcanic eruptions have been affecting mankind since beginning of civilization.
- These are believed to account for up to 4% of total annual deaths.
- Distribution of casualties due to natural disasters is, however, not evenly distributed around the globe.
- The impact of these disasters is more severe in developing countries which have higher population densities.
- Globally, the landslides, a prominent natural disaster, are estimated to cause approximately 1000 deaths annually apart from damaging property worth millions of US dollars.

- The landslides can be rapid or slow and occur in varied geological environs including underwater.
- The landslides account for considerable loss of life and cause damage to human settlements, civil structures, hydro projects, communication routes, and agricultural and forest land.
- The secondary effects of landslides are also disastrous. These include the damage by impact of waves generated by landslides entering water bodies, formation of landslide dams resulting from blockade of drainage courses by landslides and consequent floods due to breaching/overtopping.
- Coseismic landslides are induced by earthquakes. Assam Earthquakes of 1897 & 1950, Kangra Earthquake of 1905, Uttarkashi Earthquake of 1991 and Chamoli Earthquake of 1991 induced widespread landslides.

Corrective Measures

- Profile Modification–suitable modification of soil and rock profile for reducing the risk of slump and /or slide. Decreases the shear stress.
- Drainage–Draining through runoff of accumulated water to avoid saturation of water.
- Stabilization of Landslides by Vegetation – It substantially increases the cohesiveness of subsurface material, prevents surface erosion and shallow mass failures.
- Restraining structures-To arrest the movement of rocks and soil in the affected area. Increases the shear strength.
- Permeable walls-To arrest the movement of rocks and soil together with dewatering of the affected area.
- Piles–Stabilizes the mobile part of the affected mass.
- Ground Anchors–This gives support to the mobile mass and arrests its further movement.
- Miscellaneous Methods:
    - o Electro-osmosis–for drainage of low permeable soils

- o Grouting
- o Hardening of soil by thermic treatment
- o Breaking of slip surface by blasting

Tsunami

What is Tsunami?

A tsunami (pronounced su-nah-me) is a wave train, or series of waves, generated in a body of water by an impulsive disturbance that vertically displaces the water column. Earthquakes, landslides, volcanic eruptions, explosions, and even the impact of cosmic bodies, such as meteorites, can generate tsunamis. Tsunamis can savagely attack coastlines, causing devastating property damage and loss of life.

Tsunami-the Killer Waves:

Tsunami waves, which hit India for the first time today wrecking havoc across the southern coastline, is a known phenomenon in the Pacific Ocean region stretching from Chile in Latin America to Japan in far East Asia. Tsunami, in Japanese means 'tidal waves' and pronounced as "Su-namee".

The waves, which were caused by a massive earthquake on the Indian ocean and claimed thousands of lives in India and 6 other countries, are usually triggered by seismic disturbances-coastal earth quakes, volcanic eruptions or undersea landslides-that jolt the ocean floor.

Often, tremors displace ground surface, sending an entire column of water in motion outward from an earth quake region-often with disastrous results thousand of Kilometres from their region. The difference between tsunami waves and tidal waves is that while the former hit only the harbors and coastal areas even as other parts of the sea remain calm, the latter make the sea rough.

The result is a deep wave that reaches from the sea's surface to the floor and travels horizontally at speeds up to 500 miles per hour and reaches heights between 50 to 100 feet. The waves travel faster in deeper water and when it approaches shore, they rise further. It is the sharp elevation of the ocean floor near the coast that slows the bottom of the wave while the top keeps moving at the original speed. Vast quantity of water is then piled up into a vertical wall that finally crashes over the sea shore with amazing force.

Man-Made

Despite adequate warning signals most of the states failed to gear up to the crisis. The knee-jerk reaction now has only compounded the people's misery.

With the uncanny foresight of an astrologer, the Rajasthan Government's Relief Department had predicted six months ago the tragedy that is now unfolding across 23,406 of the state's 34,693 villages. In its "memorandum of scarcity" presented to the Central Government in November 1999 for additional funds to combat the situation, the department had reeled out figures of the expected calamity: Close to two-thirds of the people affected, foodgrain production down by half, massive fodder shortage and acute drinking water problems.

With such forewarnings, the state should have been forearmed. Right? Wrong. To provide drinking water, for instance, the state Government made elaborate plans to rejuvenate existing handpumps, construct new ones and also ready tankers for emergency supply of water. All this remained a pipe dream. The state minister in charge of relief, Gulab Singh Shaktawat, unabashedly admits that of the 70,000 handpumps, 50,000 are still non-functional. For cattle, at least 6,000 fodder depots were to be opened by May. But only a third of them have been set up. Similarly, to supplement income, as many as eight lakh people were to be employed in relief work. But so far only half the number have been engaged. The result of the apathy: a man-made disaster in Rajasthan.

Yet, depressingly, Rajasthan is not an exception. Much the same story is repeated in the 11 other states now staggering under severe drought conditions. In neighbouring Gujarat, the fact that two-thirds of his state was drought-affected didn't deter Chief Minister Keshubhai Patel from proceeding on a nine-day visit to the US, ostensibly to woo foreign investors.

Never mind that just a week before there were near water riots in Patel's native town of Rajkot. Anticipating the water scarcity, the Gujarat Water Supply and Sewerage Board (GWSSB), had found a water source near Halvad, 110 km away from Rajkot. The board drilled 123 borewells to supply additional water to the town. But the Rajkot Municipal Corporation failed to lay its own pipelines for distribution till the end of March. And only when the situation got out of hand did it finally go ahead.

Shortage of funds is the common refrain in most of the affected states. And they all point to an unsympathetic Centre as the problem. But it is primarily the responsibility of the state government to undertake immediate relief measures in the wake of natural calamities from the allocation under the Calamity Relief Fund (CRF). The contributions to the fund are in a ratio of 3:1. The Centre's share of 75 per cent is released in four quarterly instalments. Rajasthan's allocation under the CRF for 1999-2000 totalled Rs 207 crore. Chief Minister Ashok Gehlot says he asked for additional funds but was given only a tenth by the Centre. Gehlot's charge would have stuck if his Government had spent even Rs 63 crore — already available in its coffers — and then demanded more. Something as simple as repair of handpumps, which required only Rs 10 crore, has not been undertaken.

In Gujarat, the state Revenue Department should have arranged for adequate quantity of fodder when signs of a worsening situation on the drought front were evident late last year itself. Gujarat is one of the major producers of grass in western India and exports it to other states. But the Government made no move to stop the auctions of fodder and sold it at Rs 2 per kg. Now the Government is buying from the depots of Punjab and Haryana at the rate of over Rs 5 per kg. Says Madhusudhan Mistry, general secretary of Eklavya Sanghathan, an NGO working for the uplift of tribals: "It is a drought of ideas and implementation more than anything else."

There are larger reasons why the misery in the states have only multiplied. Despite having successively good monsoons, simple and cheap water-harvesting techniques were never implemented at the panchayat level. Much of India's rain water runs off into the sea because of this. On the other hand, there is a reckless over-exploitation of groundwater resources during years of drought that has seen water tables drop drastically.

In Gujarat, for instance, in areas were digging would have struck water at 150 ft, farmers now have to drill as deep as 1,000 ft. Way back in 1987, the Centre had drafted a model bill to prevent over-exploitation of water resources. It fixed such parameters as the number of wells that can be dug per square kilometre and called for water conservation measures. But so far no state has passed such a law. The real problem, as a senior Central official points out, is that: "We always do firefighting in India, never fire prevention. We always talk of disaster management, never mitigation."

There are no dearth of examples of how some villagers in these states have solved their water problems instead of relying on the state. Yet there is a marked reluctance to decentralise expenditure on such relief work. Because of a multiplicity of departments dealing with the drought there is a serious lack of accountability and coordination among them. Between the ministries of irrigation, rural development, environment and agriculture there is an enormous amount of buck-passing and the result is that very little trickles down to the needy.

There is knee-jerk reaction to the crisis when what is required is a sustained campaign. A couple of years ago the National Dairy Development Board (NDDB) had studied how Australia provided fodder for its cattle during drought. The NDDB used a mixture of molasses and urea to produce nutrient substitutes at a cost of just Rs 2 per kg, compared to the prevailing price of Rs 30 a kg. But the scheme never got implemented because bright ideas are rarely welcomed. Only now are Rajasthan and Gujarat making efforts to popularise it. But the fear is that it is already too late. Typically, no heads will roll for the neglect.

Technological

Manmade or technological disasters are unpredictable, can spread across geographical boundaries, may be unpreventable, and may have limited physical damage but long-term effects.

Some disasters in this class are entirely manmade, such as terrorism. Other technological disasters occur because industrial sites are located in communities affected by natural disasters, equipment failures occur, or workers have inadequate training or fatigue and make errors. The threat of terrorism is categorized as a potential technological disaster and includes bioterrorism, bombings, civil and political disorders, riots, and economic emergencies.

Technological disasters include a broad range of incidents. Routes of exposure are water, food and drink, airborne releases, fires and explosions, and hazardous materials or waste (e.g., chemical, biological, or radioactive) released into the environment from a fixed facility or during transport. Fires, explosions, building or bridge collapses, transportation crashes, dam or levee failures, nuclear reactor accidents, and breaks in water, gas, or sewer lines are other examples of technological disasters.

Risk of Morbidity and Mortality

Communities in which industrial sites are located or through which hazardous materials pass via highway, rail, or pipeline are at risk for technological disasters. Injuries can occur to workers at the site, to responders bringing the incident under control and providing emergency medical care, and to residents in the community. Those with preexisting medical conditions, such as lung or heart disease, could be at increased risk for negative health outcomes if exposed to toxic releases. Burns, skin disorders, and lung damage can result from exposure to specific agents. Table lists the health consequences of several classes of toxins.

Injury Prevention

Ensuring that local industry implements basic safety procedures can significantly reduce negative health outcomes from accidental releases of toxins. Emergency preparedness? including the ability of prehospital and hospital systems to care for patients exposed to industrial agents, the training of medical personnel to work in contaminated environments, and the stockpiling of personal protective equipment for responders?is key to providing care following industrial accidents or acts of bioterrorism. Government agencies, in coordination with hospitals and public health, should conduct computer simulations or field exercises to test the community's ability to evacuate those at risk and the ability of the health sector to provide care to those exposed to accidental releases. Information about the clinical management of exposure to toxins can be provided by poison control centers, CHEMTREC, and industry databases.

Public Health Interventions

- Take a visible role in community planning.
- Conduct hazard assessments.
- Review Material Safety Data Sheets for agents produced, stored, or used locally and regionally to evaluate range of potential adverse health effects.
- Conduct vulnerability analyses to identify target populations and potential adverse public health consequences.
- Conduct risk assessment to determine if specific agents will reach toxic levels in the vicinity of vulnerable populations.
- Determine minimal thresholds of exposure for specific agents that would trigger evacuation.
- Gather information on chemical neutralization, estimation models of plume-dispersion, and appropriate antidotes.
- Work with local hospitals to stockpile appropriate antidotes, medications, and supplies.
- Stockpile two pills per person of potassium iodide in communities located within ten miles of nuclear reactor sites.
- Provide emergency services and medical care to victims.
- Activate the health alert network.

Industrial

The National Disaster Management Authority conducted an Industrial disaster drill at Indian Oil Corporation Limited

(Assam Oil division's) at Digboi Refinery recently. The drill was conducted to test the preparedness of the civil administration concerned in the event of a major industrial disaster. The scenario envisaged for the disaster involved three mishaps: leakage of LPG at the LPG dispatch unit. Blast in hydrogen bullets in the refinery and leakage of chlorine due to catastrophic failure of toner, occurring almost simultaneously resulting in a large number of casualties. The District Administration, Civil Hospital, Civil Defence, State Fire Service, Police Department, Revenue Department, Indian Oil Corporation Limited (Assam Oil Divisions's) mutual aid partners such as Oil India Limited, Assam Gas Company Limited, North East Electric Power Corporation, Brahmaputra Valley Fertilisers Limited, Coal India Limited participated in the drill. NGOs like Lions Club of Digboi, Rotary Club of Digboi, also participated in the drill. At the concluding session, Brig (Dr) BK Khanna, senior specialist, National Disaster Management Authority, spoke on the various observations made by the expert panel of Brig Khanna, R Dubey, Director, National Disaster Management Institute, Bhopal and CR Deka, Chief Factories Inspector, Asom. He appreciated the response of the various organizations involved in the drill and pointed out the areas where further improvement could be effected. The session ended with vote of thanks from CR Deka, Chief Inspector of Factories, Asom. The National Disaster Management Authority was created after the enactment of the Disaster Management Act of the Government of India in December 2005 to spearhead and implement a holistic and integrated approach to disaster management in India. Since its inception, the authority has been stimulating disaster scenarios in various parts of the country and conducting detailed mock drills on disaster management, sources added.

Components

Technologists often exhibit an unexpected response when asked by management to produce a disaster recovery plan for an automated system. They get genuinely ticked off.

In the mind of a good technologist, this request is often interpreted as a signal that management does not trust them to recover in the event of a disaster. They look at the disaster recovery plan as some kind of a test to prove they know how to do their jobs!

Those responsible for technical systems in virtually any organization are capable of recovering from a disaster under virtually any type of circumstance. This may sound like a very surprising statement, especially coming from someone who writes disaster recovery plans for a living; it is however, quite true. The technical service staffs in most companies are very capable of recovering from many types of outages. After all, these are the very people who designed and built the system in the fist place! They know where every wire in the organization runs (well, usually) and have more committed to memory about their company than most of us could learn in a decade.

But what happens when key personnel are either incapacitated by the disaster, or maybe don't report for work ever again. After all, most have families which will be the primary concern after a major disaster. Would you come to work if your family was home alone, and your home was in danger of being looted?

One of my personal favorite ways to check the disaster recovery plan is to come into an organization and kill the LAN administrator. (No, not really – remember, it's just a test!)

The reason I like to pick on the LAN manager is that this key person phenomena is especially troublesome in distributed LAN environments. The point is, what happens to an organization's response when these key people are not available in a disaster? It's really interesting to see how the organization responds after the loss of a key player.

In light of these thoughts, it is important you present disaster recovery to your staff, not as some type of a quiz or test to prove they know their jobs, but in light of these facts, that other coworkers may be called to execute this plan. This means everything needs to be documented in a format designed to be easily followed by an outside technical person supporting the recovery efforts. Hint: Use a lot of pictures, a lot of diagrams, and spell out where everything is!

It's important for the people coordinating the recovery and response to know what was installed. Therefore, an important component to any recovery plan is an equipment inventory. At a minimum this should include:

- a listing of all equipment by type and model number;
- associated software packages, with version number;
- date of purchase; and
- original cost.

Other items are helpful as well, such as:

- name, address and telephone number of the manufacturer;
- and the local distributor or depot for the equipment.

Using this approach, quick command decisions are possible, even in the heat of the moment during a disaster. The more information on hand in a digestible format to provide rationale for these decisions, the better for the company and the decision maker.

Another item to consider is the software inventory, encompassing all software required for operation of all missing critical equipment. This inventory should include:

- the purpose of the software;
- the acquisition date of the software;
- the original cost of the software
- the license number; and
- the version number.

Other items which may find a useful place in an equipment inventory include such things as the location of third-party equipment suppliers. Since much of your equipment may be a few years old, it may already be seeing activity on the secondary market and be more easily acquired there.

Any mission-critical piece of equipment should have a disaster recovery plan, it behooves all to get this recovery plan from the vendor first. Such equipment should include things like mission-critical servers, mainframe computers, bridges, routers and gateways. The higher the price tag, the greater the likelihood your vendor may work with you. In any event, it is much more cost-effective to negotiate disaster recovery services with a vendor while they are actively after your business than to try to add these services later.

"Importing" Data for the Plan

The best method for keeping track of equipment inventories, as well as other components necessary for the recovery process is through a process called "importing" data.

Importing means finding databases and repositories of information within the organization which you can reasonably expect to stay up to date, and then acquiring them for the plan, either manually, via magnetic media, or most preferably over a LAN. For example, when a piece of equipment is purchased, a document or file for the equipment is archived. Often times, the contract and the documentation to the equipment goes to accounting, where it's stashed away by the bean counters to be amortized. If you are lucky, documentation is stored on a LAN which may be accessible to you. The key is to locate and identify these repositories of equipment inventory data so they can be imported gracefully into the recovery plan.

Organizations which make heavy use of internetworked LANs have an advantage in importing data. Here it becomes relatively straightforward to import data from other departments connected to the same LAN. In this fashion, any time a file is updated, for example, in an accounting department, showing a new piece of equipment, there are a number of ways this could be automatically transferred without human intervention to a critical file within the recovery plan.

Object-linking Microsoft Word files, for example, is one way of doing this. By keying in on a specific file name, in this case in the accounting department, a technical service manager can be assured every time that department updates an equipment-list repository file, the file in his recovery plan will also be similar updated.

Maintaining up-to-date telephone numbers for personnel and critical equipment vendors is absolutely essential to the successful implementation of the plan, and similar methodology must be employed to ensure accuracy. Once again, this means importing data from reputable sources.

Consider home telephone numbers for employees. There are many places within the organization you can go to find a home telephone number for key employees; such as human resources and the company telephone directory. Human resources may be the best place to get this information. However, you may also find an employee who has worked for the company for 20 years still has the same address on file he had when hired. The company telephone directory may be a better bet in this case. The key is to identify, verify, then import.

Speaking of numbers, many others will be needed in the plan. These include telephone numbers for key equipment vendors and suppliers. Oftentimes, these can be found in the network control center, help desk, or other operational environments with day-today contact with these vendors. When telephone numbers for key vendors and suppliers change, these people are the first to know. Importing is best performed through object linking files together, perhaps in a LAN environment. It can also be accomplished through use of a Sneaker net and floppy disk. The important thing is it be done regularly, and preferably, without human intervention.

Consider importing components of the corporate-wide recovery plan. It makes little sense for a technical recovery planner to write procedures for such broad-based concerns as loss of a building, physical security, fire procedures, bomb threats, and other items which are company-wide in effect and scope. Indeed, as far as the make-up of the recovery plan, your recovery plan itself will probably end up being imported into a corporate-wide recovery plan for execution by an emergency management team. It works both ways.

What Goes in the Plan?

We have used the concept of the Eight R's in many of our disaster recovery discussions. It serves as a good thought jogger and helps the technologist put tasks in perspective. It is also helpful to include a section of appendices at the back of your plan. This part of the plan is reserved for notes, detailed information, and things you will need but do not want cluttering up the main part of the plan. These can include:

- emergency call lists of management and recovery teams;
- vendor call out and escalation lists;
- inventory and report forms;
- carrier call out and escalation lists;
- maintenance forms;
- hardware lists and serial numbers;
- software lists and license numbers;
- team member duties and responsibilities;
- network schematic diagrams;
- equipment room floor grid diagrams;
- contract and maintenance agreements;
- special operating instructions for sensitive equipment;
- cellular telephone inventory and agreements; and
- miscellaneous (pictures of the kids?).

Broad-based Document

There are a lot of good reasons for documenting a disaster recovery plan, and they will manifest themselves throughout the document. Your recovery plan will be a broad-based document, and will cover details which are company-wide in scope. It will contain statements which speak to the issue of:

- protecting life;
- minimizing risk to the company;
- recovery critical applications;
- safeguarding against litigation and shareholder suits;
- protecting competitive positions; and
- preserving customer confidence.

Disaster recovery plans are complex, and can ultimately take two years or more to complete. For this reason, don't be ashamed to ask for some outside help. While this can be taken in one way as an advertising plug from a disaster recovery consultant, it also comes from experience. In today's busy operational environments, disaster recovery planning usually becomes kitchen table work, if it gets done at all. Regardless of who does the work however, by understanding the components of a successful plan, and devoting an enthusiastic outlook to the project, you will be secure in the knowledge that you are not only protecting the interests of the company, but your long term future as well. Good luck.

The Eight R's of a Successful Recovery Plan

1. *Reason for Planning:* Think of all the reasons your organization has for planning. There are many. Some common themes or sentiments can include:
   - protect human life;
   - recover critical operations;
   - protect competitive position;
   - preserve customer confidence and good will; and
   - protect against litigation.
2. *Recognition:* What happens if someone spots water coming under the door to your equipment room at 3 a.m.? It probably will not be one of your people at that time of night. Do the security guards know who to call and how to report trouble? These are the kinds of concerns to address in the recognition phase:
   - initial reaction procedures to a disaster report;
   - notification procedures for police, fire, medical; and
   - notification procedures for management.
3. *Reaction:* Once someone sounds the alarm, what then? Who handles security? Who talks to the media? Who is an employee and who is a looter? Careful planning here helps address these questions.
   - mobilizing the EMT (executive management team);
   - filing of initial damage assessment reports to the EMT;
   - assisting EMT in preparation of statements; and
   - opening a critical events log for audit purposes.
4. *Recovery*
   - modified signing authority for equipment purchases;
   - procedures for getting cash;

- procedures for maintaining physical security;
- procedures for arranging security at the damaged site;
- procedures for finding and getting to the recovery center (maps!); and
- procedures for arranging security at the recovery center

5. Restoration
   - coordination of restoration of the original site;
   - restoration of electronic equipment;
   - reloading of software;
   - restoration of power, UPS, common building systems;
   - replacement of fire suppression systems;
   - rewiring of the building;
   - restoring the LAN; and
   - restoring the WAN connections.
6. Return to Normal
   - testing procedures for new hardware and software;
   - what constitutes a successful test (before recommitting production);
   - training operations personnel;
   - training employees;
   - scheduling migration back to original site; and
   - coordinating return to original site.
7. Rest and Relax
   - schedule compensatory time off; and
   - make visits to employees in rehab from stress.
8. Re-evaluate and Re-Document
   - review your critical events log;
   - evaluate vendor performance;
   - recognize extraordinary achievements;
   - preparing final review and activity report; and
   - aid in liability assessments.

Impact on Environment—General

For over a decade, Orissa has been teetering from one extreme weather condition to another: from heatwaves to cyclones, drought to floods. The state has been declared disaster-affected for 95 of the last 105 years. Why is this happening? Is it the result of global warming and climate change? Richard Mahapatra, who has been awarded the CCDS-InfoChangeIndia Fellowship for development reportage, explores these questions in the first of a series of articles.

Long before Gunadhar lost his father to a heatstroke in early spring last year, and a devastating cyclone swept through nine coastal districts of Orissa for 25 hours, six years ago, the state of Orissa had already begun to show symptoms of climate change. Gunadhar knew it, though he was only in the second standard when his father died. His father, a regular migrant to Raipur in Chhattisgarh after chronic drought rendered his land uncultivable, had explained to Gunadhar during the long train journey back to the village, once the monsoons set in, that there were six seasons. And that the *koel* in the mango tree in the backyard sang throughout the day during the monsoons.

But Gunadhar can count only three seasons (summer, monsoon and winter—the transition period between the rains and the summer). And the *koel* no longer sings during the monsoons; it sings in winter. As the winters have begun to warm up, people say it sings during summer too.

- Sea levels are rising: People's perceptions and scientific projections
- Falling off the map: Orissa's submerged villages
- Death of the seasons

For old-timers, the state's new profile of seasons is confusing. Most farmers have always used the traditional *panjika* to forecast weather. The system bases its forecast on the assumption that 120 days of rain are normal, spread over six seasons. "However that is not the case now. The number of rainy days has come down to around 90 days," says Artabandhu Mishra, a life scientist who has studied the indigenous method of weather forecasting.

Caught between the past and an uncertain future, life for the ordinary Oriya is a puzzle. Besides the disasters that strike the state with frightening frequency, the change in climate is stark, affecting everything from the economy to when marriages are held.

The Disaster Dossier

For over a decade, Orissa has been teetering from one extreme weather condition to another: from heatwave to cyclone, from drought to flood. The state has been declared disaster-affected for 95 years out of the last 105 years: floods have occurred for 50 years, droughts for 32, and cyclones have struck the state for 11 years. Since 1965, these calamities have not only become more frequent, they are striking areas that have never experienced such conditions before. For instance, a heatwave in 1998 killed around 2,200 people—most of the casualties were from coastal Orissa, a region known for its moderate climate. Since 1998, almost 3,000 people have died due to heatstroke.

The 1999 super cyclone affected places like Bhubaneswar and Nayagarh, which were never traditionally cyclone-prone. While the 2001 drought parched fields in coastal districts, the unprecedented floods of 2001 submerged 25 of the state's 30 districts. Many of these areas had never witnessed floods before. Orissa has experienced around 952 small and big cyclones and 451 tornadoes between 1891 and 1970. From 1901 to 1981 there were 380 cyclones, of which 272 resulted from depressions in the Bay of Bengal. Twenty-nine of these cyclones were devastating.

A conservative study of the effects of natural disasters reveals that between 1963 and 1999, Orissa experienced 13 major disasters, which killed 22,228 people (state government figure; non-government figure puts the toll at around 40,000), and rendered 34,21,000 people homeless.

During the Ninth Plan period (1997-2002), Orissa was in the grip of a series of disasters. On the eve of the Tenth Plan (2002-03), the entire state was going through a severe drought. The total loss of livelihood and damage to capital stock due to calamities between 1998-99 and 2001-02 stands at Rs 13,230.47 crore, according to the Tenth Plan document, Government of Orissa. This is close to 60% of the state's total plan outlay of Rs 19,000 crore for the Tenth Five-Year Plan.

Natural calamities have seriously affected livelihoods in the state and the income level of households. An important fallout has been the serious setback suffered by the capital formation process in the economy. Consequently, the state's Gross Domestic Product (GDP) has been substantially depressed, says the *State Human Development Report* of 2003.

The impact of disasters on Orissa's economy is evident. The state's per capita income declined fast in the second half of the 1990s, disaster-wise the worst phase. It is now half the national average. An average of 900,000 ha of agricultural production are lost every year due to disasters. Similarly, between 1980 and 2000, agriculture's contribution to the state GDP fell by 16%.

Such disasters have resulted in a type of poverty known as 'conjectural poverty'. Vaidyananth Mishra, an Orissa-based economist, says: "Disasters have made Orissa the poorest state. What is more disheartening is that nobody cares to study this."

Economic

Economies of countries can be classified based on parameters such as ownership of means of production and levels of economic development. Based on the ownership of the means of production, economies can be classified into capitalist economy, socialist economy, and mixed economy. Capitalism is an economic system characterized by private ownership of productive goods and services.

Socialism is an economic and political system in which private property is abolished and the means of production (i.e., capital and land) are collectively owned and operated by the state. In a mixed economy, some of the means of production are owned by the government while some is held by private individuals. Based on their level of development countries can be classified into "developing countries" and "developed countries."

The World Bank relies on income levels to classify countries into these two categories. GDP is the value of the total final output of all goods and services produced in a single year within a country's boundaries. GNP is GDP plus incomes received by residents from abroad minus incomes claimed by nonresidents. Inflation is a general price rise in prices across the economy. It is different from the rise in price of a particular good or service. WPI is an index of the prices of products and services consumers buy. The amount of inflation in the economy depends on the level of monetary demand in the economy, and amount of demand in the economy relative to available supply of goods and services. The interest rate is the rate charged or paid for the use of money, normally expressed as a percentage.

The unemployment rate is the number of unemployed people as a percentage of the total labour force. The amount of foreign currency held by a nation's banking system as a reserve base, or financial backup, for its international transactions and payments is referred as foreign exchange reserves. Regional trade agreements (RTAs) are usually entered into by two or more countries from the same region. The most visible objective behind these agreements is to reduce trade barriers among member countries.

Based on the level and nature of integration, RTAs can be classified into four categories: free trade area, customs union, common market, and economic union. A free trade area is a cooperative arrangement among two or more nations, whereby trade barriers are removed among the members. A customs union is formed when two or more countries agree to remove all barriers to free trade with each other, while establishing a common external tariff against other nations.

A common market is a regional grouping of countries that levies common external duties on imports from nonmember countries, but which eliminates tariffs, quotas, and other miscellaneous government restrictions on trade among member countries. An economic union is an agreement between two or more countries that allows the free movement of capital, labour, all goods and services, and involves the harmonization and unification of social, fiscal, and monetary policies.

Social

When a firm operates in an international business environment, as an individual is bound by the society in which he lives, it needs to understand the importance of society. Social class is an important part of the society. In most western societies, these classes are classified as upper, middle and lower. The level of perception of each class and their frequency of buying goods differ from one country to another. In countries like India perception and trends of the consumers have been changing owing to the liberalization and the changes in lifestyles. Another important aspect of society is the group. The performance of groups differs in individualistic and collectivist societies. The family is an important part of the social environment. It is a primary group and influences the consumption and buying behavior of consumers. The traditional family life cycle has been changing owing to the differing lifestyles. So, marketers have to analyze these trends and bring in products that are suitable to these changing consumer segments. Also jobs and workplaces have to be designed according to the changing lifestyles.

The nature of population has also been changing in many countries due to cross-border migration. In many countries because of migration, the population now consists of various races and classes. This is reflected in the workforce as well. There is also diversity in the workplace because of the changing age structure. All these have to be managed by organizations and they have to cater to the needs of these changing employees. The other important aspect that firms operating in international business environment have to consider is the effects of their products on the environment. Environmental laws may differ from one country to another. But firms should take it as a responsibility and work towards the wellbeing of the environment by manufacturing environmentally friendly products.

Political

There are many issues on the minds of politicians and voters these days: terrorism and military operations overseas, the economy and jobs, health care. Environmental issues do not seem to rank very high on the Concern-O-Meter, but to a large extent, that is a self-fulfilling prophesy due to the underreporting of environmental problems by the mainstream corporate media. But that aside, even when politicians do get around to discussing important environmental issues with us—the air that we breathe, the water we drink, the food we eat, and the natural world we live in with the rest of the earth's creatures—the falsehoods fly. In some cases, a politician's rhetoric may be heart-felt, but in other cases it may merely be spin, covering up for the fact that the politician is willing to sacrifice what is good for the environment and the general populace for a narrower benefit, such as the interests of his big campaign contributors. But there is a little-talked-about reason that politicians sometimes lie to us about environmental issues: We can't handle the truth.

Yes, those are the famous words uttered by Jack Nicholson's Colonel Jessup in the movie "A Few Good Men." The concept was that we, the general public, are either unable to stomach certain aspects of reality or are happier being blissfully ignorant. In the case of the environment, most politicians don't want to address issues of pollution, global warming, the deteriorating web of life, the growing piles of nuclear waste, farm-animal welfare, invasive species, habitat loss, species extinction, and ever-increasing levels of human population on the planet. But why not? Each politician may have his or her reasons for stating untruths or lying by omission. Many may see the real solutions to some environmental issues as too complicated to explain to us unwashed masses, or they may view the solutions as striking at the heart of the American way of life and, therefore, political suicide to bring up.

There is some truth to both of these notions. The facets of our existence that are wasteful or unsustainable are indeed threatened by sensible solutions. But the proper explanation of issues and solutions can't easily be distilled down to 60-second sound bites, and politicians know that's about all the attention they can expect from us in these days of hyper-busy lives and hair-trigger channel changing. If we are disengaged as voters, we can't really expect politicians to talk to us as though we were paying close attention.

UNIT-II

Tsunami

Tsunami

A tsunami (pronounced su-nah-me) is a wave train, or series of waves, generated in a body of water by an impulsive disturbance that vertically displaces the water column. Earthquakes, landslides, volcanic eruptions, explosions, and even the impact of cosmic bodies, such as meteorites, can generate tsunamis. Tsunamis can savagely attack coastlines, causing devastating property damage and loss of life.

What does "Tsunami" Mean?

Tsunami is a Japanese word with the English translation, "harbor wave." Represented by two characters, the top character, "tsu," means harbor, while the bottom character, "nami," means "wave." In the past, tsunamis were sometimes referred to as "tidal waves" by the general public, and as "seismic sea waves" by the scientific community.

The term "tidal wave" is a misnomer; although a tsunami's impact upon a coastline is dependent upon the tidal level at the time a tsunami strikes, tsunamis are unrelated to the tides. Tides result from the imbalanced, extraterrestrial, gravitational influences of the moon, sun, and planets.

The term "seismic sea wave" is also misleading. "Seismic" implies an earthquake-related generation mechanism, but a tsunami can also be caused by a non-seismic event, such as a landslide or meteorite impact.

Detection

Each Deep-ocean Assessment and Reporting of Tsunamis (DART) gauge is designed to detect and report tsunamis on its own, without instructions from land. The tsunami detection algorithm in the gauge's software works by first estimating the amplitudes of the pressure fluctuations within the tsunami frequency band and then testing these amplitudes against a threshold value.

The amplitudes are computed by subtracting predicted pressures from the observations, in which the predictions closely match the tides and lower frequency fluctuations. The predictions are updated every 15 seconds, which is the sampling interval of the DART gauges.

Background oceanic noise determines the minimum detection threshold. Based on past observations, a reasonable threshold for the North Pacific is 3 cm (or 30 mm). If the amplitudes exceed the threshold, the gauge goes into a rapid reporting mode to provide detailed information about the tsunami. It remains in this mode for at least four hours.

Form of the Tsunami Detection Algorithm

The tides and lower frequency signals are predicted within a few millimeters using a cubic polynomial that is fit to bottom pressure observations over the past three hours

$H_p(t')= ?\ w(i)\ H\ (t\text{-}idt)$

$i=0$

Where the asterisk denotes 10-min averages and dt = 1 hr. The prediction time t' is set to 5.25 minutes, which is half the 10 minute averaging interval plus the 15-second sampling interval for the gauges. The coefficients w(i) come from Newton's formula (II) for forward extrapolation. Using these temporal parameters, the w-coefficients are:

w(0) = 1.16818457031250

w(1) =-0.28197558593750

w(2) = 0.14689746093750

w(3) =-0.03310644531250

A tsunami is detected if the difference between the observed pressure and the prediction Hp exceeds the prescribed threshold in magnitude (30 mm in the North Pacific).

The gauges could use the most recent pressure observation to test against the prediction. However, the next earlier value is used so that the gauges can screen the pressure values for instrumental spikes that might falsely trip the algorithm. The threshold for these spikes is set at 100 mm.

Theoretical Pressure Series

The application of the algorithm to a theoretical pressure series. The series consists of an M2 tide with an amplitude of one meter and a short pulse that has an amplitude of 5 cm and a duration of 15 minutes. The pulse affects the difference both directly and through its indirect effect on the prediction. Following the first and largest differences, pulses continue to occur each hour with diminishing amplitude until the pulse no longer influences the predictions.

The difference exceeds the threshold at the beginning of the theoretical series. This is due to the mismatch between the time series and the constant values placed initially in the H array. This phenomenon will also occur during field deployments of DART gauges as they fall through the water column toward the bottom. However, the difference will stabilize at sub-threshold values 4-5 hours after the gauges reach the bottom. Then, the H arrays contain only on-bottom pressure values, and the gauges are in thermal equilibrium with the bottom waters. As shown in software flag is set to-1 each time the difference exceeds the threshold. In turn, this exceedance flag controls a reporting flag that puts the DART gauge into its rapid reporting mode. The reporting flag is set to-1 as soon as the threshold is exceeded and remains equal to-1 until four hours has passed since the last time the threshold was exceeded. The gauge then returns to its monitoring mode.

Frequency Response

The pressure difference has a response near unity over the tsunami band, which spans the periods from 2 to 90 minutes.

At lower frequencies, the attenuation increases rapidly with decreasing frequency. Hence, tsunami and higher-frequency signals dominate the pressure difference.

Observed Tsunami

Shows small-amplitude tsunamis observed by internally recording gauges in the North Pacific. Relative to the high-passed data, the background noise in the difference series is either equal in amplitude or slightly enhanced. Neither tsunami is high enough in amplitude to set a DART gauge into rapid reporting mode.

Observed Rayleigh Waves

Shows pressure differences observed at an internally recording pressure gauge in the northern Gulf of Alaska. The two groups of high-frequency fluctuations are seismic Rayleigh waves caused by the 1996 Andreanof Island earthquakes in the Alaska-Aleutian Subduction Zone. The first group was generated by the main shock, while the second was generated by a smaller aftershock that occurred about eleven hours later. A DART gauge would be set into rapid reporting mode by the first group of Rayleigh waves.

Warning Systems

India has developed its own tsunami warning system, barely three years after it was caught off guard when the sea waves spawned by a massive earthquake wreaked havoc along its southern coastline.

The National Early Warning System for Tsunami [Images] and Storm Surges in the Indian Ocean, a project of the Ministry of Earth Sciences, has taken shape at the Indian National Centre for Ocean Information Services (INCOIS) in Hyderabad.

Tsunami warning system by September 2007.

The system is likely to be inaugurated by Earth Sciences Minister Kapil Sibal on October 15.

Scientists last week installed two bottom pressure recorders (BPR), key sensors that indicate the generation of tsunami, off the Gujarat coast in the Arabian Sea.

A set of four BPRs have already been installed in the Bay of Bengal region and were put to test on September 12 when a massive undersea earthquake hit southern Sumatra.

"There are two 'tsunamigenic' zones in our vicinity ýÿ the Andaman-Sumatra trench in the Bay of Bengal and the Makran coast in the Arabian Sea," said INCOIS Director Shailesh Nayak explaining the need to install BPRs in the two regions.

INCOIS, in association with Tata Consultancy Services [Get Quote], has generated simulations of possible 550 scenarios of tsunami after massive earthquakes.

"The information about magnitude, location and depth at which an earthquake has occurred is fed into computers which picks up an appropriate scenario and simulate formation of tsunamis," he said.

"We are able to issue tsunami alerts within 30 minutes of an earthquake," Nayak said.

According to the plan, 12 BPRs, including 10 in the Bay of Bengal, are planned to be installed as part of the network.

Asked how the system would function with only six BPRS, Nayak said: "All critical locations from the point of view of validating tsunami by monitoring sea level changes have been covered."

Twelve BPRs were planned keeping in view the redundancy factor. "In case of a malfunction, we cannot repair the BPRs immediately as they are installed on the sea bed at a depth of few kilometers," he said.

Besides the BPRs, tide gauges installed along the coastline including the Andaman and Nicobar Islands will give further confirmation on generation of tsunami, Nayak said.

INCOIS has been receiving earthquake information from India Meteorological Department, Japan Meteorological Agency and the Pacific Tsunami Warning Centre and also is digitally connected to seismic stations across the world.

"We could validate the September 12 earthquake off southern Sumatra within 12 minutes," Nayak said adding that the tsunami warning centre swung into action and issued an red alert in the next 13 minutes, which was downgraded to orange in less than two hours.

"We did not issue a tsunami warning like the Pacific System, which would have required evacuation of people from coastal areas," he said:

> *A red alert requires the citizens and the administration to be prepared for evacuation and in the event of an orange alert the administration has to remain vigilant. Nayak said the effectiveness of the system was proved in the last high-magnitude undersea earthquakes in the Indian Ocean region.*

Preparedness

The year-end havoc caused by Tsunami tidal waves in India's coastal areas has raised question marks over the country's preparedness to tackle natural disasters of this magnitude. Nearly 15,000 people are reported killed in the Tsunami waves which devastated the Andaman and Nicobar Islands and the coastal areas of Tamil Nadu, Kerala, Andhra Pradesh and Pondicherry.

Even as relief operations were being mounted to provide succour to the large number of people affected by the Tsunami killer waves, which hit the coastline on December 26, panic was created by an entirely unfounded alert of another impending Tsunami strike. The communication triggered a wave of panic in the southern coastal areas and the Andaman and Nicobar islands. Disaster-stricken people fled in panic, disrupting the rescue and relief efforts. The armed forces, acting on the false alert, started mass evacuation on the Nicobar Islands which is one of the areas worst hit by the Tsunami of December 26.

The goof up led to the Opposition attacking the UPA Government for what it called "casual handling of the Tsunami tragedy." The Opposition said that the episode showed poor coordination in the Government where a warning put out by one Ministry (Ministry of Home Affairs) was dismissed by another Ministry (Ministry of Science and Technology) as a rumour. The warning brought relief work in the affected areas to a grinding halt till the confusion ended.

Political Fallout

The political fallout of the goof up led to the summoning of the Science and Technology Minister by UPA Chairperson Sonia Gandhi. Though none of the Ministers talked to the Press later, sources in the Congress admitted that an explanation was indeed sought by 10 Janpath. The Congress, of course, downplayed the controversy with party spokesman Abhishek Singhvi dismissing the suggestion of a "row involving Shivraj Patil and Kapil Sibal" as incorrect.

Defending both the Ministers, Singhvi said : "In the face of such a gigantic disaster, it is entirely possible that the Home Ministry would have certain apprehensions and projections based on various inputs, which eventually did not turn out to be true-given the elements of prediction and chance, the error was bona fide." Singhvi said Sibal (Science and Technology Minister) did not run down the Home Ministry over the false Tsunami alarm. "When it was ascertained that the warning was unfounded, Sibal refuted it to allay any further panic."

Institutional Arrangements for Disaster Management

The crisis created by the unwarranted alert is all the more regrettable as the Government of India had put in place a new approach to disaster management after the devastation caused by the supercyclone in Orissa in October 1999 and the Bhuj earthquake in Gujarat, in January 2001. These disasters had underscored the need to adopt a multi-dimensional endeavour involving diverse scientific, engineering, financial and social processes. It included the adoption of a multi-disciplinary and multi-sectoral approach and incorporation of risk reduction in the developmental plans and strategies.

The new approach to disaster management proceeds from the conviction that development cannot be sustainable unless disaster mitigation is built into the development process. Another corner stone of the approach is that mitigation has to be multi-disciplinary spanning all sectors of development. The new policy emanates from the belief that investments in mitigation are much more cost effective than expenditure on relief and rehabilitation.

Disaster management occupies an important place in the country's policy framework as it is the poor and the under-privileged who are worst affected on account of calamities/ disasters.

The approach has been translated into a National Disaster Framework (a road map) covering institutional mechanisms, disaster prevention strategy, early warning system, disaster mitigation, preparedness and response and human resource development. The expected inputs, areas of intervention and agencies to be involved at the National, State and district levels have been identified and listed in the road map.

Ministries and Departments of Government of India, and the State Governments and Union Territory Administrations have been advised to develop their respective road maps taking the national road map as a broad guideline. There is, therefore, now a common strategy underpinning the action being taken by all the participating organisations/stakeholders.

The States have also been asked to set up Disaster Management Authorities under the Chief Minister with Ministers of relevant Departments (Water Resources, Agriculture, Drinking Water Supply, Environment & Forests, Urban Development, Home, Rural Development etc.) as members. 10 States and Union Territories-Tamil Nadu, Arunachal Pradesh, Uttaranchal, Orissa, Gujarat, Kerala, Nagaland, Delhi, Andaman and Nicobar Administration and Chandigarh Administration have notified the authority. The other States are in the process of setting up similar authorities.

India not Part of the Tsunami Warning System

Another fact which came to light was that lives could have been saved if India had been a member of the Tsunami Warning System. Within 15 minutes of the earthquake which led to the Tsunami deluge in several Asian countries, scientists running the Tsunami Warning System of the Pacific had issued a cautionary from their Honolulu hub to 26 participating countries. India was not among them.

The Tsunami warning by Honolulu stated : "Revised magnitude based on analysis of mantle waves (8.5). This earthquake is located outside the Pacific. No destructive Tsunami threat exists for the Pacific Basin. There is the possibility of a Tsunami near the epicentre."

The last part of the warning was crucial to India as it was this very "possible Tsunami" that ravaged the east coast.

The irony could not have been sharper. For, one of the people who helped set up the Pacific Tsunami Warning System three decades ago was a Canada-based Indian, Tad Murty, now attached to the University of Manitoba, Winnipeg.

Tad had approached the Indian Government several times for setting up a Tsunami Warning System for the country, but New Delhi had said that funds were not available for the purpose. They probably thought that there was very little likelihood of Tsunami striking Indian coasts.

All Party Meeting to Discuss the Tragedy

The principal opposition party, the BJP, has assured its support to the Government in its efforts to provide relief to the victims of the Tsunami. Former Prime Minister Atal Bihari Vajpayee and leader of the Opposition L.K. Advani met the Prime Minister to discuss the aftermath of the disaster. Dr. Manmohan Singh has called an all party meeting in which various issues pertaining to disaster management and relief work will be discussed. The meeting is likely to be held in a couple of days.

The Prime Minister as well as the UPA Chairperson Sonia Gandhi have toured several of the Tsunami affected areas to oversee the relief and rescue operations. The Prime Minister has announced a cash compensation of Rs.250 crores to Tamil Nadu and Rs. 100 crores to Andhra Pradesh for relief and rehabilitation of the victims. The next of kin of those who lost their lives in the tragedy are to be given an ex-gratia amount of rupees one lakh each. The Housing and Urban Development Corporation, HUDCO, has set apart Rs.10,000 crores for the reconstruction of damaged houses in the affected areas.

The nation celebrated the dawn of the New Year on a subdued note because of the Tsunami disaster. The President,

Dr. A.P.J. Abdul Kalam donated the money meant for New Year celebrations to Tsunami victims. "All the money which was slated for New Year celebration has been given to the Prime Minister's Relief Fund", said Press Secretary to the President. It has also been announced that the country's Tsunami Forecasting System would be linked to the Pacific Warning System to make it more effective.

Reports are still being received spelling out the damage caused by the Tsunami waves to the country's coastline. Indira Point, India's southernmost edge, has almost been washed off. he 100 sq. kilometre island, just 140 km. from Sumatra, and 51 km. from Campbell Bay, appears to have borne the full force of the Tsunami.

Luckily, the Government has allayed fears relating to the Kalappakam Atomic Power Station, near Chennai. Sixty-one people were killed in the vicinity of the station, but the reactors and basic capacities of the plant remained safe. According to National Security Advisor J.N. Dixit, there is no radiation whatsoever at the atomic power station. The station is likely to be put back on stream shortly.

Island Tribes Safe

After fears about the fate of the small tribes in the Andaman and Nicobar islands after the Tsunami, the Centre on December 31 said that reports till then indicated no indigenous tribes have been wiped out.

The region-particularly the Nicobar group-is nearest to the epicentre, Sumatra, of Tsunami earthquake. Some of the smaller islands appeared totally submerged and there were fears that a few of them might not be seen again.

Similar fears were expressed about the tribes with minuscule population. Apart from the massive loss of lives, an ethnographic disaster had been predicted. The Government says that it had been able to establish contact with four primitive tribes in the Andaman and Nicobar islands. A special relief package is being prepared by the Union Tribal Affairs Ministry and will be announced soon. A team from the Ministry will visit the islands for a thorough assessment of the damage.

According to the Ministry, the fate of the 100-strong Shompens, who live in Campbell Bay, and the Sentinelese, inhabitants of North Sentinel island, is not known. All bridges to these areas have been washed away and the areas have to be surveyed by boats. The Jarawas, who inhabit the Middle Andaman, are unlikely to be affected because they live on hilly terrain and forest areas and the Andamanese live on a bigger land mass, the Strait Island. A Ministry spokesman said that food was being sent to the Andamanese, and 40 or so Onges had been rescued. The Onges-only 100 in number-live in Dugong Creek and efforts are on to trace the others.

Precautions

Children who live on the streets like to do what they feel like that moment. Within a few days of coming on the street they find that they can get meals free in various parts of the city and they can earn enough to purchase their meagre needs or watch movies which is their reigning passion. They travel where they wish to go, they either go by themselves or with a friend, and since they travel ticketless through the whole city.

The main occupation of almost all children is scavenging. Children walk from one end of the city to the other and collect paper, plastic and sell these and make money

1. How would you treat a person who is electrocuted?
    - Cut off power supply
    - Remove the victim using non-conducting material
    - Carry out DRABC
    - Cover the affected area with clean dressing
    - Seek medical help
2. What are the precautions to be taken in case of snakebite?
    - Keep the bitten limb below the level of the heart, check DRABC
    - Allow the area to bleed freely for 15-30 seconds
    - Wash the affected area with soap and disinfectant
    - Treat it with a pressure immobilization bandage

3. What are the signs and symptoms of fractures and sprains?
   - Pain at or near the area of injury
   - Movement may be difficult or impossible
   - Swelling and bruising of the injured part
   - Deformity at the site of fracture
4. What is a heat stroke? What are its signs and symptoms?
   - When the body's cooling system fails and body temperature rises it is known as Heat stroke
   - Body temperature is very high
   - Body becomes dry
   - Skin becomes red with no sweating
   - Fast pulse rate and dilated pupils
5. What is ORS? How is it useful?
   - ORS is Oral Rehydration Solution
   - It is a mixture of water and a pinch of salt and sugar
   - It is useful when a person suffers from dehydration due to vomiting, heat stroke etc.It helps in restoring electrolytic balance in our body and rehydrate the body
6. If bitten by a dog, how can we reduce the risk of infection?
   - Wipe the saliva away from the wound using a clean cloth
   - Wash the wound thoroughly with plenty of soap and water
   - Cover the wound with dry sterile dressing
   - Get medical aid as soon as possible
7. Describe the composition of a rescue team.
   - They must be honest, emotionally sound, and decisive and have good physical condition
   - Have capacity and willingness to work in an emergency
   - They must be above 18 years and min. education
   - Preference is given to ex-military or army personnel

Survival Skills

Survival skills are techniques a person may use for an indefinite duration in order to survive a dangerous situation (also see bushcraft). Generally speaking, these techniques are meant to provide the basic necessities for human life: fire, water, food, shelter, habitat, and the needs to think straight, to signal for help, to navigate safely, to avoid unpleasant interactions with animals and plants, and for first aid. In addition, survival skills are often basic ideas and abilities that ancient humans had to use for thousands of years, so these skills are partially a reenactment of history. Many of these skills are the ways to enjoy extended periods of time in remote places, or a way to thrive in nature. Some people use these skills to better appreciate nature and for recreation, not just survival.

Such skills are presented as useful in situations such as storms or earthquakes or in dangerous locations such as desert, mountains, and jungle. Every different situation or location is said to present a different range of dangers-(see hazards of outdoor activities). Techniques to fit most situations are suggested by sources on the topic.

Secondary sources on survival skills, including those produced by the United States Army, and the Boy Scouts of America (priorities for an individual or group in a survival situation), formulate lists of needs to be met in order to survive.

The needs for survival are differently conceptualized between sources; they may give six, or seven, or ten "needs" or "priorities." Furthermore, those sources often differ as to the relative priority of survival needs in a given survival situation. Some sources expressly acknowledge what seems manifest: that the order of priority of survival needs shifts according to the immediate situation faced.

One widely circulated concept to help set priorities is called the "Rule of Three": Employed a mnemonic device, the Rule of Three states:

1. Humans cannot survive more than three hours exposed to extreme low-temperature.

2. Humans cannot survive more than three days without water.
3. Humans cannot survive more than three weeks without food.

The Rule of Three is often otherwise formulated and is viewed by commentators as a rough guide. An aircrew reportedly lasted 8 days without water in a liferaft. People have survived without food for over twenty-one days.

The Boy Scouts, in addition to listing seven priorities, use a mnemonic device, "STOP", to address the mental aspects of survival. "STOP" stands for "Stop, Think, Observe, Plan."

Shelter

Airmen of the United States Air Force construct a survival shelter during Arctic Survival Training in Alaska.

Shelter is any thing that protects a person from his/her environment, including dangerous cold and heat and allow restful sleep, another human need.

Shelter ranges from natural shelter such as a cave or thickly-foliaged tree, to intermediate forms of man-made shelter such as a debris shelter or a snow cave, to completely man-made structures such as a tarp, tent, house, or clothing.

Fire

The ability to start a controlled fire is recognized in the sources as to significantly increase the ability to survive. The skills required to light a fire without a lighter or matches, such as by using natural flint and steel with tinder, is a frequent subject of both books on survival and in survival courses. There is an emphasis placed on practicing fire-making skills before venturing into the wilderness.

Fire is presented as a tool meeting many survival needs. The heat provided by a fire allows the body to be warmed, wet clothes to be dried, water to be disinfected, and food to be cooked. Not to be overlooked is the psychological boost and the sense of safety and protection it gives. Fire may deter wild animals from interfering with the survivor, or wild animals may be attracted to the light and heat of a fire. The light and smoke emitted by a fire can also be used to work at night and can signal rescue units.

Water

A human being can survive an average of three days without the intake of water, assuming sea-level altitude, room temperature and favorable relative humidity.[In colder or warmer temperatures, the need for water is greater. Need for water also increases with exercise.

A typical person will lose 2-3 litres of water per day under ordinary conditions, and more in hot, dry, or cold weather. Four to six litres of water or other liquids are generally required each day in the wilderness to avoid dehydration and to keep the body functioning properly. The U.S. Army survival manual recommends that you drink water whenever thirsty. Other groups recommend rationing water through "water discipline".

A lack of water causes dehydration, which may result in lethargy, headaches, dizziness, confusion, and eventually death. Even mild dehydration reduces endurance and impairs concentration, which is dangerous in a survival situation where clear thinking is essential. Dark yellow or brown urine is a diagnostic indicator of dehydration. To avoid dehydration, a high priority is typically assigned to locating a supply of drinking water and making provision to render that water as safe as possible. Many sources in survival literature, as well as forums and online references, list the ways in which water may be gathered and rendered safer for consumption in a survival situation, such as boiling, filtering, chemicals, solar radiation + heat/SODIS, and distillation. Such sources also often list the dangers, such as pollutants, microorganisms, or pathogens which affect the safety of backcountry water.

Recent thinking is that boiling or commercial filters are significantly safer than use of chemicals, with the exception of chlorine dioxide.

The issues presented by the need for water dictate that unnecessary water loss by perspiration be avoided in survival situations.

Food

Most commentators note that food is not usually urgently needed in survival situations because a human can survive for several weeks without it. However, they also note that in extreme cold lack of food can be dangerous, and in other situations hunger, like gradual dehydration, can bring about many consequences long before it causes death, such as:

- Irritability and low morale
- Weakness
- Loss of mental clarity, such as confusion, disorientation, or poor judgment
- Weakened immune system
- Increasing difficulty maintaining body temperature (see Heat exhaustion and Hypothermia)

Many commentators discuss the knowledge, skills, and equipment (such as bows, snares and nets) necessary to gather animal food in the wild through animal trapping, hunting, fishing, and how to gather plant food to maintain a balanced diet. Some survival books promote the "Universal Edibility Test". Allegedly, one can distinguish edible foods from toxic ones by a series of progressive exposures to skin and mouth prior to ingestion, with waiting periods and checks for symptoms. However, many other experts including Ray Mears and John Kallas reject this method, stating that even a small amount of some "potential foods" can cause physical discomfort, illness, or death. An additional step called the scratch test is sometimes included to evaluate the edibility of a potential food.

Focusing on survival until rescued by presumed searchers, The Boy Scouts of America especially discourages foraging for wild foods on the grounds that the knowledge and skills needed are unlikely to be possessed by those finding themselves in a wilderness survival situation, making the risks (including use of energy) outweigh the benefits.

First Aid

First aid (wilderness first aid in particular) can help a person survive and function with injuries and illnesses that would otherwise kill or incapacitate him/her. Common and dangerous injuries include:

- Lacerations, which may become infected
- Bites or stings from venomous animals, such as: snakes, scorpions, spiders, bees, stingrays, jellyfish, catfish, stargazers, etc.
- Bites leading to disease/septicemia, such as: mosquitoes, fleas, ticks, animals infected with rabies, sand flies, komodo dragons, crocodilians, etc.
- Infection through food, animal contact, or drinking non-potable water
- Bone fractures
- Sprains, particularly of the ankle
- Burns
- Poisoning from consumption of, or contact with, poisonous plants or poisonous fungi.
- Hypothermia (too cold) and hyperthermia (too hot)
- Heart attack
- Hemorrage

The survivor may need to apply the contents of a first aid kit or, if possessing the required knowledge, naturally-occurring medicinal plants, immobilize injured limbs, or even transport incapacitated comrades.

Navigation

These two pictures of the same tree trunk in the Northern Hemisphere are an example of a navigational terrain feature. The left picture shows the northern side of a trunk, where darker and more humid micro climatic conditions favour moss growth. The right picture is south, with sunnier and drier conditions, less favourable for moss growth.

Survival situations are sometimes resolved by finding one's way to safety, or one may need to move to find a more suitable location to wait for rescue. The sources observe that to do either of these safely requires some navigation equipment and skills. Types of navigation include:

- Celestial navigation, using the sun and the night sky to locate the cardinal directions and to maintain course of travel
- Using a map and compass together, particularly a topographic map
- "Navigation by observation" of terrain features on a map or otherwise known
- Using a GPS receiver, if one is available

Communication Systems

Importance of Communication During Disasters

During any major disaster or emergency situation, the communication links are totally disrupted. Therefore it is crucial to have functional communication links among government authorities at various levels to provide adequate

Assistance to the Affected Population

Modes for emergency communication:

Radio communications:

- During these emergencies any wireless communication link based on the radio waves using the terrestrial or satellite systems.
  1. Amateur (HAM) radio—As amateur radio operation does not use the ground –based infrastructure, has limited power requirements it can be successfully used when no other communication works.
  2. Wireless sets—electronic machines which send message in sound, especially over long distance by radio-waves around the earth

Satellite based Communication Systems: Satellites are launched in different orbits for different applications-

- *Geo-stationary Orbit Satellites:* These satellites are positioned at typically around 36000 km above the equator and they remain stationary above the earth.
- *Asynchronous Orbit Satellites:* They are positioned in the lower orbits around the earth they continuously change their position with respect to earth.

Question Bank

Q.1. Mention the prime communication network of government of India.

- National Informatics Centre
- Bharath Sanchar Nigam Limited

Q.2. What is Amateur radio communication? How does it work?

- It implies the use of radio communications for non-commercial purposes
- It works under a special set of rules, which apply, to certain frequencies as defined by the International Telecommunication Union (ITU) AND REGULATED BY Wireless Planning and Coordination Wing.

Q.3. Why Amateur (HAM) radio can work successfully during any kind of natural calamity?

As Amateur radio operation does not use the ground-based infrastructure, and has limited power requirements it can be successfully used during any kind of natural calamity.

Q.4. What is meant by alternative communication system? Give examples.

During an emergency, the normal communication likes are disrupted and damaged. Power supply is also disrupted.

In such situations for emergency communications we need other reliable sources of communication. Such Sources are known as alternative communicationsystem. They include wireless radio communication, HAM radio, Satellite phones etc.

Q.5. Discuss the importance of wireless radio communication in an emergency.

- Wireless radio communication network is limited to the region of operation. It is based on the radio waves either making use of the satellite or terrestrial systems. It is comparatively easy to install and operate .It can be easily installed and very useful in relief works.

Q.6. What makes the satellite based communication systems more reliable in case of large-scale emergencies?

— Communication satellites being established in space are not affected by disasters on earth.

— Small portable and easy to install satellite antennas can easily establish global links.

— Information can be send very fast in any part of the world

— They can help effectively in early warning of disasters.

Sharing Responsibilities

1. Who form the village level disaster management committee?
   - The sarpanch –village headman (pradhan) as chairman and
   - Members from community, students, youths, NGO'S, and panchayat representatives
2. Who constitute the district level disaster management committee?
   - District magistrate as chairman
   - Health deptt, irrigation deptt. Veterinary deptt. Water sanitation deptt.. Police and fire services.
   - Representatives from national and international NGO'S
2. What are the functions of district administration in disaster management?
   - District administration plays an imp. Role in managing disasters
   - They help by early warning systems, relief distribution, medical assistance and shelter to victims.
3. Who are the standard bodies for disaster management at central level?
   - Union cabinet headed by the prime minister
   - Group of ministers (GOM) HEADED BY THE PM
   - National crisis management committee (NCMC)

4. What function does the UNDMT perform?
   - To respond effectively when required
   - To implement disaster preparedness
   - To mitigate the ill effects of any disaster
   - To strengthen government capacities effectively
5. What are the aims of civil defence in disaster management?
   - Civil defence embraces the whole society including all services
   - A holistic approach is applied to use resources created
   - It aims at saving life and minimizing damage
   - Maintaining continuity of industrial production

Government Agencies

The Tata Institute of Social Sciences (TISS) completed an assessment of loss to lives, property, livelihoods, environment and infrastructure; rehabilitation and development needs; and psychosocial counseling with affected women and children in Tamil Nadu. This assessment covered about 100,000 families in 279 villages spread over 11 tsunami-affected districts and was done in collaboration with 29 Colleges of Social Work in Tamil Nadu, involving about 1,500 post-graduate student volunteers and over 100 teachers.

Village-specific reports, along with data, are being provided to government and non-government agencies engaged in reconstruction and rehabilitation work. The TISS proposes long-term involvement in the villages selected by the Tata Relief Committee for housing and livelihood rehabilitation. Possible areas of support are facilitating community participation in decision-making; implementation of housing and livelihood programmes; psychosocial support; and other initiatives.

In the Andaman & Nicobar Islands, most islands in the Nicobar area were devastated by the tsunami waves. The Institute was involved in relief work in Katchal Island, following whichit carried out an assessment of resources and livelihoods affected by the tsunami in Car Nicobar, Nancowry Group of Islands, and Katchal Island. This was carried out in collaboration with the National Institute of Disaster Management, Government of India; and Pondicherry University. The TISS's long-term plan in this area includes provision of psychosocial recovery support to affected people in two islands — Katchal and Teressa.

The Institute is also collaborating with Butterflies, a child rights organisation, for conducting a training programme on child rights-based development work in the Islands. It aims at training the youth from the affected community with basic knowledge, attitudes and skills to work for the community's development with specific focus on child rights. Further, the TISS will work to create a cadre of development workers in each of these islands by organising training to educated youth in the islands to plan, implement and monitor development and welfare programmes. They will work with the people to link resources available from government and non-government agencies.

Sri Lanka

To support the tsunami-affected people in Sri Lanka, the TISS deputed 5 faculty members over a period of 3 months to train volunteers in psychosocial support and trauma counseling in the affected areas all over the country. In the coming months, the TISS will be deputing 2 faculty members to strengthen Sri Lanka's capacity to provide long-term psychosocial support to women and children, as well as to strengthen institutional capacity to effectively respond to disasters.

Voluntary Organizations

Volunteerism has played important role in human civilization. The people of the north east region especially tribal are seen expanding their voluntarism beyond their periphery and today they have built global network from their areas. After the advent of the Christianity in the north east, the people of north east have picked up the thread of volunteerism with the outside world particularly the Western countries.

Volunteerism is about people helping, learning and actively participating in communities. Volunteerism has no borders. It is a cross-cutting social phenomenon that involves all groups in society and all aspects of human activity. It can take many different forms, depending on cultural and economic realities of countries and communities. The volunteerism is also participation or civic engagement. This refers to the role played by individuals in the governance process, from representation on government consultation bodies to use involvement in local development projects. As a form of volunteering, it is found in all countries, although it is most developed in countries with a strong tradition of civic engagement.

Mutual aid in many parts of the world constitutes the main system of social and economic support. It often plays a primary role in the welfare of communities in developing countries, from small informal kinship and clan groupings to more formal associations and welfare groups. It also plays an important role in industrialized countries, particularly in the health and social welfare field, providing support and assistance to those in need. Philanthropy or service to others is distinguished from mutual aid in that the primary recipient of the volunteering is not the member of the group him or herself, but an external third party, although most people would acknowledge that philanthropy includes an element of self-interest. This type of volunteering takes place typically within voluntary or community organizations, although in certain countries there is strong tradition of volunteering within the public sector and a growing interest in volunteering in the corporate sector. There is also longstanding tradition of volunteers being sent from one country to another to offer development and humanitarian assistance, both North to South and South to South.

Advocacy or campaigning is also a form of volunteerism which may be a change in legislation affecting the right of people with disabilities, or introduction of anti-discrimination measures. Through advocacy and campaigning, volunteers have paved the way for the introduction of new welfare services in the field of HIV/AIDS, have raised public consciousness about human rights and the environment and have been active in the women's movement.

Voluntarism is an ancient and global phenomenon. Since the beginning of civilization, a fundamental human value has been people helping people and, in the process, helping themselves. Most cultures have names to describe it: Baranguay in the Philippines ; benevolat and volontariat in France ; gotong royong in Indonesia ; harambee in Kenya ; shrmadana in India; mingu in Andean countries; and al taawun wal tawasul in many Arab States. The act is familiar even where the word "volunteer' is not. Volunteerism is strongly influenced by the history, politics, religion and culture of communities. What may be valued as volunteerism in one country may be dismissed as low-paid or labour-intensive work in another. Despite the wide variety of understandings, it is possible to identify some core characteristics of what constitutes voluntary activity.

India is yet to formulate legal framework and still many voluntary organizations in the country and hundreds in the north east have been receiving foreign aids, most of the time directly from the donors. Thus, in the absence of a clear legal definition of what constitutes voluntary work and a volunteer, some laws and regulations can inadvertently have an impact on voluntary action. States should pay careful attention to the way in which international and domestic regulations can affect volunteerism in their country. The Ministry of External Affairs has recently notified that all the funds coming from foreign countries to voluntary organizations whether Governmental or Non-Governmental Organizations in the country should be properly screened by the Ministry and they should accordingly apply for approval.

Numerous Voluntary organizations including Christian ones are mushrooming in the region; many of them are purely for monetary benefits. Voluntary activity is not undertaken primarily for financial reward. It is undertaken voluntarily, according to an individual's own free will. Voluntary activity brings benefits to people other than the volunteer, although it is recognized that volunteering brings significant benefit to volunteers as well. It is high time to check such bogus Voluntary Organizations.

UNIT-III

Strategies and Management

Meaning

According to the Indian National Disaster Management Act 2005, disaster management means a continuous and integrated process of planning, organizing, coordinating and implementing measures which are necessary or expedient for (1) prevention of danger or threat of any disaster (2)mitigation or reduction of risk of any disaster or its severity or consequences (3) capacity building (4)preparedness to deal with any disaster (5) prompt response to any threatening disaster situation or disaster (6)assessing severity or magnitude of effects of any disaster (7) evacuation rescue and relief and (8) rehabilitation and reconstruction. The High Powered Committee defined Disaster Management as "a collective term encompassing all aspects of planning for and responding to disasters, including both pre and post disaster activities. It may refer to the management of both the risks and consequences of disasters". Clearly the term management has emerged as an umbrella term that encompasses the entire disaster cycle, including mitigation. This needs careful noting and wide spread awareness because traditionally the term management was restrictively used to address only post disaster operations. Unless the old mindsets get changed, the cause of disaster mitigation will continue to suffer at the hands of traditional disaster managers.

Disaster Mitigation

According to the Indian Act 2005, "mitigation means measures aimed at reducing the risk, impact or effects of a disaster or a threatening disaster situation". There is the urgent need to ensure that disaster mitigation strategies get enmeshed and integrated with the very development process.

Strategies—Four Phases of Activities

The Unesco programme on Man and the Biosphere (MAB) brought together an expert panel in Salzburg, Austria, in 1973 to discuss the impact of human activities on mountain ecosystems. As a part of the final report of the discussions the panel characterised mountain regions as those in which there exists an altitudinal gradient of barometric pressure, radiation, temperature and precipitation. This gradient results in vertical zonation of soils, flora, fauna and ecosystem types. Accordingly, man's way of life, his habitat and land ways and exploitation patterns, are differentiated vertically (Unesco 1973).

The Unesco project and many other initiatives such as the symposium on Himalayan, Andean and Alpine mountain ecosystems organised by the American Anthropological Association in 1973 and published in *Human Ecology*, the Munich Conference on Development Problems in Mountain Environments, 1974, IUCN'S Conference on the Management of High Mountain Resources, held in Christchurch, New Zealand, in 1976, the International Symposium on the Earth Sciences, Ecology, and Ethnology of the Himalayas at Paris (CNRS, 1977), the United Nations University Project on Highland-Lowland Interaction Systems in 1978, the inauguration of the International Centre for Integrated Mountain Development (ICIMOD) in Kathmandu in 1983 under the aegis of Unesco, and so on, were a response to the expression of great concern in the late 1950s and 1960s about progressive environmental degradation and the realisation that 'all is not well in the mountain regions of the world' (Ives 1985).

There was a spate of studies of Alpine, circum-Alpine, Andean and Himalayan mountain ecosystems during the past three decades, with growing interest in mountain environments and the human populations inhabiting them. Most of these studies were focused on the subsistence strategies employed by mountain inhabitants for survival in rugged and inhospitable regions.

Despite the strenuous and hazardous conditions, the mountains have a mystical attraction for humankind, so much so that a sizeable number, adding up to a tenth of the world's population, lives in the mountain regions. The Himalaya are the most popular and are inhabited by nearly 120 million people over a 2,500 km stretch from Afghanistan to Myanmar.

Because of this demographic reality and because of the distinctive subsistence strategies of mountain populations, their comparative and analytical study became a major focus of attention (Brush *et al.* 1974; Rhoades *et al.* 1975; Hoffpauir 1978; Goldstein and Messerschmidt 1980; Guillet 1983). Most of these studies were in agreement with the vertical zonation of life support resources in mountain ecosystems as underlined by the Unesco project. However, since most studies were undertaken in the Nepal Himalaya, so far as the Himalayan ecosystem is concerned mention must be made of the pioneering study of Pant (1935) and recently that of Nitya Nand and Kumar (1989) in the Uttarakhand region of the Indian Himalaya. S.D. Pant's *Social Economy of the Himalayans* is, as a matter of fact, a path-breaking endeavour employing the ecosystem approach in analysing the subsistence strategies of the people inhabiting the Kumaon region.

It has generally been recognised that the basic characteristic of mountain life is the vertical stratification of life support resources with immense altitudinal and seasonal variations. Life sustenance therefore is totally dependent on successful adaptation to the mountain environment. Mountain populations have apparently responded with efficient utilisation of resources in conformity with altitudinal variations and the annual cycle of seasonality. The main feature of mountain life thus emerges as adaptation to the constraints of the environment, through time and space, with the application of indigenous ecological knowledge.

However, increasing awareness of the fragility of mountain ecosystems highlighted by a series of ecological disasters the world over, in which human intervention may create serious resource degeneration, have raised apprehensions about the well-being and survival of mountain populations and their immediate neighbours. In recent years serious environmental degradation of the Himalayan ecosystem and fears of impending disaster have drawn worldwide attention. In this connection two publications, Eric Eckholm's *Losing Ground* (1976) and John Lall's *The Himalaya: Aspects of Change* (1981), specially the former, have had a popular impact the world over. Eckholm, with the support of Dr Maurice Strong and World Watch, made a challenging and emotional appeal to the effect that the world's mountains, and especially the Himalaya, were facing imminent catastrophe.

This, recently reinforced by Sandra Nichols' spectacular film *The Fragile Mountain*, has become standard news media fare, to such an extent that we have almost come to expect the collapse of Nepal and of much of the Himalayan system by AD 2000, with devastating consequences for the teeming millions of the Indo-Gangetic plain (Ives 1985 in Tejvir Singh and Jagdish, eds.).

There is no doubt that human intervention resulting in large-scale deforestation, leading in turn to depletion and degeneration of life support resources, is the main cause, but what is ironical is that the mountain inhabitants are the prime suspects in bringing it about. A set of pet assumptions, the chief being that uncontrolled population growth in the Himalaya induces deforestation for the procurement of fuelwood and the expansion of subsistence agricultural land, point an accusing finger towards the mountain inhabitants, completely disregarding the fact that commercial exploitation in the wake of the industrial revolution in the West is the major culprit in deforestation all over the world, including mountain ecosystems.

The 'fact' that the 'growing demand for fuelwood induced by population growth' in the Himalaya 'is the cause of deforestation' is rather astonishing in view of a small observation made by Nitya Nand and Kumar (1989) that in 1976-78 timber production in Garhwal was 3.05 million cubic metres whereas fuelwood collection during the same period was 0.8 lakh cubic metres. It is to be noted that timber production (commercial activity) is from cutting fully grown trees whereas fuelwood collection (subsistence activity) is only from dead wood, branches and twigs. No tree is ever cut down just for the procurement of fuelwood.

Now the question arises, how are the altitudinally differentiated vertical life zones in mountain ecosystems integrated by mountain populations in the adaptation of alternative subsistence strategies for resource utilisation? Is there any built-in mechanism, developed over generations of living in the mountains, directed towards the regeneration and conservation of resources? An attempt is made here to address these questions by examining the subsistence strategies in a micro situation in the Garhwal Himalaya.

Four Process Phases

The Unified Process consists of cycles that may repeat overthe long-term life of a system. A cycle consists of four phases: Inception, Elaboration, Construction and Transition. Each cycle is concluded with a release, there are also releases within a cycle. Let's briefly review the four phases in a cycle:

Inception Phase : During the inception phase the core idea is developed into a product vision. In this phase, we review and confirm our understanding of the core business drivers. We want to understand the business case for why the project should be attempted. The inception phase establishes the product feasibility and delimits the project scope.

Elaboration Phase : During the elaboration phase the majority of the Use Cases are specified in detail and the system architecture is designed. This phase focuses on the "Do-Ability" of the project. We identify significant risks and prepare a schedule, staff and cost profile for the entire project.

Construction Phase : During the construction phase the product is moved from the architectural baseline to a system complete enough to transition to the user community. The architectural baseline grows to become the completed system as the design is refined into code.

Transition Phase : In the transition phase the goal is to ensure that the requirements have been met to the satisfaction of the stakeholders. This phase is often initiated with a beta release of the application. Other activities include site preparation, manual completion, and defect identification and correction. The transition phase ends with a postmortem devoted to learning and recording lessons for future cycles.

Risk Assessment

Definition

A major emergency in industry is one, which has the potential to cause serious injury or loss of life. It may cause extensive damage to property and serious disruption in work inside and outside the premises. It would normally require the assistance of emergency services to handle it effectively.

It must be realized that any incident may develop into a major emergency even with the best safety measures and programmes in any industry. Hence an emergency preparedness should be planned properly and documented for ease of implementation at the time of need without loosing time and avoiding. Chaos and confusion etc. at the hour of the need by assigning specific responsibilities to persons, who will render services in meeting emergency smoothly and effectively.

Scope

An important element of mitigation is emergency planning, i.e. recognizing that accidents are possible, assessing the consequences of such accidents and deciding on the emergency procedures, both on-site and off site, that would need to be implemented in the event of an emergency:-

- To protect mines personnel and nearby private citizens.
- To prevent or minimize damage of property or the environment.
- To render help to the person at site to provide him relief.
- To restore the affected area as soon as possible.
- To review incident to evaluate and strengthen the emergency management response for future emergencies.

Objective

The objectives of DMP is to describe the company's emergency preparedness organization, the resource availability and response actions applicable to deal with various types of emergencies that could occur at the mines with organization structure being deployed in shortest time possible during the emergency. Thus the overall objectives of the emergency plan are summarized as:

(a) Rapid control and containment of Hazardous situation.

(b) Minimizing the Risk and impact of event/accident.

(c) Effective prevention of damage to property.

In order to achieve effectively the objectives of emergency planning, the critical elements that form the backbone of Disaster Management Plan (DMP) are:

a. Reliable and early detection of an emergency and immediate careful planning.

b. The command, co-ordination and response organization structure along with availability of efficient trained personnel.

c. The availability of resources for handling emergencies.

d. Appropriate emergency response action.

e. Effective notification and communication facilities.

f. Regular review and updating of DMP.

g. Protect training of the concerned personnel.

Minimizing the effects may include rescue, first aid, evacuation, rehabilitation and giving information promptly to people living nearby and scrutinized information's to media.

Identification of Hazards

The following types of Hazards are identified at Limestone Mines:

a) Fire in HEMM, Electric Panels, Oil room, Diesel storage and near magazine.

b) Inundation in rainy season due to seasonal Nallah and barrier gets breached or when impermeable barriers are removed.

c) Failure of slope of benches giving rise to slide of material on bench.

The Manal Limestone Mines of Cement Corporation of India Ltd. is an opencast mines operating on slopes of hill with multiple benches with overall pit slope of 45 O. This risk of slope failure is there subject to stratigraphic disposition of various rock formation coupled with prevailing hydrological conditions & pit design. Yes, the case of fire in equipment could be a possibility and for which emergency plan must be prepared and this be controlled to quench it immediately at the source itself and not to allow it to spread. The relief to the person who might be inside the machines or standing close by is also to be considered along with revival of machines & preventing fire to spread further.

However a team of trained persons must be kept in readiness all the time, who can deal not only with fire emergency but also other emergencies if arise inside mines or off site emergency of any sort. So to deal the above emergencies, the Emergency Plan is prepared.

Responsibility

The responsibility for establishing and maintaining DMP updated is of Head (Personnel and Administration) who is also nominated as liaison officer. He is responsible for preparation of the DMP and for ensuring that the plan and the applicable implementing procedures are reviewed and revised periodically.

Head (P&A) is also responsible for training of personnel to ensure that the adequate emergency response capabilities are maintained in accordance with the plan. He is further responsible for ensuring the adequacy of conducting mock drills outlined in DMP.

Head (Mines) is responsible for co-ordination jobs with various site mangers and through him with the emergency team members for morale boosting and better co-ordination and liaison with district and tehsil level Government Officers for seeking as well as rendering services for ON-SITE AND OFF-SITE DISASTER MANAGEMENT as may be required Prevention, Preparedness and Mitigation 4.C.1 Appropriate

Disaster Management plans will be drawn up at the State and District, Block and Village Levels to ensure coordination and holistic response to a disaster. 4.C.2. A systematic study of the risk assessment and vulnerability in respect of main hazards facing the state – earthquakes, floods landslides, fires, cyclone and hailstorms, droughts and mining/industrial/chemical disasters – will be taken up and specific action plans formulated to handle such disasters. 4.C.3. Each Government department shall prepare its plan/SOP and Emergency Support Function and have a mechanism for its half yearly review. All departments will identify in advance the tasks, which they will be expected to perform in major disasters and will prepare a detailed plan for emergency response.

The personnel/teams will be identified to perform these tasks, the equipment/stores will be kept in ready for mobilisation at the request of the nodal authority. 4.C.4. The communities are the first responders in a disaster situation and need to be empowered to manage disasters. The objective is to make the community aware about their vulnerability to natural hazard, to organize them in various teams and to train these teams in dealing with the impending disasters as first responders. Therefore, capacity building will be taken up at all levels-state, districts, blocks, villages and capacity of the communities as well as the personnel from Government, NGOs, and all agencies concerned with handling hazards/calamities shall be strengthened.

The Meghalaya Administrative Training institute has been strengthened with the establishment of disaster management cell therein. 4.C.5. The State will build specialized search and rescue teams with the support of Central Government. The Central Training Institute of the Home Guards and Civil Defence will be strengthened for imparting training to search and rescue teams. 4.C.6. The State Government will endeavour to bring its Building Codes and relevant Byelaws in accordance with the recommendations of the National Expert Committee on Techno-legal regime as consistent with the specific needs of the State. The relevant authorities (Urban Development Department/Municipal bodies/District Councils. Traditional

Institutional shall ensure that the building codes and type designs as laid down by State Government above are followed. Where buildings being constructed with government grant or aid it shall be mandatory that the construction is as per the relevant Building Codes specified by the State Government. The Hazard Safety Cell constituted by the Government shall put in place a mechanism to ensure that all future constructions both government and non-government – adhere to the specified Building Codes Appropriate training will also be imparted to local authorities responsible for enforcing safe construction standards. The masons, engineers, builders and other stakeholders in the building construction will be trained in appropriate building technologies.

4.C.7. The State Govt. will seek to retrofit lifeline buildings with available resources in a feasible time-frame. The Govt. shall also encourage retrofitting of private buildings particularly those where large number of people congregate such as Cinema Halls, shopping complexes, multi storey apartments, etc.

4.C.8. The State Government will encourage the financial institutions to review that lending guidelines to ensure adoption of safe construction practices also the requirements for insurance in case of new constructions. They will also be encouraged to loan funds for retrofitting purposes.

4.C.9. Disaster management will form an integral part of school curriculum and teachers training courses.

4.C.10. Information Technologies will be used for forecasting, prediction, early warning, dissemination, disaster database management, web-based inventorization of resources for disaster management. The IDRN network will be updated regularly.

4.C.11. Emergency Operation Centres shall be established in the State HQ and districts and communication equipments installed and networked.

4.C.12. The State Government believes that awareness generation is a key prerequisite for prevention, mitigation and preparedness by the community. Existing institutions like press, radio, television will be used extensively for the campaign. The posters, pamphlets, manuals in vernacular language will be published and distributed. The manuals for appropriate construction technologies (using local materials) will be prepared in simple and local language with drawings and will be distributed amongst the masses. The traditional institutions (village durbars etc.) will be used for disaster management extensively.

Risk Prevention

Natural disasters exert an enormous toll on development. In doing so, they pose a significant threat to prospects for achieving the Millennium Development Goals in particular, the overarching target of halving extreme poverty by 2015. Annual economic losses associated with such disasters averaged US$ 75.5 billion in the 1960s, US$ 138.4 billion in the 1970s, US$ 213.9 billion in the 1980s and US$ 659.9 billion in the 1990s. The majority of these losses are concentrated in the developed world and fail to adequately capture the impact of the disaster on the poor who often bear the greatest cost in terms of lives and livelihoods, and rebuilding their shattered communities and infrastructure. Today, 85 percent of the people exposed to earthquakes, tropical cyclones, floods and droughts live in countries having either medium or low human development.

This Report is premised on the belief that in many countries the process of development itself has a huge impact—both positive and negative—on disaster risk. It shows how countries that face similar patterns of natural hazards—from floods to droughts—often experience widely differing impacts when disasters occur. The impact depends in large part on the kind of development choices they have made previously. As countries become more prosperous, for example, they are often better able to afford the investments needed to build houses more likely to withstand earthquakes. At the same time, the rush for growth can trigger haphazard urban development that increases risks of large-scale fatalities during such a disaster. The same is true in many other areas.While humanitarian action to mitigate the impact of disasters will always be vitally important, the global community is facing a critical challenge: How to better anticipate — and then manage and reduce — disaster risk by integrating the potential threat into its planning and policies.

Preparedness

Emergency preparedness is crucial for coming out from disasters with least damage. Just the knowledge of what to do, may help save lives of you and your family. Here are collection of studies and links of documentation related to disasters preparedness also as per the type of disaster. Besides these, links to resources for forecasting disasters are also provided here. The source of the reference is also given along with them. Trauma Management:

> *Disaster stress may revive memories of prior trauma, as well as possibly intensifying pre-existing social, economic, spiritual, psychological, or medical problems. Trauma management is crucial and rescue workers as well as family members should prepare themselves to handle trauma hit members in the family. For more go to Trauma Management.*

Disaster Preparedness: Preparedness Questionnaire, ask yourself how prepared you are in the event of a disaster. This is a step towards getting yourself ready to meet eventualities which might save your, your families life in the event of disasters. Also you may be able to help your community to come out better during disasters. After going through this questionnaire explore resources listed above for preparedness in event of disasters as mentioned.

1. Do you think that your family is relatively well-prepared for a disaster such as an earthquake, tornado, cyclones, winter storm, fire, flood and other such incidents?

   This small step to understand and equip yourself about knowledge related to disaster preparedness would help you come out from a disaster unscathed. Your well-prepared family could help save the lives of others, not just yourselves. Are you and your family prepared, ask this question to yourself first?

2. Do you believe that the community you live in is relatively well-prepared for a disaster?

   Do you know about your community/ Panchayat/District, Disaster Management Plan? Is there any source of community Information system that you know of? Are you aware of any source of information to prepare yourself for disasters?

   Has your District / State DMA (Disaster Management Authority) coordinator worked with local hospitals, nursing homes, day care centers, shopping malls, schools, etc. to make sure they have a plan for what to do during an emergency?

3. Have you discussed disaster preparedness with your family?

   If you have a plan of what you will do during a disaster but you haven't shared it with your family ahead of time, your plan may not work! Each family member needs to know how to phone for help, escape out of the house, and seek safe shelter in the house. Each family member needs to know how to be safe when they are out of the home (at work, school, play). Each family member needs to know how the family plans to reunite if it becomes impossible to return to the home.

4. Do all members of your family know how to call for help?

   If you have kids, do they know how to phone for help? Do they know to dial 100 (if it is available where you live)? If you don't have 100, do you have the number of the Police, Fire, Ambulance, responsible friend/ relative, etc. near the phone? Do your kids know what sort of information they will need to give over the phone (i.e., the address of the home, their last name, etc.)? Do they know to phone from outside of the house if the house is on fire? Do they know to stay off the phone during an electrical storm?

5. Have you conducted a home hazard hunt and fixed potential hazards?

Many disasters at home can be averted with a simple hazard hunt. Is the home fire-safe-no frayed electrical cords, no overloaded outlets, working smoke detectors, if any, working carbon monoxide detectors, no flammable liquids near sources of heat or flames? Are working fire extinguishers easily available? Is the home earthquake safe—no unsecured heavy objects (mirrors, bookshelves, etc.), the water heater bolted to the wall? If there is a water tank on the top of the house, then how much water should be stored in earthquake prone zones?

6. Do you have a Family Disaster Supply Kit?

   In your supply kit you will need ALL of the things it will take to survive 72 hours. This will include food and water of course, but also medicines, blankets, flashlights, etc. Even if you don't put together an actual kit (although we encourage you to do so), think about having at least enough food, water and medicine at home with you to last 72 hours.

7. Do you have a Disaster Supply Kit for each car?

   A small box in the trunk of your car, other vehicle with blankets, a first-aid kit, cash, food, flashlight, radio, etc. could literally mean the difference between life and death. Every car should have a kit (atleast a first aid kit). You might want to change the contents of the kit for the different seasons of the year.

8. Are you trained in First-Aid (within the last 3 years)?

   Basic first-aid, for example how to stop bleeding by applying pressure, can be crucial, even life saving knowledge. First-aid courses are often offered by and local hospitals and charitable hospital for nominal charges. Think how happy you (and the victim) will be if you are able to make use of current training in an emergency situation.

9. Are all responsible family members current in First-Aid?

   Unfortunately, there is the possibility that you might be the victim! Does everyone in your family know basic first-aid?

10. Are you current in CPR (trained in the last 3 years)? CPR-Cardio Pulmonary Resuscitation is a simple technique that has saved many folks who would have otherwise been choking, drowning, smoke inhalation, or heart attack victims. When you think about a few hours of training saving a loved one's life, isn't it worth it?
11. Are all responsible family members current in CPR? Again, there is the possibility that YOU might be the victim! Or, you might not be home when the incident occurs. Be sure that everyone in your family is trained.
12. Do you have operational smoke detectors and carbon monoxide detectors?

    Having a smoke detector and/or a carbon monoxide detector in your home is NOT good enough! You need to make sure they are operational, that is, they must have working batteries. An operational smoke detector more than doubles your chance of escaping from your home alive. Two good rules of thumb are check your detectors once a month (pick a day of the month, say the 1st, and make a habit of checking the detectors every month on the 1st); when you change your clock for daylight savings/standard time, change the batteries of detectors too.
13. Do you have a charged ABC fire extinguisher?

    There are three basic classes of fires. All fire extinguishers are labeled using standard symbols for the classes of fires they can put out. A red slash through any of the symbols tells you the extinguisher cannot be used on that class of fire. A missing symbol tells you only that the extinguisher has not been tested for a given class of fire.

    Class A: Ordinary combustibles such as wood, cloth, paper, rubber and many plastics.

    Class B: Flammable liquids such as gasoline, oil, grease, tar, oil-based paint, lacquer, and flammable gas.

Class C: Energized electrical equipment-including wiring, fuse boxes, circuit breakers, machinery, and appliances

Many household fire extinguishers are *"multipurpose"* A-B-C models, labeled for use on all three classes of fire. If you are ever faced with a Class A fire and don't have an extinguisher with an *"A"* symbol, don't hesitate to use one with the *"B:C"* symbol.

WARNING: It is very dangerous to use water or an extinguisher labeled only for Class A fires on a Class B or Class C fire.

Do you know where your fire extinguisher is? Do you know if it is still fully charged (they can lose their charge over time)?

14. Do you know how to use the fire extinguisher?

    Using a fire extinguisher is not completely straightforward and the time to learn how to operate one is NOT during a fire. Follow the four-step PASS procedure. Pull the pin: This unlocks the operating lever and allows you to discharge the extinguisher. Aim low: Point the extinguisher nozzle (or hose) at the base of the fire. Squeeze the lever above the handle: This discharges the extinguishing agent. (Some extinguishers have a button instead of a lever.) Sweep from side-to-side: Moving carefully toward the fire, keep the extinguisher aimed at the base of the fire and sweep back and forth until the flames appear to be out. A good practice might be to purchase two fire extinguishers—one to keep and one to let each family member practice on.

15. Do you know how to turn off all utilities (gas, electricity, water, etc.)?

    For a variety of reasons, it may be necessary to turn off the utilities in your home. Do you know where the water main is? Do you know where the circuit breaker box or main switch is? Does everyone in your family know not to turn off the electricity if you have to stand in water to do so?

16. Do you know where your family records are?

    If your house burned down today would your insurance papers, household inventory, receipts, other important papers etc. burn too? A great place to keep your valuable papers (marriage certificate, birth certificates, passports, insurance papers, household inventory, etc.) is in a safe deposit box. It is probably not wise to keep your will in a safe deposit box though. A will is best kept with your lawyer or a close friend (if you die it will become difficult for others to access your safe deposit box, making it difficult for them to find your will).

17. Do you know where your family will meet outside your home in case of an emergency?

    If your family is separated during an emergency you should have two contingency plans in place. The first plan should be a place to meet near your home (such as across the street at a neighbor's) if the emergency is something like your house burning down. The second plan should be a place to meet in your community, away from your home, (such as a local business or friend's house) if the emergency is something like your neighborhood being evacuated. By knowing ahead of time where to rendezvous, family members can avoid needlessly worrying about members that are fine and concentrate on family members that are unaccounted for.

18. Do you know at least two exits from every room in your house in case of a fire?

    Most rooms have a door and a window. If the window is a second story window, do you have a way to escape safely (i.e., a fire ladder)?

19. Have you practiced an emergency drill in your home within the past year?

    Drills are a terrific way of making sure that everyone in the family (kids and adults) understands and has the physical/mental ability to carry out the plan your family has developed. If kids get confused about whether to stay inside or leave the house during a fire for example, the time to get them straight about it is before anything happens.

20. Do you have an out-of-area phone contact?

    Believe it or not, long distance phone calls are often easier to make immediately following a disaster than are local phone calls. Does everyone in your family knows to phone the contact to inform about there safety.

21. Do you know about disaster plans at your workplace, at your children's school or day care, etc.?

    Few of us spend 100 percent of our time at home, so we need to know about the disaster plans at the other places we (and our loved ones) spend time. Be sure that you know what the plan is and that it is a sound plan.

22. Can you list the actual cash value of every item in your home?

    You may be asked to create such a list after a fire, cyclone or flood! Obviously, a wise choice is to make that list (often times called a household inventory) well before a disaster occurs. A household inventory can provide you with some excellent information for deciding how much insurance to purchase as well.

23. Some family members have special needs, for example the elderly, mobility impaired or sick. Do you have a plan for making sure these members will be safe during a disaster?

    Check your family disaster plan and make sure it will work for everyone. For example, if the family plan is to seek shelter in the basement or community shelter during a cyclone warning, be sure everyone in the family is able to negotiate the stairs to the basement/shelter. If some members are unable to go to the basement/shelter, make sure you have a second plan in place for them (i.e., seek shelter in an interior room, under a heavy piece of furniture).

24. Do you have a plan for your pets?

    A simple sign on your door, alerting the fire department to the fact that you have pets inside, could save your pets' lives. Bringing a pet to a temporary shelter may pose health risks that the local shelter may not be willing to cope with. It's a good idea to arrange for a place ahead of time (maybe a friend or relative) where your pets could stay temporarily in case of an emergency.

Emergency Response

In emergency situations, time is usually the most crucial factor. When preserving lives comes down to the minutes and seconds it takes for help to arrive, effective emergency response management can literally be a matter of life and death. Intergraph, a world leader in disaster response management and emergency response management software, provides the next-generation solutions you need to coordinate and deploy resources when emergencies occur.

Public safety and government organizations in 24 countries around the world already trust Intergraph emergency response management software solutions. As the world's leading spatial information management provider, we can give you the power to see all facets of emergency rescue management.

- *Emergency Response Management Software:* Because we offer our emergency response management software solutions in 14 languages, Intergraph is uniquely positioned to offer products to individual nations or governing bodies that deal with emergency and disaster response management across a wide geographical range.
- *Contact Intergraph:* If you have any questions or concerns regarding our emergency response management software, please contact us. If your organization has a sales inquiry, please use our information request form and we will respond to you right away. For up-to-date information on emergency response management, we encourage you to sign up for Intergraph's e-Connection newsletter today.

Emergency Response Management Software Solutions

Look around you and you can clearly see the important role emergency response management carries on contemporary society. What can be more difficult to discern, however, is the best way to go about building an effective emergency response management plan. Intergraph provides powerful and configurable software solutions that give your organization the flexibility to create plans unique to your environment, while still being comprehensive enough to address all of your needs.

CAD Emergency Dispatch Software. In an emergency response management situation, having the most up-to-date information is key. Intergraph's Computer-Aided Dispatch (I/CAD) System combines real-time mapping, mobile resource management, call handling, and dispatch to create a coordinated response when seconds count. Our I/CAD emergency and 911 dispatch software even generates reports for review and future planning purposes.

Police Records Management. Police records software from Intergraph allows your organization to collect a myriad of related records in a central database for quick, comprehensive access.

Mobile Solutions for Public Safety. By harnessing the power of our I/CAD and records management software and making it available to public safety officers in their vehicles or via PDA, Intergraph emergency response management software promotes a truly connected, coordinated response effort.

With intelligent emergency response management software from Intergraph, your organization can be better prepared to handle emergencies with real-time information and improved communications coordination.

Disaster Response Management

As terrorism and natural disasters continue to be factors that require extensive preventive and response planning, matters of disaster response management take on increasing global relevance, especially in terms of national security. To that end, Intergraph has bundled some of our software offerings to form a consequence and disaster response management suite that includes: Computer-Aided Dispatch, GeoMedia, and Video Analyst.

Disaster and Emergency Response Management from Intergraph

When every second matters, you can count on Intergraph's disaster response management and emergency response management software to give you every advantage possible. To learn more about our emergency response management software or any of our other software offerings, contact Intergraph today.

Some Disaster and Their Management

Disasters are generally considered as sudden occurrences or events or calamities that cause damage, loss of life, economic disruption and deterioration of health and essential services on a scale sufficient to warrant an extraordinary response from outside the community or area. They are classified into two categories-Natural (e.g., earthquake, cyclone, flood, famine, landslide, volcanic eruption, etc.,) and Man-made (e.g., industrial disasters, accidents, terrorist attack, war, refugee migration, etc.,). This conceptual formulation, however, is too simplistic to comprehend the nature and magnitude of disasters seen in a holistic perspective. 'Natural' and 'Man-made' disasters can no longer be seen as separate entities as many so called 'natural' catastrophic events within the environment are man-induced or atleast made worst by the intervention of man. Humankind is an important causative faction in most disasters.

There are patterns of development and human settlement which are linked to the severity with which the disasters strike. Increase in population combined with poor resource management have resulted in the conversion of forests to pasture and arable land as a result of which less water is stored in upper reaches of catchment areas making floods more frequent and severe Desertification and unwise land use contribute to the impact of drought. Underground testing of nuclear devices creates pressure which could effect the stability of parts of earth 's crust leading to earthquakes. Removal of vegetation cover accelerates the rate of soil erosion resulting in appreciable accumulation of loose unsorted material causing landslides. Many landslides or flooding disasters are closely linked to the rapid and unchecked urbanization which forces low-income families to settle on the slopes of steep hillsides or ravines or along the banks of flood-prone rivers.

Famines, too, are not natural events alone. As Amartya Sen's celebrated study on famines and hunger shows, in the scale of deaths, the Chinese famine of 1958-61 was about five to ten times as large as the largest famine in India in this century the Great Bengal Famine of 1943 in British India. The fact that there has been no large-scale famine in India since independence is a positive contrast with the Communist China experience. The main reason for this difference was the existence of political democracy in India. Given the political system in post independence India, it was extremely hard for any government in office to get away with neglecting prompt and extensive anti-famine measures at the first signs of a famine. The contrast with China is striking in this respect. Given its system of public distribution, China did not lack a delivery and redistribution mechanism to deal with food shortages as the famine threatened in 1958 and later. What was lacking when the famine threatened China was a political system of adversarial journalism and opposition. The Chinese famine raged on for three years without it being admitted in public that such a thing was occurring and without there being an adequate policy response to the threat. In fact, the precise feature of absence of adversarial politics and open journalism that contributed to the occurrence, magnitude and duration of Chinese famine in 1958-61 are also present in most Sub-Saharan countries today.

Hence, Disasters are the consequences of the way societies structure themselves, economically politically and socially, the ways that societies and states interact and the ways that relationships between the decision makers are sustained. The traditional distinction between natural and human-induced disasters has to give way to emphasis on the interdependence of human activities and natural events in shaping the frequency and intensity of disasters.

The disastrous consequences of environmental pollution are being increasingly debated and discussed. Global warming, due to accumulation of 'greenhouse' gases in the atmosphere

& depletion of ozone layer due to excessive release of CFCs are examples of disasters-in-the-making. Their immediate impact in terms of casualities and damage may be less dramatic in comparision to natural phenomenon like earthquakes and cyclones but their long term impact cannot be ignored in any disaster planning. In fact, the scope of human rights has been widened to include the right to a healthy & ecologically balanced environment as a 'third generation' right and the scope of disaster management has to be widened to include such 'slow-onset' disasters also.

There is yet another category of disasters which are simply over looked. They may be termed as invisible disasters. Thus, according to World Development Report 1992 (World Bank) about one billion people in developing countries do not have access to clean water and 1.7 billion lack access to sanitation. The effect on their health is shocking. This contributes to some 900 million cases of diarrheal diseases every year which cause the deaths of more than three million children.

Development and Disasters

The desirability of development is universally recognised-no society can afford to stay in a state of stagnation. But the adoption of any model of development is not a universally accepted ready-made recipe for progress, it has its pitfalls and pose serious dilemma . A long number of natural resources in the world are limited, non-renewable and may be exhausted if the present consumption levels of industrial system continue. A cautionary note in this regard was sounded by a report titled ' The Limits to Growth' produced by Massachusetts Institute of Technology for a project of 'Club of Rome'. The report contained, inter-alia, an interesting table which showed the known global reserves, the rate of consumption and projected growth etc for 19 non-renewal natural resources of vital importance to industrial societies. The report concluded that "Given present resource consumption rates and projected increase in these rates, the great majority of the currently important non-renewable resources will be extremely costly 100 years from now".

Moreover, developmental projects implemented without taking into account long term environmental hazards may prove disastrous. In other words, development process should be 'sustainable' in the long run. The term "Sustainable Development" was brought into common use by the World Commission on Environment and Development (the Brundtland Commission) in its seminal 1987 Report, Our Common Future. The idea of sustaining the earth has proved a powerful metaphor in raising public awareness and focussing of the need for better environmental stewardship.

The crux of the concept, according to the Commission, is "meeting the needs of the present generation without compromising on the needs of the future generation". Making the concept of sustainability precise, however, has proved difficult. It is not plausible to argue that all natural resources should be preserved. Successful development will inevitably involve some amount of land clearing, oil drilling, river damming and swamp draining. Some here argued that natural capital should be preserved in some aggregate sense with losses in one area replenished elsewhere. This approach has helpfully focussed attention on the need to estimate the value of environmental resources and on the importance of protecting certain essential ecological systems.

On a more practical plane, the debate over large dams presents an important issue of development process vis-à-vis its disaster potential. In India, the acrimonious controversy over the Narmada Project refuses to die down. For the supporters of the project, it will be the lifeline of Gujarat with immense potential of meeting the immigration and energy needs of the region. The opponents of the project regard it as an unmitigated environmental and human disaster resulting in submergence of large areas of forest wealth and displacement of lakhs of tribals uprooted from their ancient habitat where they lived for centuries. Even the technical feasibility of the large dams is questioned by these critics who vouch for the superiority of 'small' projects. Needless to say, there are no clear cut answers to such dilemma. The opponents of the dam clearly overstate their case when they dismiss totally the need for large dams, romanticize the idyllic simplicity of the tribals traditionally living in harmony with nature and espouse the cause of small dams in tune with the ideal of ' small is beautiful ' (which was the title of E.F. Schumacher famous book). At the same time, the inadequacy of rehabilitation measures and their disastrous consequences for the displaced people cannot be overlooked. Each case has to be decided on its merits keeping in view the whole issue in totality with minimum suffering for the affected people. Disaster Prevention has to be integrated as part of developmental planning.

Industrial Disaster Management

It goes without saying that industrial growth is an important index of the progress of the nation. At the same time, the environmental pollution caused by many industrial undertakings is also beyond doubt. Nuclear Plants have the potential to cause disaster of frightening consequences in more than one way. A Chernobyl type disaster could be bad enough but worst possibilities exist. Some nuclear experts fear that deepening economic and political upheaval in Russia has increased the likelihood that financially desperate specialists with access to nuclear material may be tempted to sell it in the nuclear black market as the security at nuclear sites will continue to corrode as fast as the beleaguered economy. Once the smuggled Uranium or Plutonium is sold to the highest bidder there is the possibility, terrorists or outlaw nations detonating a primitive nuclear device. Such fears may be exaggerated but not baseless.

Non-nuclear installations, however, are not free from disaster potential. A large number of industrial units hold noxious gases which on leakage in large quantities can cause serious damage as in case of Bhopal Gas Tragedy. A Steel Plant in Bhilai has a LD Gas Holder containing huge quantity of Carbon Monoxide Gas, a colourless & odourless gas which, if inhaled can cause paralysis of lungs and death. A fertiliser plant at Phulpur has a Ammonia tank whose leakage in large quantity would make the place another Bhopal. Innumerable such examples can be cited. While adequate safety measures would be taken in such plants, the possibility of such vulnerable points subject to sabotage or bomb explosion by a terrorist cannot be ruled out. It would be an effective way for a terrorist to wreck havoc & destruction to thousands of people living in the vicinity.

The disaster management plans of such industries suffer from two serious drawbacks in India. Security personnel, particularly at the lower level do not have adequate working knowledge of the production process of the plants, its safety requirements and vulnerable points. The plant safety and security wings function as separate entities with little coordination between the two. Lack of a working technical knowledge would reduce the effectiveness of a security personnel both in preventing disasters and in tackling it. Integration of Security & Safety wings is the crying need of the hour.

The second lacuna is the lack of knowledge of hazards among the local population living in the vicinity of the industrial township. Most of the disaster management plan rehearsals are done by the plant management & workers in a routine manner within the premises of the industry and no serious effort is made to educate the local people who can become hapless victims of disasters. Community participation is necessary for effective industrial disaster management.

Role of Government

The frequent natural calamities in India and the huge loss of life and property that ensues have forced the government to revise its approach towards disaster management.

India is prone to multiple natural disasters, such as floods, earthquake, drought, landslides, cyclone, etc. This is due to various factors like the geo-climatic conditions, increase in population density, improper urbanization, deforestation and desertification.

According to government data, about 60 per cent of the Indian landmass is prone to earthquakes of varying intensities, over 40 million hectares is prone to floods, around eight per cent of the total area is prone to cyclones and 68 per cent of the area is susceptible to drought. In the last decade, the damage in terms of human suffering, loss of life, agriculture productivity and economic losses has been astronomical.

At the government level, there has been considerable concern over restricting socio-economic damage. Substantial scientific and material progress has been made in this field for more than five decades. However, the loss of human life and property due to natural and man-made disasters has not decreased.

The cyclone in Orissa in 1999, the earthquake in Gujarat in 2001 and the tsunami in South India in 2004 has highlighted the need to adopt a multi dimensional endeavour involving various scientific, engineering and social processes. The need to adopt multi disciplinary and multi sectoral approach and incorporation of risk reduction in the developmental strategies has also been underlined.

The basic responsibility of response mechanism, like undertaking rescue, relief and rehabilitation measures in the event of a disaster, rests with the state governments. And, the center supplements the efforts by extending logistics and financial support.

The government has formed a National Disaster Framework covering institutional mechanisms, disaster prevention strategy, early warning system, disaster mitigation, preparedness and response and human resource development.

The government has set up National Crisis Management Committee and Crisis Management Group. There is a National Committee on Disaster Management to suggest necessary institutional and legislative measures necessary for an efficient and long-term strategy to manage natural disasters. Another committee – High Powered Committee on disaster management plans was constituted in 1999 to prepare comprehensive model plans for management of disasters at the national, state and district levels.

The state governments have set up state crisis management groups headed by chief secretaries, institutes of relief commissioners and state/district contingency plans. There is a

Calamity Relief Fund (CRF) for each state. 75 per cent of the CRF is contributed by the central government and the rest contributed by the various state governments.

The disaster management policy of the government stresses on forecasting and warning using advanced technologies, contingency agricultural planning to ensure availability of food grains, and preparedness and mitigation through specific programmes. The central sector scheme for disaster management focuses on setting up National Centre for Disaster Management, disaster management faculties in states and programmes for community participation and public awareness.

Disaster Management in India

Considering how huge a country India is, with varied geographical features ranging from miles of coastline to the highest mountains in the world, natural disasters are understandably frequent at some part or another. India has had more than a fair share of earthquakes, cyclones, drought, landslides and floods. Some of the major disasters in the past few years are the December 2004 tsunami that hit the Indian Ocean, leaving more than a 300,000 people dead, the 2001 Gujarat earthquake, and the 1999 Orissa cyclone. Each of these disasters, and the many others that have struck the country, leave thousands of deaths in its wake, and due to their unexpected nature, put great pressure on government and civil society relief efforts.

The most recent natural disaster to strike India and other parts of Asia was the December 26, 2004 tsunami or tidal wave. Government, international organizations and non government organizations (NGOs) such as Oxfam and ActionAid, along with local NGOs, had to be mobilized on short notice to provide relief and assistance. Apart from the loss of life and property, many more people lost their means of livelihood and face long-term starvation.

One of the first steps in relief and recovery following a disaster is to restore the livelihoods of the affected people. While aid in the form of food, clothing and shelter is often made readily available, little is done for disaster victims, especially those of the economically marginalized groups, who look ahead to a bleak future because of their sole means of earning being completely destroyed. In such situations, it is the condition of women that is especially the most precarious, especially if their husbands or fathers, who are often the sole earning members of the family, have been victims. In desperation, survivors often migrate to cities and other regions, adding to the migrant labour population. Survivors also run a great health risk in the form of epidemics after coming in contact with contaminated food, water and air in the wake of a large-scale disaster that has claimed a lot of lives.

In many cases of natural disasters, it is only the event that is natural. The accompanying loss of life and destruction of property can often be minimized by proper planning and application. More often than not, it is the poor and the marginalized who suffer the most in the event of a natural disaster. Taking all this into account, governments world over, including the Indian government, have of late incorporated and in fact prioritized multi-disciplinary disaster mitigation into its development paradigm, because development cannot be sustainable if it is disaster-prone. It is not post-disaster relief and recovery measures that is the answer, it is the preventive measures that stop the disaster from happening in the first place that saves more life and assets. Expenses on disaster mitigation, for one, are far more economical that on relief and rehabilitation. The key to making it work is to involve local communities in the system, be it in post-disaster relief and recovery, or in mitigation.

The government has penned a National Disaster Framework that seeks to chalk out possible sources of involvement in disaster mitigation at national, state and district levels. Foremost among them are early warning systems, human resources, infrastructure and preparedness.

The main areas that require intervention in disaster mitigation are earthquakes, floods, cyclones and landslides. For earthquakes, building laws and by-laws, retrofitting and training in earthquake engineering and architecture have already been envisaged. Coastal plantation belts, shelters and preemptive warning systems can minimize the damage from cyclones to a great extent. Numerous flood control measures are already in operation to prevent the kind of floods that wreak havoc in states like West Bengal, Assam and Bihar. Geological surveys, hazard zonation and monitoring go a long way towards reducing the risk from landslides. Above all, what is required is awareness among all citizens of the possible dangers from various disasters, be they natural or human-made.

With each disaster, along with the death and misery, there is also something to learn that equips us to deal better with the next one. Greater research needs to be conducted into the patterns of disaster occurrence and their outcomes, and also possible further victimization during relief and rehabilitation. For many survivors, a disaster is only a long chain of events the outcome of which is not immediately apparent. It is only through the involvement with the local community, those who have been hit hardest by the disaster, that appropriate measures can be taken and networks set up for the survivors' housing and livelihood needs.

Finally, it is not only natural disasters that can wreak havoc on people's lives. Human-made disasters, such as war and riots have the same effects.

UNIT-IV

Risk Management Process

Hazards

Natural hazards impact on every Australian State and Territory. These hazards include bushfires, cyclones, earthquakes, floods, landslides, severe weather, tsunami, and volcanoes. The phenomena threaten lives and damage private and public assets as well as disrupt water, power, transport, and communication services. These hazards and their associated impacts also can seriously affect employment and incomes to industry, agriculture, commerce and public administration.

In Australia, natural hazards are estimated to cost an average of A$1.25 billion annually (BTE, 2001), but the cost of individual hazards can be much greater. For example, in 1989 an earthquake cost the community in the New South Wales city of Newcastle an estimated A$4.5 billion.Natural hazards cannot be averted, but their consequences can be minimised by implementing mitigation strategies and reducing the potential impact to areas which are most vulnerable.As part of its extensive work on natural hazard risk research, Geoscience Australia monitors and assesses earth-surface processes which pose a risk to Australia. It gathers data and develops tools for use by governments and other authorities to help them make Australia as safe as possible from natural hazards.

Vulnerability Factors

SINCE the 1970s, there has been a substantial increase in the external debt of several low income countries. Recently an

IMF team, after making a detailed study of ten such countries, made some observations from their experience. The ten countries includ e those with high external debt burdens (Congo, Nicaragua); those with more sound debt management (Ghana, Kenya); countries with a high fiscal burden of debt (Niger, Cameroon) those with relatively low ones (Bolivia, Kenya); countries with a highly conce ntrated export base and vulnerability to commodity price shocks (Uganda, Niger, Zambia); those with less export concentration (Bolivia, Cote d'Ivoire, Kenya) and countries with considerable debt to private creditors (Cameroon, Cote d'Ivoire).

Evolution of External Debt burden

The debt burden increased significantly between the late 1970s and the early 1990s in all the ten countries. In the late 1970s, their external debt-to-exports ratio stood at relatively moderate levels, at about 200 per cent or below, with the exception o f Bolivia at 260 per cent. For Cameroon, Ghana, Niger, and Uganda, the ratio was at about 100 per cent. By the early 1990s, most sample countries' debt-to-exports ratio increased by three-four times. Nicaragua and Uganda had the largest increase in the d ebt-to-exports ratio between 1976-80 and 1991-95 because of a big jump in the nominal debt stock, some 600 per cent in dollar terms.

Kenya kept its debt at manageable levels and experienced one of the smallest increases in the debt-to-exports ratio between 1976-80 and 1991-95, reflecting its success in achieving high export growth, about 55 per cent in dollar terms, in tandem with sub stantive borrowing, its debt stock increasing by 215 per cent over this period. Bolivia's debt-to-exports ratio peaked earlier, increasing more than four-fold, between 1976 and 1987, as the country's debt grew by 450 per cent, while exports, after increa sing rapidly through 1980, declined to close to their initial level.

In the early 1990s, for most countries, the net present value (NPV) of the debt-to-export ratio was lower than the nominal ratio because a significant share of debt was concessional. Given that the share of concessional debt increased over time, the stud y notes that the NPV ratio would not have increased as quickly as the nominal ratio.

Though a lack of NPV data for the earlier period makes it difficult to judge the extent of this change, the present value ratio was still above 220 per cent in 1991-95 f or five sample countries despite the sizeable share of concessional debt.

According to the study, a combination of several elements listed below was responsible for the increase in the sample countries' external debt burden:

Exogenous Factors: All countries under review suffered adverseterms-of-trade shocks of varying degrees during 1975-95 and — toa lesser extent — adverse weather conditions. Countries with the least diversified export bases were hardest hit, particularly Niger, Uganda, and Zambia which, in the early 1980s, obtained more than 80 per cent of their exports from one commodity — uranium, coffee, and copper, respectively.

Lack of Sustained Adjustment Policies: This factor, particularly in the face of erogenous shocks, gave rise to sizeable financing needs and failed to strengthen the debt-servicing capacity. In most cases, inadequate progress was made with structural refo rms that would promote sustainable growth of output and exports. The lack of appropriate policies was a particular problem in Cameroon, Congô, Cote D'Ivoire, Nicaragua, and Zambia, and to a lesser degree in Kenya and Niger.

Non-concessional Lending Terms: Largely non-concessional lending and refinancing through the mid-1980s, and capitalisation of interest contributed to the debt build-up. Recognising the limited debt-servicing capacity of these countries, creditors and don ors have, since the late 1980s, moved increasingly to provide financing through concessional reschedulings involving debt reduction and grants.

Lack of Prudent Debt Management: This factor was partly driven by excessive optimism among creditors and debtors about the prospects for increasing export earnings and building debt-servicing capacity.

Lack of Careful Management of the Currency Composition of Debt: Exchange rate changes among major currencies also contributed to the increase in the debt burden. Most countries did not appear to consider the currency composition of debt important in the management of their external debt, and placed little emphasis on matching the currency composition of debt with that of export earnings.

Political Factors: These included civil war and strife. Civil strife was a major factor affecting the debt burden in Nicaragua and Uganda, and to a lesser extent, in Congo and Niger. In Nicaragua, the armed conflict throughout the 1980s eroded the export base and led to a very large buildup of external debt to finance both military and non-military imports. In Uganda, civil strife in the 1970s and the early 1980s, destroyed the country's infrastructure and left large areas of fertile land uncultivated. As a result, by the mid-1980s, there was virtually no non-coffee export.

Lessons to Learn

The study identifies several important lessons for the sample countries' future adjustment and external debt strategies, and for poor countries and creditors, more generally.

Strong and sustained implementation of sound macroeconomic and structural adjustment policies, particularly in response to exogenous shocks, is crucial in limiting the need for financing, especially of the public sector, and in creating an environment co nducive to export growth. Bolivia's export earnings doubled between 1987 and 1995, not withstanding a sharp deterioration in the export price of gas in the early 1990s, because of a successful diversification of the export base. Ghana and Uganda were mor e successful than other countries in adjusting to sizeable terms-of-trade shocks by achieving some export growth as a result of sound policy implementation over an extended period. Exchange and trade liberalisation, supported by tight financial policies, appeared to be the key ingredients for export growth in these countries. Countries which failed to put in place a sustained record of strong policies—Cameroon, Cote d'Ivoire, Nicaragua, Niger, and Zambia—also failed to encourage the broad-based ex port growth that would have strengthened their debt-servicing capacity and reduced their financing needs.

The study notes that a diversified export base, with limited reliance on commodities subject to large price swings, is important in reducing the vulnerability of export receipts to commodity price shocks. Kenya, for example, was able to offset large term s-of-trade shocks through its reasonably well-diversified export base and export growth, particularly following fundamental exchange and trade regime reform. Bolivia, Ghana, Nicaragua, and Uganda were also successful in reducing their vulnerability to sh ocks by diversifying their export base. According to the study, the lack of prudent debt management and risk assessment created difficulties in Bolivia, Cameroon, Congo, Cote d'Ivoire, Nicaragua, Niger, and Zambia.

In the late 1970s and the early 1980s, the countries undertook sizeable borrowing on non-concessional terms with relatively short maturities—often from private sources. The study advises that while it is difficult to define prudent debt management, it should be geared to keeping external o bligations at sustainable levels. This would call for debtors and creditors alike to focus on contracting highly concessional loans and to place more emphasis on the use to which resources are put.

A more prudent strategy would also include taking greater care to assess the most appropriate currency composition of debt, so as to avoid large cross-currency fluctuations adversely affecting debt-servicing capacity. More cautious assumptions about debt-servicing capacity can help limit loan financing and encourage more adjustment. In many of the sample countries, sizeable borrowing was based in part on the erroneous assumption of a recovery in export earnings.

Further, large increases in commodity pri ces may have given rise to an inappropriate assessment of a country's permanent capacity to generate income and, thus, to excessive borrowing. The study concludes there is a need for more in-depth risk analysis, based on a country's vulnerability to shoc ks. (The author was Special Secretary, Finance Department (NFC & TFC) and later Finance Secretary, Government of

Tamil Nadu. The views represented are personal and not those of the State Government.).

Coping Capacity

Successful adaptation to climate change and sea-level rise depends greatly on coping capacity or adaptive capacity, that is, the ability of an affected (human or natural) system, region, or community to cope with or adapt to the impacts and risks of climate change induced sea-level rise.

While the concept of coping capacity is more directly related to an extreme event (e.g. a flood or a winter storm), the concept of adaptive capacity refers to a longer time frame and implies that some learning either before or after an extreme event is happening. The higher the coping capacity and adaptive capacity, the lower the vulnerability of a system, region, community or household. Enhancement of adaptive capacity is a necessary condition for reducing vulnerability, particularly for the most vulnerable regions and socioeconomic groups.

Adaptive capacity in natural systems tends to be more limited than adaptive capacity in human systems. As to human systems, Yohe & Tol (2002) analyse adaptive capacity in terms of different determinants which include a variety of system, sector, and location specific characteristics:

1. The range of available technological options for adaptation,
2. The availability of resources and their distribution across the population,
3. The structure of critical institutions, the derivative allocation of decision-making authority, and the decision criteria that would be employed
4. The stock of human capital including education and personal security
5. The stock of social capital including the definition of property rights
6. The system's access to risk spreading processes (e.g. insurance systems)

7. The ability of decision-makers to manage information, the processes by which these decision-makers determine which information is credible, and the credibility of the decision-makers, themselves, and
8. The public's perceived attribution of the source of stress and the significance of exposure to its local manifestations.

Some of the determinants of adaptive capacity operate on the structural macro-level in which institutional actors play the most significant role, but other determinants function on the micro-level, where the capacities of households and individuals are central to adaptation. Thus, successful adaptation requires coordination across these scales.

In the SEAREG methodology, the notion of coping capacity was operationalised in the following manner:

1. Identification of "hotspots" of sea-level rise (impact assessment)
2. Linking of these hotspots to a network of relevant actors
3. Assessment of the capacities of these stakeholders
   * awareness of the Sea-level rise as an problematic issue
   * knowledge of the SLR and related phenomena such as flooding
   * resources available for mitigation efforts
4. Assessment of the regional coping capacity "between actors", i.e. regulations and roles of institutions that are not related to single actors that have to be evaluated
   * co-operation between relevant actors
   * strength of institutions
   * guidance of planning instruments
   * trust in decision-makers
5. The combination of these results in an overall assessment of the regional coping capacity.

The assessment was devised as a qualitative exercise due to 1) the difficulty of aggregating the different elements of coping capacity and 2) it's pedagogical value for the stakeholders involved in the assessment excercise. The idea of the coping capacity assessment is to estimate the current possibilities of planners and decision makers to define appropriate mitigation strategies. The methodology thus provides a starting point for participatory assessment processes.

Output from Risk Assessment

Depending on the nature of the project, several outputs from the process are possible. Among the most common are the following:

- Expected value analyses of cost and duration with probability values for other potential outcomes.
- Value of information and control.
- Contingency assessments for cost and duration.
- Sensitivity analysis for individual risks.
- Risk management mitigation plans and strategies.
- Risk-based analyses of preferred project contracting/ procurement approach.
- Risk allocation decisions that align team members with customer-oriented performance measures.

These outputs will be explained later in this document, including examples of best practices from throughout the transportation community and elsewhere. There are indeed some excellent examples from WSDOT, Caltrans, FTA, and DOE. Effectiveness of the process as a management decision aid is most often linked to the clarity of its communication.

The simplest representations often work best. While the analysis may be supported by a complex, rigorous, and probabilistically sophisticated model, it is of little value if its outputs are obscured in jargon or overly complicated in their representation.

Similarly, simple qualitative analyses that are easily understood by the decisionmakers can have a powerful influence on the risk measures taken. Communication is very much a key in using these outputs to their full potential.

Risk Assessments

Threats and vulnerabilities need to be known so information assets can be properly protected. The ultimate concern for an organization is that of an exposure. An exposure is the coupling of a threat and vulnerability. For example, if you have an attacker scanning your web server, that is threatening behavior to your environment. If you also have a system vulnerability on that web server, and the attacker both finds and leverages that vulnerability, you have an exposure. This is where risk assessments come into play. A risk assessment looks at both the threats and the vulnerabilities that exist within your environment. To illustrate some of the risks to organizations, the *2003 CSI/FBI Computer Crime and Security Survey* identified the following risk that accounted for financial loses to organizations:

- Theft of Proprietary Information
- Sabotage of Data on Networks
- Telecom Eavesdropping
- System Penetration by Outsider
- Insider Abuse of Network Access
- Financial Fraud

Denial of Service

In addition to looking at risks, a properly conducted risk assessment also looks at controls that are currently in place to determine the overall level of risk to your organization. Based on this information, a risk assessment requires more resources than either a threat or vulnerability assessment. Illustration A provides an overview of the risk assessment cycle. A risk assessment begins by identifying and characterizing key systems within an environment. Once key systems are identified, threats and vulnerabilities for those systems can be assessed. Current controls must also be identified. Based on a listing of threats, vulnerabilities and controls, a likelihood and impact evaluation can be calculated. The impact is composed of both the sensitivity and the criticality of the data stored by the systems. Based on all information gathered, an overall risk prioritization can be assigned. Items identified with the highest level of risk must immediately receive some level of mitigation. Mitigation steps should be recommended as part of the risk assessment, and the results of this analysis are reported.

Global Insecurities and their Linkages to Disaster Risk Management Process

The WAGE Governing Global Insecurities Collaborative focuses on new insecurities the process of globalization has created for states and societies, with special emphasis on the globalization of violence and ecological risk, and offers concrete proposals for institutional and policy reforms to address these concerns.

Project Overview: The end of the Cold War witnessed the passing of many conceptual and institutional anchors in the international system. Most significant, assumptions about "national security" encountered a powerful set of new challenges. The expanding range of transnational flows in people, capital, and knowledge seriously undermined the ability of any single state policy-making body to manage its nation's interactions with the wider world. Globalization contributed to a growing contradiction between the path dependent institutional structures of state authority and the proliferating sources of power that diminish the leverage of the state.

Governing Global Insecurities is an interdisciplinary collaborative project that will analyze the sources and implications of this contradiction, and offer concrete proposals for institutional and policy reform. The group will examine central issues of security in light of the new vulnerabilities created by globalization. Specifically the project will interrogate two prime areas where globalization undermines the dominant paradigm of "national security." These two areas are the globalization of violence and the globalization of ecological risk. The project will also investigate the normative concerns for democratic theory that arise with globalization and various policy responses. In the end, the project will lay out an agenda for replacing assumptions about "national security" with a more effective notion of "global governance."

Disaster Risk Management

Bhadrak district lying between 20 deg.44' and 21deg.15' North Latitude and 86 deg.16' and 86 deg.58' East Longitude comes within the long coastal area (480km) of Orissa has suffered enormous loss of lives, livelihoods and damage of public property due to its typical geographical features which is extremely vulnerable to several natural hazards.

Immediate response from government and many non-government agencies resulted in rescue and evacuation that thus saved lives and properties.Nevertheless, the unprecedented and undesirable repercussions of "Super Cyclone-99" revealed many more painful truths specially the lack of coordinated effort in the whole system which brought a lot of changes in the thought & actions of the Government of Orissa and resulted in the formation of OSDMA (Orissa State Disaster Mitigation Authority).OSDMA along with the funding and technical support from UNDP (United Nations Development Programme) implemeted CBDP (Community Based Disaster Preparedness Programme) in the 10 most affected blocks of 7 coastal districts of Orissa on pilot basis.

The success of the pilot programme brought Government of India (Ministry of Home Affairs) and UNDP to sign an agreement to cover the blocks of disaster prone districts (125 most vulnerable districts in 12 states of India) under the DRM (Disaster Risk Management) Programme.

The programme seeks to involve Communities, PRIs, NGOs, CBOs, educational institutions and Govt. functionaries in this multi-stake holder disaster mitigation approach, where the community and other local stake holders will come together to prepare their Disaster Management Plans through Resource, Hazard and Vulnerability Analysis. Govt. functionaries /PRIs/ NGOs will provide necessary support for Orientation, Capacity Development, Skill Up-gradation, Awareness Generation and other Technical Inputs as would be required.

Goal : Sustainable reduction in disaster risks in all the 7 blocks,2 ULBs (urban local body),193 GPs and 1356 no of revenue villages of the district.

Objectives: Capacity building support to the district administration.

Environment building, education, awareness programmes and strengthening the capacity at all levels in natural disaster risk management and sustainable recovery.

Multi-hazard preparedness, response and mitigation plans at the district, ULB,block, grampanchyat,revenue village and /ward levels

Networking knowledge on effective approaches, methods and tools for natural disaster risk management, developing and promoting policy frameworks.

OSDMA would carry the above objectives through district administration.

Progress : Information Education & Communication :

Hundreds of posters regarding preparedness during Sunstroke, Flood, Cyclone, Drought, Earthquake and Fire has been distributed thru Blocks, Panchayat Office, Angan Wadi Centers and local Non-Government Organisations through out the district. Number of leaflets regarding implementation of DRM Programme as well as Community Based Disaster Risk Reduction and Recovery has been produced and distributed. Wall Painting on Dos and Don'ts on Disaster is in progress.

Awareness Generation: More than 200 numbers village sensitize meetings, regarding community level disaster preparedness and DRM Programme has been made. All the 193 nos of Grampanchayat Disaster Management Committees (GPDMC), 7 nos of Block Disaster Management Committees (BDMC) & 1 District Disaster Management Committees (DDMC) headed by Collector and District Magistrate, Bhadrak have been formed and thoroughly oriented on DRM Programme in the district. State Disaster Preparedness Day (29th October) is being observed in the district each year, where besides meetings, seminars number of competitions among school children regarding Disaster Risk Management held, specially trained village volunteers organized Mock Drills.

Trainings : Total 22 nos of Govt. as well as NGO members have undergone specialized training on DRM in SIRD, Bhubaneswar jointly by OSDMA, SIRD & UNDP. Orientation thru Video Conferencing and Workshops for Administrative Heads in the state level organized. All the 7 BDMCs, 85 nos of GPDMCs and selected NGOs, VLWs, AAWs, SHG members have under gone specialized training on DPDM and Contingency Plan preparation. 70 nos of volunteers have undergone specialized training on First Aid and Search & Rescue by professional organizations such as St. Jones Ambulance and Civil Defense.

Disaster Management Plans : Total 143 no of Community Contingency Plans-CCP (village plan),10 no of GPDM Plans, 3 nos of Block DM Plans and District DM Plan have been prepared.

District Control Room : District Control Room or District Disaster Management & Information Center has been strengthened with the advent of VHF Set, Fax, Computer with Internet facility etc. All most all the Blocks are directly accessible thru VHF Sets. Process is on to have the same facilities in the other vulnerable areas over and above the 7 blocks. One SAT Phone has been supplied to District Administration by OSDMA. IDRN (India Disaster Resource Network) a newly developed website has been launched by Deputy Prime Minister, Govt. of India, on September 1st, which contains inventory of resources available throughout the State as well as the Nation is definitely a boon for those who are directly involved in the field of Disaster Management.

UNIT-V

Policy Framework Strategies

Global Disaster Risk Situation

In 2001 after the Gujarat earthquake in India, and in 2004 after the tsunami recovery was invariably faster when individual enterprise was matched with an enabling environment.

According to the International Disaster Database, Brussels, Asia is the most disaster-risk vulnerable continent. Asia is also the most vibrant disaster-risk reduction continent in terms of diversity of public and private initiatives. The report of the office of the special envoy for tsunami (Bill Clinton) noted in 2005 that more than one-third of the $15 billion pledged for recovery after the December 2004 earthquake and tsunami in Asia is committed to local NGOs directly or through international NGOs.

Thus, the Second Asian Ministers' Conference to be held in New Delhi this week must set its own agenda, not follow global trends that average out Asia's vulnerabilities and capacities. To set the agenda, Asian agencies must find ways to reinstill the full trust of disaster victims in their governments. These victims, often poor and low income, running microenterprise or small businesses, are the engines of recovery when they find opportunities to work with the government.

In 2001 after the Gujarat earthquake in India, and in 2004 after the tsunami in India, Sri Lanka, Indonesia and Thailand, recovery was invariably faster when individual enterprise was matched with an enabling environment. Over the years, this trust has been eroded by the poor, delayed and inadequate performance of the relief and rehabilitation administration.

Loss assessments often ignore the loss of informal sector housing of the poor as well as lost livelihoods and income. Compensation takes too long and is notoriously below market rates. Coordination is agency-centric and top-down. Most significantly, relief measures leave out risk reduction, exposing the affected citizens to repeated disasters, as seen in the July 2007 floods in India, Nepal and Bangladesh.

Next, disaster risk reduction institutions need to be made more democratic by serving the efforts of local civil society bodies without taking over their mandate. The newly established National Disaster Management Authority in India, Earthquake Reconstruction and Rehabilitation Authority in Pakistan, and Disaster Management Centre in Sri Lanka are examples of such institutions.

Asia's local organizations are the first to respond and the last to remain in the field when international agencies have left. With direct links to local communities, they are apt for identifying potential threats and vulnerabilities, assessing damage, and mobilizing people's capacities between two disasters. They have demonstrated, expanded and mainstreamed risk reduction measures, and challenged development that they believe to induce risk. Asia must make these efforts a priority for governmental and multilateral authorities and agencies.

Asia must also rapidly raise its spending on disaster-risk reduction operations over the next five years. These are critical to making the ongoing tsunami, earthquake and other recoveries safer. These are also critical in context of the fact that Asian countries are driving global economic growth in some areas. The risks of floods, droughts, cyclones and earthquakes can slow the pace of growth and negate past gains.

Further, Asian agencies must initiate civil society oversight for each national and international humanitarian response situation to ensure that the response is inclusive and sustainable. Repeatedly, women, tribals, Dalits, minorities and species. This is a dynamic process that drives the creation of moral and ethical standards. Every human action inspires a corresponding reaction whether subtle in nature or violent. Some people are more emotionally reactive than others. Emotions can get out of control if not regulated by laws, customs, moral codes, professional codes and even the rules of etiquette. Rules are a stabilizing force that enhance the survivability of individuals, families and nations. Mathematically, the initial point* evident in human behavior is the survival of the species. It is defined and redefined in many ways, such as a concern for public safety. The complexity of this process cannot be understated, and it is best described by cybernetic science. There is a considerable difference between the static term "moral standards" and the cybernetic process that creates them. A basic understanding of this process can be conveyed through a series of illustrations:

> *For example, the evolution of traffic laws demonstrates the creation of standards of vehicular conduct directly related to public safety. Public safety itself is dedicated to increasing human survival on the highways. If an action on the highway consistently leads to unnecessary pain, suffering and death, it is an action discouraged by new rules and regulations designed to prohibit it. Thus, by the destructive consequences of human actions, the notion of "right" and "wrong" evolves.*

The standards of vehicle codes integrate seamlessly into cultural morality as illustrated by the example of consuming alcohol while driving an automobile. Here, the standards of behavior are statistical in nature. The probability that any outcome will occur is ranked from the first standard deviation to the fourth. Some of the facts surrounding alcohol abuse go back thousands of years. Alcohol has long been known to have a profound affect on human thinking. The destructive tendencies alcohol motivates is compounded in multiples if you add the simultaneous emotions that, for example, come from the breakup of a romantic relationship—or stress from the workplace. Put job and family problems together with a fifth of 100-proof alcohol and a fast car traveling 10 miles across crowded city streets, and you have the formula for a very likely accident. This destructive behavior conflicts with a fundamental value—self-preservation—and the preservation of others in society. So in time, rules evolve to restrict drinking and driving. Every time there is a tragedy produced by alcohol abuse, it reinforces and perpetuates a long history of the moral sentiments and laws relating to the use of alcohol.

There is larger dimension to the creation of laws prohibiting drinking and driving: There are economic considerations that drive the creation and implementation of new laws based on survival. Economics is a primary force in human cultures; it is a powerful expression of the will to survive. Economics sometimes overrides ethical concerns because the survival as a person, nation or world demands it.

If a society allows intoxicated people to drive on the highways, there is a statistical certainty many unnecessary deaths will occur. Property will also be destroyed, the flow of goods and services will be interrupted and the healthy spirits of people will be damaged. All of these factors, if allowed to go unchecked, will affect the health and efficiency of an economy. Maximizing economic health requires the evolution of behavioral standards that avoid pain, suffering and death and embrace the values of peace, prosperity and productivity. There must be an uninterrupted flow of goods and services and minimal accidents and dislocations sufficient to evoke a societal spirit and willingness to work hard. That is how, in theory, a particular economic or social system survives when others have failed.

The UN, both as an organisation and as individual states, has affirmed its clear commitment to democracy and good governance in numerous declarations over the years.

Importantly, what is essential is not just the formal expressions of democracy. regular elections and parliamentary processes. but substantive, *participatory* democracy. What this means, in practice, is that democratic government needs to be not only *for* the people, but *of* the people and *by* the people. It is not enough that people are able to exercise their vote every few years.

Meaningful democracy requires that people are supported and encouraged to actively engage in their own governance.

Civil society (i.e. non-governmental organisations (NGOs), the media, academics and many other community sector groups) has a vital role to play in this context. While it is true that many civil society groups focus primarily on providing services to the community, experience has shown that civil society groups have also often been key facilitators of government-citizen dialogue as well as having an important monitoring role of government activities. Civil society group.s strength and importance to democracy stem from the fact that they provide a key means for channelling the views and needs of the broader public due to the power that collectivity and solidarity can give to individual voices. Civil society groups often act as a medium for individuals who may either not be comfortable engaging directly with government or who may just not know how to have the views put forward to policy-makers.

There are many issues that affect the livelihood and effectiveness of civil society. Generally, the main restrictions on civil society are caused by the laws that regulate the various branches of civil society. Government procedure, bureaucracy and inefficiency of public officers can also be as damaging to NGOs as a restrictive law. The attitude of governments around the Commonwealth towards civil society varies greatly and, consequently, so do the laws they enact to regulate it.

There are various laws that can restrict civil society, such as restrictions on the media and on NGO registration, as well as restrictions on the freedom of expression and freedom of assembly.

The subject matter can be very wide and it is important to keep this in mind in order to understand the large extent to which civil society is affected in so many areas by so many varying aspects of the law.

One area, which deserves to be examined in particular, is that of laws, rules and regulations that affect NGOs. these could be either specific NGO Acts or other legislation which directly or indirectly affect the livelihood and work of NGOs.

Whilst the term. civil society organisation. (CSO) encompasses many more different types of organisations than non-governmental organisations (NGOs), this paper focuses primarily on laws that affect NGOs. This choice was made in order to narrow down the focus of the discussion to one that is more easily manageable.

Application of Sociology in the Classroom Situation

In recent decades, calls for improvement of the undergraduate experience have addressed the need for attention to what best fosters student learning on college campuses. Recognizing that learning hinges on student experiences both within and outside the classroom, educators need to commit to build a campus community that maximizes student learning (Boyer, 1987; Chickering & Gamson, 1987; Gabelnick, MacGregor, Matthews, & Smith, 1990; Study Group on the Conditions of Excellence in American Higher Education, 1984; Watson & Stage, 1999). By considering the classroom environment itself as a community setting, this chapter provides a view of the classroom through a sociological lens. We focus on what social factors either advance or inhibit student learning. Considering how social factors affect the teaching and learning exchange between faculty and students and among peers in a classroom enables educators to address structural inequities and promote learning for students of varying backgrounds.

Education as a Social Experience

American higher education provides a means to fulfill several social purposes: transmit knowledge to succeeding generations, reproduce cul- tural traditions and norms, discover new knowledge, and develop an educated citizenry in a democratic society (Brubacher & Rudy, 1968). Dewey (1916/1966) emphasized education as a "vitally social or vitally shared" (p. 6) experience, through which social groups maintain their existence.

Dewey added, "It is [also] the aim of progressive education to take part in correcting unfair privilege and unfair deprivation, not to perpetuate them" (1916/1966, pp. 119–120). Although higher education offers avenues of social mobility through which individuals can improve their occupational and economic status, educators have a responsibility to address intentional inequities so all students can take advantage of its resources. Students who enter colleges and universities differ in their backgrounds; likewise, their experiences in the college environment vary. Evidence of these differences can be observed in the persistence rates of students whose parents did not attend college versus those students whose did. First-generation college student status has a negative association with students' academic preparation and persistence (Warburton, Bugarin, & Nunez, 2001). Meanwhile, minority students experience inequities on predominantly White campuses (Watson & Terrell, 1999), and minorities inhabit substantially different academic, social, and psychological worlds than their White counterparts (Pascarella & Terenzini, 1991). In another example of how students can experience college differently, Canada and Pringle (1995) identified a theme in the feminist literature that in many college communities women are treated as "second-class citizens" (p. 166).

Based on the plethora of literature on college student persistence, there is strong interest in learning how students succeed in college and what factors impede their progress. Although copious efforts have been directed at improving nonacademic areas of institutions, work remains in responding to the research to adjust the academic experiences of students (Tinto, 1998). Because faculty–student and peer interactions influence many college effects on students (Pascarella & Terenzini, 1991), the college classroom is a logical focal point.

Sociology of the Classroom

Palmer (1998) offered that knowing and learning are communal acts shared among individuals. Because most college classes are held with the same participants over several weeks or months, one can consider them groups. Even groups that have a short duration have characteristics, such as beliefs, leaders, and norms, that may shape members' actions (Fassinger, 1997). Further, because all class participants belong to the larg- er college community, it follows that the classroom setting has the potential to become a site of community itself. As students and faculty develop relationships over time through interaction and common goals, social forces emerge that either facilitate or impede learning. These social influences can be considered the sociology of the classroom.

Sociologists often focus on how social status, role relationships, and structural inequalities affect individuals in a social context (Thoits, 1995). In the context of a college classroom, social status can include the gender, race, age, and social class of the students and the instructor. For example, students with lower status backgrounds may experience more difficulty adjusting to college life than their higher status peers do. The college environment reflects the social relationships of upper-level, white-collar work (e.g., faculty and students are free from constant supervision; Mickelson, 1980). In this milieu, while some from blue-collar, minority, or disadvantaged backgrounds manage to quickly grasp the tacit rules, they may still feel like outsiders. Bourdieu and Passeron (1977) maintained that students are not equally equipped to attend college, as only some students benefit from higher levels of cultural capital (such as ways of thinking, types of dispositions, and cultural mores of the higher status groups).

Families that are not as connected to sources of cultural capital may not prepare their students adequately for the transition to college. Role relationships can be discerned by observing interaction patterns between the instructor and students and among student peers. In each classroom, rules and norms influence interactions among class participants. These norms of discourse shape the patterns of participation, that is, who participates and who does not (Sykes, 1990), whether one feels free to disagree with the instructor or other students, how to deal with conflicts, what kinds of questions are acceptable, and, in general, how to act appropriately in a classroom.

Falchikov (1986) noted that students hold an unequal position of power, and this structural inequity can inhibit the students' development of responsibility and autonomy.

Traditionally, professors hold an asymmetrical power position in the classroom by designing the syllabus, assigning work, and evaluating students' performance. Ways in which faculty exercise or share their authority influence how students learn through pedagogical strategies, and they affect the classroom environment. With their authority, instructors can decide how to structure the class participants' interactions by reinforcing some behaviors and deterring others.

Faculty teaching role performance norms are guided by the goal of serving the welfare of clients, such as students and the academic discipline (Braxton & Bayer, 1999). In the classroom, the teaching norms provide a framework within which faculty interact with individual students and with students as a group. Braxton and Bayer (1999) specified seven normative patterns in college teaching that are deemed unacceptable by faculty: condescending negativism, inattentive planning, moral turpitude, particularistic grading, personal disregard, uncommunicated course details, and uncooperative cynicism. Defined briefly in their relation to faculty–student interaction, condescending negativism occurs when a faculty member publicly demeans a student; inattentive planning indicates a lack of appropriate preparation or structure for students to learn; moral turpitude means relating to students in an unprofessional, immoral manner; particularistic grading is evaluating students in unfair or unmeritorious ways; examples of personal disregard are being routinely unprepared for class, arriving late to class, and frequently using profanity; uncommunicated course details include failing to inform students about changes in class time and location; and uncooperative cynicism reflects a cynical attitude toward teaching and a refusal to participate in teaching-related departmental matters. These seven norms support faculty–student interaction that is genuine, caring, fair, moral, and well considered.

Research also indicates that student peers have a significant effect on the norms of the classroom, both by how individuals choose to interact and how they hinder or encourage their classmates' involvement (Colbeck, Campbell, & Bjorklund, 2000;

Fassinger, 1997; Hallinan & Smith, 1989). It follows that both faculty and students affect the characteristics of the classroom environment, which in turn influences student learning.

Classroom Climate and Interaction

Classroom climate refers to the kind of learning environment that exists in a classroom. Instructors can influence classroom climate by emphasizing the type of learning environment, such as valuing achievement, love of learning (Hallinan & Smith, 1989), competition, collaboration, or caring. Teachers structure the learning environment by making pedagogical choices, and both instructors and students play an active role in defining the interactions among classroom participants. What characteristics of a classroom environment support or hinder student learning?

What characteristics have differential effects depending on the students' characteristics? These questions are considered by assessing research findings on the interaction between faculty and students and the interaction between student peers.

Student–Faculty Interaction

Research on classroom interaction and its effects on learning supports the assumption that a student's level of classroom participation is related to intellectual skill development (Terenzini, Theophilides, & Lorang, 1984). Student learning is also associated with the perception that faculty are devoted teachers, as evidenced by intellectually challenging classes and encouraging students to discuss their perspectives in class (Volkwein & Cabrera, 1998). Students' perceptions of the instructor influence the amount of academic effort students exert. For example, students who perceive gender equity from the instructor experience an increase in their sense of responsibility for their own learning (Colbeck, Cabrera, & Terenzini, 2000) and a higher level of confidence in their abilities. In a different study, students who perceived high levels of faculty concern and interaction with student peers reported the most beneficial class experiences (Volkwein & Cabrera, 1998).

Evidence of deleterious effects of classroom climate exists also. In contrast to the positive classroom influences previously discussed, Pulvers and Diekhoff (1999) found that students who admitted to cheating described their classes as significantly less personalized, less task oriented, and less satisfying than did noncheaters. Further, the students justified their deviant behavior in part because of their perceptions of the classroom climate. In addition to the three characteristics just mentioned, those who were academically dishonest perceived their classes as less involving, less cohesive, and less individualized. Thus, faculty–student interactions can also impede student learning.

Hall and Sandler (1982) describe differences in how some professors discriminate against women students compared to men classmates, spurring the chilly climate for women in the classroom as a focus of research efforts. The authors hypothesize that by treating students differ- ently by gender, professors negatively affect the success of women students. The research findings about this issue are mixed. For example, ear-lier work by Karp and Yoels (1976) affirmed that students' classroom behavior is different with a man or a woman as professor. Women students participated more actively with instructors of the same gender, and men professors were more likely to call on men students. More recently, Fassinger (1995) compared students' perceptions of their instructors by gender. The gender of the faculty member had little effect on men students' perceptions of themselves. In the only significant indicator, men perceived that they were more likely to comprehend course material when taught by women instructors versus men instructors. In contrast, several women students' perceptions of themselves (e.g., confidence, comprehension of class material, and class participation) were higher when taught by women professors. No self-perceptions of either men or women students favored men instructors. Fassinger suggests that both men and women students might experience a chillier climate in men professors' courses at the institution in which the study was conducted (p. 89).

Canada and Pringle (1995) also examined gender issues and faculty–student classroom interactions by studying mixed-sex and all-women college classrooms. They found that faculty–student interaction patterns changed when comparing all-women classes with mixed-sex classes. Men students acted differently than women students, and women students and professors of both sexes behaved differently in mixed-sex classes. In all-women classrooms, men and women professors initiated contact with students with similar frequencies. In mixed-sex classrooms, however, men professors initiated contact less frequently, and women professors initiated contact more often. In mixed-sex classes with higher percentages of men students, women students initiated follow-up interactions less frequently, and men students initiated follow-up contact more often. Although the nature of faculty–student interaction has some different effects on men and women students in some studies, in others, men and women students perceived their instructors as treating both genders equally (Colbeck, Cabrera, et al., 2000) and having no influence on their classroom participation (Karp & Yoels, 1976).

Goodwin and Stevens (1993) studied the influence of gender on faculty perceptions of good teaching. Overall, few gender differences were found, but women professors showed higher mean averages than men professors on four characteristics of good teaching: (a) concern about improving students' higher order thinking, (b) concern about students' self-esteem, (c) encouraging student interaction via small-group activities, and (d) seeking a variety of learning levels via exams and discussions. Men professors seem to value student evaluations more than women, whereas women appear more interested in seeking outside assistance to improve their teaching.

The inconsistent findings discussed on the effects of gender on facultystudent interaction indicate that there is potential for instructors to influence student learning through the type of environment they encourage (and discourage) through their interactions. Research shows that the pedagogical approaches faculty take in structuring courses also influence the classroom climate. Faculty who include collaborative and active learning strategies in their teaching, offer feedback to and interact with students, are clear and organized, and treat students equitably help mediate the negative effects of a competitive classroom climate (Colbeck, Cabrera, et al., 2000). Not surprisingly, the researchers also found that poor teaching and competitive classroom atmospheres served as barriers to participation of engineering and science students for both men and women (Colbeck, Cabrera, et al., 2000).

Given the research findings on classroom interactions, informed instructors can make intentional pedagogical choices that positively affect student learning. For instance, academics can ease the transition for students with working-class backgrounds who attend college. Green- wald and Grant (1999) described the position of having a working-class background and teaching at a college as "existing between the borders of both worlds, feeling fully at home in neither" (p. 28). Working-class students also felt alienated—a barrier to their success. Professors who recognize the situation can purposefully include course material or examples that reflect real-life, diverse experiences. For example, choosing texts that reflect a wide range of experiences helps demonstrate the diversity within ethnic and class groups (Esposito, 1999). By engaging in the classroom environment, working-class students create a place for themselves in the academy (Greenwald & Grant, 1999). Providing ways for students to integrate their experiences and inviting them to take responsibility for their learning is an example of empowering students to bridge the two environments. Students who value their own backgrounds and experiences can see them as a source of strength rather than weakness as they progress in college (Heathcott, 1999).

Other cultural aspects influence student learning. Many students experience a gap between their natural learning style and how material is presented in class. Anderson (1988) posited that learning styles differ among ethnic and racial groups, given that they reflect different cultural, social, and environmental backgrounds. Learning styles are the "ways students begin to concentrate on, process, internalize, and remember new and difficult academic information" (Dunn, 2000). These learning style differences are expressed in the classroom. With some notable exceptions (e.g., tribal colleges, historically Black colleges and universities) the American higher education system reflects the dominant, Euro-American, Western cultural norms. Characteristics of the Western worldview include emphasizing competition, individual achievement, a nuclear family, and a task orientation. Student (and faculty) populations who have a non-Western orientation, such as Native Americans, Hispanic Americans, African Americans, and Asian Americans, are more likely to emphasize group cooperation and achievement, have an extended family, and be socially oriented. Some rural and White women identify more closely with the non-Western worldview. Where the Western orientation dovetails with the culture of higher education, the non-Western style often conflicts with the traditional learning environment. As a result, many students experience a gap between their natural learning style and how material is presented, contributing to a feeling of not fitting in, or alienation. For example, Mexican American and African American students are sometimes criticized for their "symbolic, affective, reality-based" style of learning, even being labeled as deficient (Dunn, 2000).

Dunn and Griggs's (1995) work affirms that cultural differences exist in learning styles among the five major cultural groups in the United States: African Americans, Asian Americans, Hispanic Americans, Native Americans, and Euro-Americans. Noting the large differences in learning style preferences within groups as well as between groups, the authors stressed the need for multiple learning style perspectives in classrooms. Professors who are familiar with different learning styles can aid students in connecting to course material in ways that are meaningful to them, thus helping them learn more effectively.

Dunn and Griggs's (1995) learning-style approach identifies five stimulus areas that affect how an individual learns effectively. Personal knowledge of reactions to these stimuli can enhance understanding of new and challenging concepts. Similarly, instructors who understand that individuals learn best in different ways can design courses that allow diverse learning opportunities. The five stimuli are environmental, emotional, sociological, physiological, and psychological. Although a full discussion of learning styles is beyond the scope of this chapter, Whitley and Littleton (2000) provided examples of how professors can integrate one aspect of learning styles in their teaching by attending to physiological preferences. Instructors can attend to various perceptual preferences by providing both oral and written directions for completing assignments for auditory and visual learners. Using charts and graphs helps visual learners conceptualize abstract ideas. Providing physical models, experiential learning exercises, or demonstrations offer ways for tactual and kinesthetic learners to grasp difficult concepts. Cultural differences also interact with learning styles. For example, Euro-Americans tend to prefer auditory learning, Native Americans and Hispanic Americans prefer visual stimuli, and African Americans are more likely to be kinesthetic learners (Dunn & Griggs, 1995).

A second learning style area focuses on sociological aspects. Students' sociological preferences include working alone, in pairs, or in larger groups; learning with an authoritative versus a collegial instructor; and learning with a routine structure or with a variety of social groupings (Dunn, 2000). Euro-Americans tend to prefer learning alone, whereas Native Americans tend to be more peer oriented (Dunn & Griggs, 1995). As stated earlier, each of the groups of students includes wide withingroup variations. Faculty who understand different learning styles and integrate a variety of teaching techniques to address them will likely help a diverse student body learn more effectively in the classroom.

Student–Student Interaction

Although faculty–student interactions affect the classroom climate and student learning, peer interactions also help shape the classroom climate, especially in courses that involve group collaboration (Colbeck, Campbell, et al., 2000), and they may facilitate or limit student learning (Hallinan & Smith, 1989). Because students are part of the classroom community, they share responsibility for class interactions.

Colbeck, Cabrera, et al. (2000) studied engineering students' perceptions of their interactions with their instructor and their peers. Men and women students' perceptions of how men treated women differed significantly. Women were more likely to perceive that men occasionally treated them differently from how the men treated their men peers. This perception difference was even stronger when the students were asked about their small-group interactions. Put differently, women students perceived gender discrimination from their men peers but not from faculty (Colbeck, Cabrera, et al., 2000).

Students' perceptions of the friendliness of their peers contributed to how often they were willing to speak in class, whereas their perceptions of the instructor had less impact on their participation (Fassinger, 1997). When women students were praised and perceived a supportive class- room environment, they felt more encouraged to participate than did their men peers (Reynolds & Nunn, 1997). Examining both students' and professors' contributions to classroom interaction, Fassinger (1995) found that student traits (e.g., confidence) and class traits (e.g., supportive classmates) were better predictors of stu- dents' participation or silence than instructor traits, such as approachability, discussion style, and expertness. Based on this work, Fassinger suggested that professors can have the greatest impact on classroom interaction through their course designs, such as involving students in ways that build their confidence and developing more assignments in which students work cooperatively.

Seven variables shed light on why students participate verbally in class: confidence, class size, how often students speak with each other (rather than their teacher) in class, interest in subject matter, contributing positively affects one's grade, the emotional climate of the class, and the gender of the student (men participate more) (Fassinger, 1997). What might be reasons for students to choose to not participate in class? Stu- dents may be frustrated with domineering peers, fear appearing stupid, have low confidence levels, be shy, arrive unprepared, experience uncom- fortable feelings about the topic, be sleep deprived, not understand the material in the manner it was presented, perceive that the professor does not really want discussion, or feel anxiety about being singled out as a model member of a group. For example, students may want to avoid the position of having to speak for all members of their religious or ethnic group. Research on cultural traditions indicates that some Native Ameri-can students and Asian students may not participate actively in the class-room out of respect for the instructor and his or her authority (Vasquez &Wainstein, 1999).

This list does not exhaust the possibilities of why a student chooses tobe silent in class; still, it provides clues to the complex dynamics of class-room interaction. It is possible for any or a combination of the precedingsituations to influence a particular student on a particular day. Clearly,many of the reasons are solely the students' responsibility, such as arriv-ing with adequate preparation and rest. With others, an instructor's in-tervention may encourage a classroom climate that supports respectfuldiscourse among classmates and advances other effective learning condi-tions for diverse populations.

Approaches to Promote Student Learning in the ClassroomMany research studies cited in this chapter refer to approaches to pro-mote student learning. The pedagogical methods described here—collab-orative learning and cooperative learning—fit under the umbrella term*active learning*. Active learning maximizes student involvement in learn-ing with other students and promotes students' responsibility for theirintellectual growth (Davis & Murrell, 1993).Collaborative learning methods offer an alternative to traditional, lecture-style, authority-oriented classrooms. With the shift from ateacher-centered to a learner-centered environment, the collaborativeclassroom becomes an interdependent community (Smith & MacGregor,1992). Students and instructors share a common goal: working togetherto increase understanding. Collaborative learning is significantly andpositively associated with increases in student self-perceptions (Col-beck, Cabrera, et al., 2000).

Cooperative learning refers to a set of learning strategies that encour-ages students to work together on a structured task in a collaborative,noncompetitive manner (Davis & Murrell, 1993). Smith and MacGregor(1992) identified cooperative learning as the most structured on the col-laborative learning continuum. In a cooperative learning approach, stu-dents typically work on specific tasks in small groups, and each personcontributes to complete the task, project, or problem. Through the interde-pendent process, many students feel a sense of community develop fromcooperative learning activities. The positive peer relationships promote alearning environment, which supports diverse student learning styles(Kreke, Fields, & Towns, 1998) and develops intergroup (e.g., race or ethnicity) friendships (Slavin, 1985).

Although collaborative and cooperative learning are pedagogicalmethods, the learning community model is a structural approach toimprove the curriculum (Davis & Murrell, 1993). Put differently, learningcommunities are a "purposeful restructuring of the curriculum to linktogether courses so that students find greater coherence in what they arelearning and increased interaction with faculty and fellow students" (Gabelnick et al., 1990). Though there is wide variation in how cam-puses design learning communities, there are two common goals: Provideintellectual coherence and block scheduling so students share an academ-ic and social community"(Smith & MacGregor, 1992).

DiscussionResearchers recommend ways to create a classroom environment thatsupports student learning. Gould (2000–01) suggests seven strategies thatbuild classroom communities: (a) demonstrate the process of a democrat-ic classroom, (b) treat the students with respect, (c) provide a safe base forconversation, (d) model emotional support, (e) encourage real conversa- tions, (f) encourage students to challenge themselves and each other, and (g) ask students to design meaningful and interesting tasks. Findings from a different study encourage a nonhierarchical, mutually supportive classroom dynamic that supports differences (Gardner, Dean, & McKaig, 1989). From a review of teaching improvement literature, Braxton, Eimers, and Bayer (1996) identified six recommendations to improve undergraduate teaching and learning: (a) encourage faculty and student contact, (b) advise through a systematic programme, (c) offer feedback on student performance, (d) learn about students, (e) foster egalitarianism

Herman E. Daly argues that sometimes the terms internationalization and globalization are used interchangeably but there is a significant formal difference. The term "internationalization" refers to the importance of international trade, relations, treaties etc. owing to the (hypcthetical) immobility of labour and capital between or among nations.

History

The term "globalization" has been used by economists since the 1980s although it was used in social sciences in the 1960s; however, its concepts did not become popular until the latter half of the 1980s and 1990s. The earliest written theoretical concepts of globalization were penned by an American entrepreneur-turned-minister Charles Taze Russell who coined the term 'corporate giants' in 1897.

Globalization is viewed as a centuries long process, tracking the expansion of human population and the growth of civilization, that has accelerated dramatically in the past 50 years. Early forms of globalization existed during the Roman Empire, the Parthian empire, and the Han Dynasty, when the Silk Road started in China, reached the boundaries of the Parthian empire, and continued onwards towards Rome.

The Islamic Golden Age is also an example, when Muslim traders and explorers established an early global economy across the Old World resulting in a globalization of crops, trade, knowledge and technology; and later during the Mongol Empire, when there was greater integration along the Silk Road.

Globalization in a wider context began shortly before the turn of the 16th century, with two Kingdoms of the Iberian Peninsula-the Kingdom of Portugal and the Kingdom of Castile.

Portugal's global explorations in the 16th century, especially, linked continents, economies and cultures to a massive extent. Portugal's exploration and trade with most of the coast of Africa, Eastern South America, and Southern and Eastern Asia, was the first major trade based form of globalization. A wave of global trade, colonization, and enculturation reached all corners of the world.

Global integration continued through the expansion of European trade in the 16th and 17th centuries, when the Portuguese and Spanish Empires colonized the Americas, followed eventually by France and England. Globalization has had a tremendous impact on cultures, particularly indigenous cultures, around the world. In the 15th century, Portugal's Company of Guinea was one of the first chartered commercial companies established by Europeans in other continent during the Age of Discovery, whose task was to deal with the spices and to fix the prices of the goods.

In the 17th century, globalization became a business phenomenon when the British East India Company (founded in 1600), which is often described as the first multinational corporation, was established, as well as the Dutch East India Company (founded in 1602) and the Portuguese East India Company (founded in 1628). Because of the large investment and financing needs and the high risks involved with international trade, the British East India Company became the first company in the world to share risk and enable joint ownership of companies through the issuance of shares of stock: an important driver for globalization.

Globalization was achieved by the British Empire (the largest empire in history) due to its sheer size and power. British ideals and culture were imposed on other nations during this period.

The 19th century is sometimes called "The First Era of Globalization." It was a period characterized by rapid growth in international trade and investment between the European imperial powers, their colonies, and, later, the United States.

It was in this period that areas of sub-saharan Africa and the Island Pacific were incorporated into the world system. The "First Era of Globalization" began to break down at the beginning of the 20th century with the first World War. Said John Maynard Keynes,

"The inhabitant of London could order by telephone, sipping his morning tea, the various products of the whole earth, and reasonably expect their early delivery upon his doorstep.

Militarism and imperialism of racial and cultural rivalries were little more than the amusements of his daily newspaper. What an extraordinary episode in the economic progress of man was that age which came to an end in August 1914."

The "First Era of Globalization" later collapsed during the gold standard crisis and Great Depression in the late 1920s and early 1930s.

In late 2000s much of the industrialized world entered into a deep recession. Some analysts say the world is going through a period of deglobalization after years of increasing economic integration. Up to 45% of global wealth had been destroyed by the global financial crisis in little less than a year and a half.

Modern Globalization

Globalization, since World War II, is largely the result of planning by politicians to breakdown borders hampering trade to increase prosperity and interdependence thereby decreasing the chance of future war. Their work led to the Bretton Woods conference, an agreement by the world's leading politicians to lay down the framework for international commerce and finance, and the founding of several international institutions intended to oversee the processes of globalization.

These institutions include the International Bank for Reconstruction and Development (the World Bank), and the International Monetary Fund. Globalization has been facilitated by advances in technology which have reduced the costs of trade, and trade negotiation rounds, originally under the auspices of the General Agreement on Tariffs and Trade (GATT), which led to a series of agreements to remove restrictions on free trade. Since World War II, barriers to international trade have been considerably lowered through international agreements-GATT. Particular initiatives carried out as a result of GATT and the World Trade Organization (WTO), for which GATT is the foundation, have included:

- Promotion of free trade:
    - o elimination of tariffs; creation of free trade zones with small or no tariffs

- o Reduced transportation costs, especially resulting from development of containerization for ocean shipping.
- o Reduction or elimination of capital controls
- o Reduction, elimination, or harmonization of subsidies for local businesses
- o Creation of subsidies for global corporations
- o Harmonization of intellectual property laws across the majority of states, with more restrictions.
- o Supranational recognition of intellectual property restrictions (e.g. patents granted by China would be recognized in the United States)

Cultural globalization, driven by communication technology and the worldwide marketing of Western cultural industries, was understood at first as a process of homogenization, as the global domination of American culture at the expense of traditional diversity.

However, a contrasting trend soon became evident in the emergence of movements protesting against globalization and giving new momentum to the defense of local uniqueness, individuality, and identity, but largely without success.

The Uruguay Round (1986 to 1994) led to a treaty to create the WTO to mediate trade disputes and set up a uniform platform of trading. Other bilateral and multilateral trade agreements, including sections of Europe's Maastricht Treaty and the North American Free Trade Agreement (NAFTA) have also been signed in pursuit of the goal of reducing tariffs and barriers to trade.

Global conflicts, such as the 9/11 terrorist attacks on the United States of America, is interrelated with globalization because it was primary source of the "war on terror", which had started the steady increase of the prices of oil and gas, due to the fact that most OPEC member countries were in the Arabian Peninsula.

World exports rose from 8.5% of gross world product in 1970 to 16.1% of gross world product in 2001.

Measuring Globalization

Looking specifically at economic globalization, demonstrates that it can be measured in different ways. These center around the four main economic flows that characterize globalization:

- Goods and services, e.g. exports plus imports as a proportion of national income or per capita of population
- Labour/people, e.g. net migration rates; inward or outward migration flows, weighted by population
- Capital, e.g. inward or outward direct investment as a proportion of national income or per head of population
- Technology, e.g. international research & development flows; proportion of populations (and rates of change thereof) using particular inventions (especially 'factor-neutral' technological advances such as the telephone, motorcar, broadband)

As globalization is not only an economic phenomenon, a multivariate approach to measuring globalization is the recent index calculated by the Swiss think tank KOF. The index measures the three main dimensions of globalization: economic, social, and political.

In addition to three indices measuring these dimensions, an overall index of globalization and sub-indices referring to actual economic flows, economic restrictions, data on personal contact, data on information flows, and data on cultural proximity is calculated. Data is available on a yearly basis for 122 countries, as detailed in Dreher, Gaston and Martens (2008).

According to the index, the world's most globalized country is Belgium, followed by Austria, Sweden, the United Kingdom and the Netherlands. The least globalized countries according to the KOF-index are Haiti, Myanmar the Central African Republic and Burundi.

A.T. Kearney and *Foreign Policy Magazine* jointly publish another Globalization Index. According to the 2006 index, Singapore, Ireland, Switzerland, the Netherlands, Canada and Denmark are the most globalized, while Indonesia, India and Iran are the least globalized among countries listed.

Food Security

Food security refers to the availability of food and one's access to it. A household is considered food secure when its occupants do not live in hunger or fear of starvation. According to the World Resources Institute, global per capita food production has been increasing substantially for the past several decades. In 2006, MSNBC reported that globally, the number of people who are overweight has surpassed the number who are undernourished-the world had more than one billion people who were overweight, and an estimated 800 million who were undernourished. According to a 2004 article from the BBC, China, the world's most populous country, is suffering from an obesity epidemic.

Worldwide around 852 million people are chronically hungry due to extreme poverty, while up to 2 billion people lack food security intermittently due to varying degrees of poverty (source: FAO, 2003). As of late 2007, increased farming for use in biofuels, world oil prices at more than $100 a barrel, global population growth, climate change, loss of agricultural land to residential and industrial development, and growing consumer demand in China and India have pushed up the price of grain. Food riots have recently taken place in many countries across the world.

It is becoming increasingly difficult to maintain food security in a world beset by a confluence of "peak" phenomena, namely peak oil, peak water, peak grain and peak fish. More than half of the planet's population, numbering approximately 3.3 billion people, live in urban areas as of November 2007. Any disruption to farm supplies may precipitate a uniquely urban food crisis in a relatively short time. The ongoing global credit crisis has affected farm credits, despite a boom in commodity prices. Food security is a complex topic, standing at the intersection of many disciplines.

A new peer-reviewed journal of *Food Security: The Science, Sociology and Economics of Food Production and Access to Food* is to be published from 2009. In developing countries, often 70% or more of the population lives in rural areas. In that context, agricultural development among smallholder farmers and landless people provides a livelihood for people allowing them the opportunity to stay in their communities. In many areas of the world, land ownership is not available, thus, people who want or need to farm to make a living have little incentive to improve the land.

In the US, there are approximately 2,000,000 farmers, less than 1% of the population. A direct relationship exists between food consumption levels and poverty. Families with the financial resources to escape extreme poverty rarely suffer from chronic hunger; while poor families not only suffer the most from chronic hunger, but are also the segment of the population most at risk during food shortages and famines.

Two commonly used definitions of food security come from the UN's Food and Agriculture Organization (FAO) and the United States Department of Agriculture (USDA):

- Food security exists when all people, at all times, have physical and economic access to sufficient, safe and nutritious food to meet their dietary needs and food preferences for an active and healthy life. (FAO)
- Food security for a household means access by all members at all times to enough food for an active, healthy life. Food security includes at a minimum (1) the ready availability of nutritionally adequate and safe foods, and (2) an assured ability to acquire acceptable foods in socially acceptable ways (that is, without resorting to emergency food supplies, scavenging, stealing, or other coping strategies). (USDA)

The stages of food insecurity range from food secure situations to full-scale famine. "Famine and hunger are both rooted in food insecurity. Food insecurity can be categorized as either chronic or transitory. Chronic food insecurity translates into a high degree of vulnerability to famine and hunger; ensuring food security presupposes elimination of that vulnerability. [Chronic] hunger is not famine. It is similar to undernourishment and is related to poverty, existing mainly in poor countries."

Global Water Crisis: Water deficits, which are already spurring heavy grain imports in numerous smaller countries, may soon do the same in larger countries, such as China or India. The water tables are falling in scores of countries (including Northern China, the US, and India) due to widespread overpumping using powerful diesel and electric pumps. Other countries affected include Pakistan, Afghanistan, and Iran. This will eventually lead to water scarcity and cutbacks in grain harvest. Even with the overpumping of its aquifers, China is developing a grain deficit.

When this happens, it will almost certainly drive grain prices upward. Most of the 3 billion people projected to be added worldwide by mid-century will be born in countries already experiencing water shortages. After China and India, there is a second tier of smaller countries with large water deficits—Afghanistan, Algeria, Egypt, Iran, Mexico, and Pakistan. Four of these already import a large share of their grain. Only Pakistan remains self-sufficient. But with a population expanding by 4 million a year, it will also likely soon turn to the world market for grain.

Land Degradation

Intensive farming often leads to a vicious cycle of exhaustion of soil fertility and decline of agricultural yields. Approximately 40% of the world's agricultural land is seriously degraded. In Africa, if current trends of soil degradation continue, the continent might be able to feed just 25% of its population by 2025, according to UNU's Ghana-based Institute for Natural Resources in Africa.

Land Deals

Rich governments and corporations are buying up the rights to millions of hectares of agricultural land in developing countries in an effort to secure their own long-term food supplies. The head of the Food and Agriculture Organisation (FAO), Jacques Diouf, has warned that the controversial rise in land deals could create a form of "neocolonialism", with poor states producing food for the rich at the expense of their own hungry people. The South Korean firm Daewoo Logistics has secured a large piece of farmland in Madagascar to grow maize and crops for biofuels. Libya has secured 250,000 hectares of Ukrainian farmland, and China has begun to explore land deals in Southeast Asia. Oil-rich Arab investors, including the sovereign wealth funds, are looking into Sudan, Ethiopia, Ukraine, Kazakhstan, Pakistan, Cambodia and Thailand.

Climate Change

Agriculture

According to a UN climate report, the Himalayan glaciers that are the principal dry-season water sources of Asia's biggest rivers-Ganges, Indus, Brahmaputra, Yangtze, Mekong, Salween and Yellow-could disappear by 2035 as temperatures rise. Approximately 2.4 billion people live in the drainage basin of the Himalayan rivers. India, China, Pakistan, Afghanistan, Bangladesh, Nepal and Manmar could experience floods followed by severe droughts in coming decades.

In India alone, the Ganges provides water for drinking and farming for more than 500 million people. The west coast of North America, which gets much of its water from glaciers in mountain ranges such as the Rocky Mountains and Sierra Nevada, also would be affected. Glaciers aren't the only worry that the developing nations have, sea level is also reported to rise as climate changes progresses, reducing the amount of land available for agriculture.

In other parts of the world a big effect will be low yields of grain according to the World Food Trade Model, specifically in the low latitude regions where much of the developing world is located. From this the price of grain will rise, along with the developing nations trying to grow the grain. Due to this, every 2-2.5% price hike will increase the number of hungry people 1%. And low crop yields is just one of the problem facing farmers in the low latitudes and tropical regions. The timing and length of the growing seasons, when farmers plant their crops, are going to be changing dramatically, per the USDA, due to unknown changes in soil temperature and moisture conditions.

Children

On 2008-04-29, a UNICEF UK report found that the world's poorest and most vulnerable children are being hit the hardest by the impact of climate change. The report, "Our Climate, Our Children, Our Responsibility: The Implications of Climate Change for the World's Children," says access to clean water and food supplies will become more difficult, particularly in Africa and Asia.

Wheat Stem Rust

An epidemic of stem rust on wheat caused by race Ug99 is currently spreading across Africa and into Asia and is causing major concern. A virulent wheat disease could destroy most of the world's main wheat crops, leaving millions to starve. The fungus has spread from Africa to Iran, and may already be in Pakistan.

The genetic diversity of the crop wild relatives of wheat can be used to improve modern varieties to be more resistant to rust. In their centers of origin wild wheat plants are screened for resistance to rust, then their genetic information is analysed and finally wild plants and modern varietes are crossed through means of modern plant breeding in order to transfer the resistance genes from the wild plants to the modern varieties.

Achieving Food Security

"The number of people without enough food to eat on a regular basis remains stubbornly high, at over 800 million, and is not falling significantly. Over 60% of the world's undernourished people live in Asia, and a quarter in Africa. The proportion of people who are hungry, however, is greater in Africa (33%) than Asia (16%). The latest FAO figures indicate that there are 22 countries, 16 of which are in Africa, in which the undernourishment prevalence rate is over 35%."

In its "The State of Food Insecurity in the World 2003", FAO states that:

> *'In general the countries that succeeded in reducing hunger were characterised by more rapid economic growth and specifically more rapid growth in their*

agricultural sectors. They also exhibited slower population growth, lower levels of HIV and higher ranking in the Human Development Index'.

As such, according to FAO, addressing agriculture and population growth is vital to achieving food security. Other organisations and people (eg Peter Singer, ...) too have come to this conclusion and advocate improvements in agriculture, and population control.

USAID proposes several key steps to increasing agricultural productivity which is in turn key to increasing rural income and reducing food insecurity. They include:

- Boosting agricultural science and technology. Current agricultural yields are insufficient to feed the growing populations. Eventually, the rising agricultural productivity drives economic growth.
- Securing property rights and access to finance.
- Enhancing human capital through education and improved health.
- Conflict prevention and resolution mechanisms and democracy and governance based on principles of accountability and transparency in public institutions and the rule of law are basic to reducing vulnerable members of society.

The UN Millennium Development Goals are one of the initiatives aimed at achieving food security in the world. In its list of goals, the first Millennium Development Goal states that the UN "is to eradicate extreme hunger and poverty", and that "agricultural productivity is likely to play a key role in this if it is to be reached on time".

"Of the eight Millennium Development Goals, eradicating extreme hunger and poverty depends on agriculture the most. (MDG 1 calls for halving hunger and poverty by 2015 in relation to 1990.)

Notably, the gathering of wild food plants appears to be an efficient alternative method of subsistence in tropical countries, which may play a role in poverty alleviation.

The Agriculture-hunger-poverty Nexus

Eradicating hunger and poverty requires an understanding of the ways in which these two injustices interconnect. Hunger, and the malnourishment that accompanies it, prevents poor people from escaping poverty because it diminishes their ability to learn, work, and care for themselves and their family members. Food insecurity exists when people are undernourished as a result of the physical unavailability of food, their lack of social or economic access to adequate food, and/or inadequate food utilization.

Food-insecure people are those individuals whose food intake falls below their minimum calorie (energy) requirements, as well as those who exhibit physical symptoms caused by energy and nutrient deficiencies resulting from an inadequate or unbalanced diet or from the body's inability to use food effectively because of infection or disease. An alternative view would define the concept of food insecurity as referring only to the consequence of inadequate consumption of nutritious food, considering the physiological utilization of food by the body as being within the domain of nutrition and health. Malnourishment also leads to poor health hence individuals fail to provide for their families. If left unaddressed, hunger sets in motion an array of outcomes that perpetuate malnutrition, reduce the ability of adults to work and to give birth to healthy children, and erode children's ability to learn and lead productive, healthy, and happy lives. This truncation of human development undermines a country's potential for economic development–for generations to come.

There are strong, direct relationships between agricultural productivity, hunger, and poverty. Three-quarters of the world's poor live in rural areas and make their living from agriculture. Hunger and child malnutrition are greater in these areas than in urban areas. Moreover, the higher the proportion of the rural population that obtains its income solely from subsistence farming (without the benefit of pro-poor technologies and access to markets), the higher the incidence of malnutrition. Therefore, improvements in agricultural productivity aimed at small-scale farmers will benefit the rural pocr first.

Increased agricultural productivity enables farmers to grow more food, which translates into better diets and, under market conditions that offer a level playing field, into higher farm incomes. With more money, farmers are more likely to diversify production and grow higher-value crops, benefiting not only themselves but the economy as a whole."

Biotechnology for Smallholders in the Sub-tropics

The area sown to genetically engineered crops in developing countries is rapidly catching-up with the area sown in industrial nations. According to the International Service for the Acquisition of Agri-biotech Applications (ISAAA), genetically engineered (biotech, GM) crops were grown by approximately 8.5 million farmers in 21 countries in 2005, up from 8.25 million farmers in 17 countries in 2004. The largest increase in biotech crop area in any country in 2005 was in Brazil, provisionally estimated at 44,000 km^2 (94,000 km^2 in 2005 compared with 50,000 km^2 in 2004. India had by far the largest year-on-year proportional increase, with almost a threefold increase from 5,000 km^2 in 2004 to 13,000 km^2 in 2005.

Current high regulatory costs imposed on varieties created by the more modern methods are a significant hurdle for development of genetically engineered crops well suited to developing country farmers by modern genetic methods. Once a new variety is developed, however, seed provides a good vehicle for distribution of improvements in a package that is familiar to the farmer.

Currently there are some institutes and research groups that have projects in which biotechnology is shared with contact people in less-developed countries on a non-profit basis. These institutes make use of biotechnological methods that do not involve high research and registration costs, such as conservation and multiplication of germplasm and phytosanitation.

Risks to Food Security

Fossil Fuel Dependence: While agricultural output increased as a result of the Green Revolution, the energy input into the process (that is, the energy that must be expended to produce a crop) has also increased at a greater rate, so that the ratio of crops produced to energy input has decreased over time. Green Revolution techniques also heavily rely on chemical fertilizers, pesticides and herbicides, some of which must be developed from fossil fuels, making agriculture increasingly reliant on petroleum products.

Between 1950 and 1984, as the Green Revolution transformed agriculture around the globe, world grain production increased by 250%. The energy for the Green Revolution was provided by fossil fuels in the form of fertilizers (natural gas), pesticides (oil), and hydrocarbon fueled irrigation.

David Pimentel, professor of ecology and agriculture at Cornell University, and Mario Giampietro, senior researcher at the National Research Institute on Food and Nutrition (INRAN), place in their study *Food, Land, Population and the U.S. Economy* the maximum U.S. population for a sustainable economy at 200 million. To achieve a sustainable economy and avert disaster, the United States must reduce its population by at least one-third, and world population will have to be reduced by two-thirds, says the study.

The authors of this study believe that the mentioned agricultural crisis will only begin to impact us after 2020, and will not become critical until 2050. The oncoming peaking of global oil production (and subsequent decline of production), along with the peak of North American natural gas production will very likely precipitate this agricultural crisis much sooner than expected. Geologist Dale Allen Pfeiffer claims that coming decades could see spiraling food prices without relief and massive starvation on a global level such as never experienced before.

However, one should take note that, (numbers taken from the CIA World Factbook), the country of Bangladesh achieved food self-sufficiency in 2002 with both a far higher population density than the USA (~1000 inhabitants per square kilometer in comparison to just 30/km for the USA-so this is more than 30 times as many) at only a tiny fraction of the USA's usage of oil, gas, and electricity. Also, pre-industrial Chinese mini-framers/gardeners developed techniques to feed a population of more than 1000 people per square kilometer (cf. e.g. F.H. King's 1911 report, "Farmers of Forty Centuries"). Hence, the dominant problem is not energy availability but the need to stop and revert soil degradation.

Price Setting

On April 30, 2008 Thailand announces the project of the creation of the Organisation of Rice Exporting Countries with the potential to develop into a price-fixing cartel for rice.

Treating Food the Same as Other Internationally Traded Commodities

On October 23, 2008, Associated Press reported the following:

> *"Former President Clinton told a U.N. gathering Thursday [Oct 16, 2008] that the global food crisis shows "we all blew it, including me," by treating food crops "like colour TVs" instead of as a vital commodity for the world's poor....Clinton criticized decades of policymaking by the World Bank, the International Monetary Fund and others, encouraged by the U.S., that pressured Africans in particular into dropping government subsidies for fertilizer, improved seed and other farm inputs as a requirement to get aid. Africa's food self-sufficiency declined and food imports rose. Now skyrocketing prices in the international grain trade—on average more than doubling between 2006 and early 2008—have pushed many in poor countries deeper into poverty."*

Stakeholder Participation and Complex Emergencies

Stakeholders

A stakeholder is any person, group or institution that has an interest in an aid activity, project or programme. This definition includes both intended beneficiaries and intermediaries, winners and losers, and those involved or excluded from decision-making processes.

Stakeholders can be divided into two very broad groups: those with some intermediary role-secondary stakeholders-and those ultimately affected, primary stakeholders, who expect to benefit from or be adversely affected by our aid. ODA is a secondary stakeholder, with its own perspective, culture and agenda. ODA-related secondary stakeholders may include consultancy companies, training institutions and British NGOs. In a typical education project, other secondary stakeholders might include the Ministry of Education, the Ministry of Planning or Finance, local government, suppliers of text books, teachers' training institutions, teachers and their trade unions, and owners of private schools. Primary stakeholders are potential schoolchildren and their parents.

Stakeholders are groups of people who share a common interest, for example "the consultancy company", "the project management", "the villagers", "the local authorities" etc. But, within any of these, there are sub-categories of stakeholders with differing interests which they may or may not be prepared to subsume in the general collective interest. Analysis might conclude that the concept of "villager" as a collective stakeholder is quite meaningless because the various groups of people living in a village have so little in common; some villagers might consider that they have more shared interest with the representatives of the local authorities than with their next door neighbours.

Similar issues arise in formal institutions, such as government ministries. Competition between departments or individuals may be stronger than commitments to the institutions as a whole. There may also be cross-cutting interests, such as on an ethnic basis, both within the institution and affecting outside relationships. Care is therefore needed in using terms like "recipient government" to recognise the variety of interests involved.

Stakeholder Participation

Participation is often used to mean a number of different kinds of activity and confusion may arise when the term is used without specifying which is meant. For example:

i. a person can be said to participate by the very fact of agreeing to interact, such as coming to meetings but remaining silent;

ii. people may participate in management or implementation of a project, through active involvement (such as in the operation and maintenance of infrastructure);

iii. people may participate in the governance of a programme or project. This could include consultation about sector objectives and setting the criteria by which project success might be measured.

This Note defines stakeholder participation as a process whereby stakeholders-those with rights (and therefore responsibilities) and/or interests-play an active role in decision-making and in the consequent activities which affect them. It encapsulates the second and third aspects listed in the preceding paragraph: within this definition, greater or lesser participation of the various stakeholders can occur at various over-lapping stages in the delivery of aid. Enhanced participation of other stakeholders in our aid programme requires a conscious and planned strategy by ODA.

Why Stakeholder Participation is Important?

The purpose of aid is to enhance the economic and social development and well-being of recipients. This means fully taking into account recipients' views on objectives and how they are to be achieved. It is a question both of principle and practice. The principle is that people should be fully involved in issues concerning themselves and the society in which they live. And effectiveness and sustainability depend practically, in part, on the commitment of interested parties (stakeholders). Thus participation is a central element in achieving aid objectives.

Participation contributes to the chances of our aid being effective and sustainable because:

- It is more effective because, in drawing on a wide range of interested parties, the prospects for appropriate project design and commitment to achieving objectives is likely to be maximised.

- It is more sustainable because people are more likely to be committed to carrying on the activity after aid stops, and more able to do so given that participation itself helps develop skills and confidence.

Evaluation findings from the Institutional Strengthening and NGO Syntheses show that the most successful projects proved to be those where the project objectives corresponded to the priorities of partner institutions and beneficiaries, and where the local institutions and beneficiaries were regularly involved in decision-making at all stages of the project cycle. Enhancing participation is an integral part of the Project Cycle Management approach.

By enhancing stakeholder participation we aim to strengthen local ownership of our aid activities-in structural adjustment programmes, teacher training projects or parastatal reform, as much as community level projects. It also means encouraging and helping our institutional partners become more participatory and responsive to the other stakeholders, particularly their clients. And in this assistance we are more credible, and therefore effective, if we practice the same principles of responsiveness, transparency and accountability with our aid recipient partners

Participation should reduce the risk of failure. But it is not a guarantee of project success. Achieving participation is not easy. In any aid activity there may be conflicting interests among recipients as well as among others involved in the project or programme. It may result in conflict, it can have significant costs in time and it means that institutions, including ourselves will have to change the way they go about their business.

Who Participates?

The extent to which ODA resources in time, people and money should be directed towards stakeholder participation should ideally always be a function of the activity itself. In practice, the conditions prevailing in the recipient country, the

Country Strategy, the economic and social characteristics of the sector and the professional resources available, both in the UK and in the country, must necessarily produce a great deal of variation between projects in this respect. Prescription as to the extent or kind of participation in relation to types of projects or sectors is not possible. Nor is it desirable, bearing in mind that the eventual decision will be based on a negotiated agreement with other stakeholders.

As there is no blueprint for participation, how do we reach a judgement about whom we think should participate (remembering that other stakeholders may have other views)? The universe of stakeholders is potentially boundless. We can set parameters by deciding that only key stakeholders should participate. *Key stakeholders are those who can significantly influence the project, or are most important if ODA's objectives are to be met.* Both primary and secondary stakeholders may be key.

Stakeholder analysis is a tool which helps us discover the key stakeholders in any aid-assisted programme or project. It is the first step in helping us decide, from our perspective, whom we believe should be encouraged and assisted to participate.

Stakeholder analysis aims to:

- identify and define the characteristics of key stakeholders;
- assess the manner in which they might affect or be affected by the programme/project outcome;
- understand the relations between stakeholders, including an assessment of the real or potential conflicts of interest and expectation between stakeholders;
- assess the capacity of different stakeholders to participate.

The outside intervention by an aid agency, bringing additional resources into an area, may in itself create *new stakeholder groups* which previously did not exist. Stakeholder analysis must be repeated at intervals during the project cycle to ensure that the involvement of such groups is adequately addressed and also to check whether the situation of original stakeholders has changed.

Stakeholder analysis differs from *institutional analysis* which is concerned with looking at the appropriateness and effectiveness of institutional arrangements and assessing the strengths, weaknesses and development needs of individual organisations. Supplementary guidance on how to do stakeholder analysis is available from the Social Development Department. Institutional analysis is described in the TN on Institutional Development.

Primary Stakeholders

In most cases, other than in field visits during review missions, it is unlikely that advisers or administrators will come into direct contact with primary stakeholders. ODA-related secondary stakeholders, such as TCOs or consultants will establish more sustained contact but even they will generally be working through others in order to achieve primary stakeholder participation.

There are no particular sectors where primary stakeholder participation is more needed than others. More important than sector is type of project. Participation of primary stakeholders is essential in projects which are expected to have a direct positive impact on defined groups of people. Included here would be slum improvement projects, rural health or population projects, agricultural projects targeting small farmers, skills training for the unemployed/landless, small scale enterprise, rural water supply projects, primary education and forestry conservation projects. Primary stakeholder participation is also essential when they are to be negatively affected by the project outcome, for example with the construction of a road or airport which may require resettlement or create a potentially dangerous environment. Sometimes primary stakeholders, who believe their interests or livelihood is threatened by the project outcome, may win the support of secondary stakeholders, such as NGOs, a local newspaper or a Member of Parliament.

Primary stakeholders may participate in a project as individuals, for example entrepreneurs in a small business promotion programme; and information and consultation can take place on an individual basis through the use of audio-visual materials, interviews and questionnaires. But if participation is stronger than this, and involves a *partnership* between primary stakeholders and the implementing agency-in a rural water supply project, for example-then some kind of alliance or association will need to be established by those sharing a common interest. This is sometimes referred to as *popular participation,* replacing the earlier usage *community participation* which implied the existence of a homogeneous community-often not the case.

Secondary Stakeholders

As with primary stakeholders, stakeholder analysis will reveal those who will benefit from the outcome and those whose interests are threatened. The focus should be on those secondary stakeholders whose influence can have a significant effect on outcomes. Our daily work in ODA involves a constant intercourse with other secondary stakeholders: UK-based consultants, representatives of the implementing agency, the relevant line ministry, the ministry of finance or planning, other donors who are co-financing the project. Others may be equally significant in terms of project feasibility but with whom we may have no direct relationship, for example fundamentalist religious leaders in a Pakistan population project, trade unions in a railway restructuring project or factory owners in a vocational training project. Our concerns for their participation may be mediated through one of the other secondary stakeholders, such as the line ministry or implementing agency. Out of sight should not mean out of mind.

In considering which secondary stakeholders we would like to participate in our aid activity, our primary consideration must be their potential for affecting the livelihoods and welfare of the activity's primary stakeholders and to influence achievement of project objectives. The box overleaf illustrates how negotiations between various secondary stakeholders (including ODA) can strengthen the project's viability, effectiveness and sustainability.

What is a Complex Emergency?

The official definition of a complex emergency is "a humanitarian crisis in a country, region or society where there is total or considerable breakdown of authority resulting from internal or external conflict and which requires an international response that goes beyond the mandate or capacity of any single agency and/ or the ongoing United Nations country programme." (IASC, December 1994).

Such "complex emergencies" are typically characterized by:

- extensive violence and loss of life; massive displacements of people; widespread damage to societies and economies
- the need for large-scale, multi-faceted humanitarian assistance
- the hindrance or prevention of humanitarian assistance by political and military constraints
- significant security risks for humanitarian relief workers in some areas

The Changing Nature of Conflict

In the immediate aftermath of the Cold War, the number of armed conflicts around the world increased – particularly those within State borders. According to one widely quoted source, the Stockholm International Peace Research Institute (SIPRI), in 1992 a total of 55 armed conflicts were recorded in 41 locations. This number declined to 33 armed conflicts recorded in 26 locations in 1997.

Statistics on refugees and other uprooted people are often inexact and controversial, with different sources citing conflicting statistics. According to just one source, the UNHCR, the total number of people of concern to them rose from 17 million in 1991 to a record 27 million in 1995. This figure includes refugees, returnees and certain IDPs. Until the Kosovo crisis in 1999 however, this number had been in decline, dropping to 22.3 million at the beginning of 1998 (a figure that still represents one out of every 264 people on earth). It is widely agreed that the proportion of IDPs within this figure had increased throughout the 1990s.

The amount of resources provided for international humanitarian assistance efforts continues to decrease. In 1994 the total requirements for the UN Consolidated Inter-Agency Appeal (CAP) amounted to US$2,778 million, of which 75.8% was met, whereas in 1998 only 53.9% of the US$2,163 million requested was met.

In today's wars, typically over 90% of the victims are civilians. At the same time assisting affected civilians in war zones has become increasingly dangerous. Between 1993 and 1999 more than 150 UN personnel lost their lives while on duty.

UNIT-VI

Preparedness Planning

Key Preparedness

The PATA workshop on Risk and Crisis Management conducted by Bert van Walbeek, the 'Master of Disaster' recently in New Delhi was surely well-timed, when India is at the threshold of a tourism boom and needs a concrete disaster management system in place. The Bangkok-based speaker who runs his boutique consulting company was hosted by PATA India Chapter.

Preparedness works. It is always advisable to take action to protect and reduce risk and crisis. Pacific Asia Travel Association (PATA) believes that a step-by-step procedure on how to prepare, respond to and recover from disasters is important. But the main task lies in identifying these symptoms of crisis and to recognise the threats and risks.

At this point of time, when the world is looking at south Asia as a potential tourist destination, it is our responsibility to be able to sustain this sudden inflow of tourists with preparation. In the Indian context, inefficient disaster management or no disaster management can be looked upon as being one of the major reasons why India gets fewer tourists in comparison to the neighboring Asian countries.

Reputation at Stake

PATA also recognises that with an effective risk management system, managing the reputation of the destination gets a lot easier as the destination would be able to meet the international standards of managing crisis. Taking care of visitors, speed and efficiency in returning to normal, and maintaining business continuity would be considered when evaluating a destination's image and reputation in the international market.

Explaining more about the various shocks and threats, and phases of crisis management, van Walbeek, a hotelier, marketer and a lecturer, gave a thorough insight on the various aspects during the seminar. According to PATA, crisis can be defined as 'any situation that has the potential to affect long-term confidence in an organisation or a product, or which may interfere with its ability to continue operating normally.'

According to van Walbeek, the first step towards avoiding a crisis is to identify various sources of risk and the possible impact it will have on the region's tourism. Then came the ideas on how to avoid the risks along with implementation and availability of adequate resources to be put in place. He added that planning will help get over risks by 70 to 80 per cent otherwise there is almost no chance. He strongly recommended keeping a running implementation cycle of identifying, analysing, planning, tracking, controlling and communicating is essential.

Agreeing to the idea, Deepak Bhatnagar, vice president of Le Passage to India, a participant at the training seminar said that such an exercise opens one's mind and makes the think-tank to work towards a proper plan to deal with crisis of different nature.

Strong Leadership

Stressing on the role played by the leaders and co-ordination among different parties, van Walbeek said that in order to do useful planning and effective implementation, strong leaders are to be looked up to. "It's their duty to effectively handle hostility and confusion and structure decisions. A strong leadership will help take through any crises," he said.

He also rated co-ordination and partnerships as essential ways to achieve tourism safety. Integration between national tourism administrations, national police, airlines and transportation companies, tour operators association and tourism safety and security-oriented research and documentation centers will have a strong impact on the way things are being dealt. With all of these coming together a crisis management centre can be developed with emergency resources, regional and national available expertise and 'stand by' experts to enhance safety or rescue for tourism stakeholders.

The core issue of the four levels of crisis management suggested by PATA was later explained by the speaker and was highlighted to be the most essential of the entire exercise. Starting with the Reduction stage, dealing with detecting early warning signals to lower the impact; the Readiness stage focusing on preparing plans and running exercises; Response stage involving executing operational and communication plans; and lastly the Recovery stage by taking the organisation to normality. These four essential stages will ensure recovery at the earliest.

Due to the continuous risks that prevails, Bhatnagar said that these sessions help a lot as normally we tend to ignore precautions in spite of knowing its importance. "These sessions must be organised on regular basis as they create the awareness and remind us the importance of having a plan to deal such issues," he said.

Media Management

van Walbeek, talking about the fourth stage of how the media and information management plays a role in making public reactions by presenting a picture in the right manner, said that communicating the crisis management plan to the media will enhance the safety perception of the destination and help plan and prepare for any potential crisis by establishing a positive relationship with the new media. It will help develop a communication database of media and stakeholders.

Avantika Dhar, assistant general manager of Tourism Finance Corporation of India, said, "Preparedness is the only way to avoid risks. With new developments come newer risks and for overcoming those risks new techniques are being developed. This is an ongoing process." Towards the end,

Bhatnagar added that it is an important tool for a big organisation and said, "Today's business is very demanding and we have to depend on various suppliers to work out the risk and crisis management manual and ensure that the entire team is made aware of the processes to deal with any crisis."

Emergency Coordination Centres

State-Wide Wall Map

Client: Rinske Poulier, Fire Management, Department of Sustainability and Environment, Victoria The Department of Sustainability and Environment's Emergency Coordination Centre (ECC) is the State's coordination centre for suppression of wildfire on public land. The ECC assists in planning and is crucial to the coordination of an appropriate response to control and suppress wildfires. Much of the Centre's focus is a 1:250,000 scale state-wide situation map mounted on the wall at the front of the room. The map is used to provide an overview of the current fire or emergency situations and encompasses the state of Victoria and at least 30 Kilometres into South Australia and New South Wales. In 2004 the ECC was moved to a new location at 8 Nicholson Street Melbourne. A new wall map was required. In the past, wall maps were prepared from published topographic base maps. This is generally no longer viable as many published maps are 10-20 years old, and quite out of date. There is also no scope for customising the information you need to show.

The new wall map prepared by Spatial Vision, utilised Vicmap Digital data to provide an up-to-date view of the infrastructure and major assets across the state. The use of a muted version of satellite imagery provides depiction of the terrain and highlights the forested / cleared areas of the state. Land managed by the various agencies is classified and depicted using an outlining technique that combines the land classifications and the imagery.

DSE's ECC now has a comprehensive large format (4.1m by 2.5m) 1:250,000 wall map customised to their specific requirements.

Early Warning Systems

The Early Warning System is based on the key figures of the Logistics Information System (LIS) and can be used for all of the applications in Logistics. You can find the Early Warning System in all of the LIS information system menus. The Early Warning System allows you to make decision-oriented selections and to check weak areas in Logistics, by enabling you to search for exceptional situations. This means that you can detect and rectify potential problems at an early stage. You can define both Exceptions [Ext.] and the conditions for follow-up processing. An exception consists of specified characteristics or characteristic values (for example customer, material), and requirements. The following requirements can be defined:

Threshold Value

For example, materials/customers whose sales are greater than 10,000 DM)

Trend

For example, materials/customers with a negative trend in sales or lead times)

Planned/Actual Comparison

For example, which customers have a plan realization for incoming orders of less than 80%)

In the planned/actual comparison, you specify the plan realization in percent and specify an operator (>, <, = etc.). This type of requirement helps you to check the plan realization and to pinpoint the weak areas between planned and actual data.

You can also carry out a forecast in the threshold value analysis and planned/actual comparison. The number of periods to be forecasted are determined by you. The forecast is carried out based on historical data.

When using the threshold value analysis you can determine, with the help of the forecast, whether or not a preset threshold value is also possible in the future based on the present actual data thereby enabling you to react in time to undesirable situations. With the help of the forecast in the planned/actual comparison you can compare planned figures with forecasted data, which result due to past developments. This allows you then to react quickly to threatening situations in the future.

Another advantage to checking for trends is that developments can be recognized early, leaving enough time for a reaction. An exception can have a variety of forms, for example, you can store requirements for various characteristic values and different key figures or you can combine a trend and threshold value analysis.

By combining exceptions into exception groups you can make a check on complex data.

There are three possible ways to check for exceptional situations:

- Standard analysis
- Exception analysis
- Periodic analysis

Displaying Exceptional Situations in the Standard Analyses

You can specify an exception when carrying out a standard analysis. In standard analyses the exceptional situations are highlighted using colour codes. Differentiation is possible in that different colours can denote different conditions. For example, you can choose red for an inventory turnover less than three, yellow for an inventory turnover greater than two and green for an inventory turnover greater than five.

These colour codes allow you to navigate selectively within the standard analyses. If exceptions occur, on the material level, for example, this will be displayed on a higher aggregation level (for example, on the purchasing organization or customer level). With the help of the drill-down function, you can then go to the line with the corresponding colour code for the exceptional situation.

Exception Analysis

You can carry out what is known as an exception analysis. The difference between this and the display of exceptions in standard analyses is that only data to which the exception applies is displayed here. The exception analysis is like a filter; only exceptional situations are displayed. Exceptional situations here are also highlighted in different colours.

Periodic Analysis

Periodic analyses release you from the burden of searching for exceptional situations. The existing dataset is searched systematically for exceptional situations,. The frequency of the search is freely definable (hourly, daily, weekly, monthly). If an exceptional situation arises, you can be informed by mail or via workflow and initialize follow-up processing. A periodic analysis can be carried out in two ways:

- *As an Event-driven Analysis:* search for exceptional situations is initialized when a change in data occurs due to a logistics event (for example, sales order, purchase order, stock movement).
- *As a System-driven Analysis:* The dataset chosen is checked for exceptional situations.

We recommend that you monitor particularly important key figures or characteristics using event-driven periodic analysis. For all other cases, a weekly check, for example, can be carried out with the system-driven periodic analysis.

Overview of the Tsunami Warning System

The Tsunami Warning System (TWS) in the Pacific, comprised of 26 participating international Member States, has the functions of monitoring seismological and tidal stations throughout the Pacific Basin to evaluate potentially tsunamigenic earthquakes and disseminating tsunami warning information. The Pacific Tsunami Warning Center (PTWC) is the operational center of the Pacific TWS. Located near Honolulu, Hawaii, PTWC provides tsunami warning information to national authorities in the Pacific Basin.

Tsunami Warning Centers

As part of an international cooperative effort to save lives and protect property, the National Oceanic and Atmospheric

Administration's (NOAA) National Weather Service operates two tsunami warning centers. The Alaska Tsunami Warning Center ATWC) in Palmer, Alaska, serves as the regional Tsunami Warning Center for Alaska, British Columbia, Washington, Oregon, and California.

The Pacific Tsunami Warning Center in Ewa Beach, Hawaii, serves as the regional Tsunami Warning Center for Hawaii and as a national/international warning center for tsunamis that pose a Pacific-wide threat. This international warning effort became a formal arrangement in 1965 when PTWC assumed the international warning responsibilities of the Pacific Tsunami Warning System (PTWS). The PTWS is composed of 26 international Member States that are organized as the International Coordination Group for the Tsunami Warning System in the Pacific.

Tsunami Watch and Warning Determination

The objective of the PTWS is to detect, locate, and determine the magnitude of potentially tsunamigenic earthquakes occurring in the Pacific Basin or its immediate margins. Earthquake information is provided by seismic stations operated by PTWC, ATWC, the U.S. Geological Survey's National Earthquake Information Center and international sources. If the location and magnitude of an earthquake meet the known criteria for generation of a tsunami, a tsunami warning is issued to warn of an imminent tsunami hazard. The warning includes predicted tsunami arrival times at selected coastal communities within the geographic area defined by the maximum distance the tsunami could travel in a few hours. A tsunami watch with additional predicted tsunami arrival times is issued for a geographic area defined by the distance the tsunami could travel in a subsequent time period.

If a significant tsunami is detected by sea-level monitoring instrumentation, the tsunami warning is extended to the entire Pacific Basin. Sea-level (or tidal) information is provided by NOAA's National Ocean Service, PTWC, ATWC, university monitoring networks and other participating nations of the PTWS. The International Tsunami Information Center, part of the Intergovernmental Oceanographic Commission, monitors and evaluates the performance and effectiveness of the Pacific Tsunami Warning System. This effort encourages the most effective data collection, data analysis, tsunami impact assessment and warning dissemination to all TWS participants.

Tsunami Warning Dissemination

Tsunami watch, warning, and information bulletins are disseminated to appropriate emergency officials and the general public by a variety of communication methods.

- Tsunami watch, warning and information bulletins issued by PTWC and ATWC are disseminated to local, state, national and international users as well as the media. These users, in turn, disseminate the tsunami information to the public, generally over commercial radio and television channels.
- The NOAA Weather Radio System, based on a large number of VHF transmitter sites, provides direct broadcast of tsunami information to the public.
- The US Coast Guard also broadcasts urgent marine warnings and related tsunami information to coastal users equipped with medium frequency (MF) and very high frequency (VHF) marine radios.
- Local authorities and emergency managers are responsible for formulating and executing evacuation plans for areas under a tsunami warning. The public should stay-tuned to the local media for evacuation orders should a tsunami warning be issued. And, the public should NOT RETURN to low-lying areas until the tsunami threat has passed and the "all clear" is announced by the local authorities.

Understanding the Importance of Damage Assessment in Continuity Planning By Pat Moore, CBCP FBCI (Ret.)

Many business continuity planners don't completely understand what damage assessment entails. You can't assume you'll get your building back the minute the fire is out, or the water is contained.

Until your local health department declares your building "safe for re-occupancy," you should not operate your business there.

Do you know what your organization's responsibilities are versus those of the municipal authorities and first responders? Who is responsible for performing a damage assessment and mitigating the loss? Where does your organization's responsibility for cleanup begin?

The National Fire Protection Association (NFPA) says that depending on the circumstances and the type of facility, most fires are extinguished in approximately four hours and most buildings are not burned to the ground. In many cases, however, it can take 12 to 72 hours until officials perform the initial damage assessment. This will take even longer if they suspect any hazardous materials and call in a HazMat team.

Your BC programme must then help you facilitate a quicker damage assessment of your facility. A well-designed and maintained site and damage assessment plan that includes pre-loss site safety audits, along with disaster avoidance, mitigation and good loss control and waste management practices should be an integral part of any organization's business continuity planning effort.

Creating a Pre-Loss Site Safety Plan

Can you really make a damage assessment quicker before disaster even strikes? You can, with some proper preplanning before a loss.

First, build a relationship with your local emergency first responders (i.e. fire, police, etc.). For example, take a first responder representative on a preloss walk through your mission critical facility or facilities. Familiarize them with your facility's drawings, including any improvements you've made. Make your Material Safety Data Sheets (MSDS) available to them. Get them to understand your time-sensitive business and service recovery needs. This process can greatly expedite the process of first responders getting you the emergency damage assessment information you need after the incident.

Next, take your facility's unique environment into account. In many cases, manufacturing operations, healthcare facilities, museums, storage warehouses and other facilities require a more complicated damage assessment and restoration than other types of facilities.

Manufacturing and distribution facilities, for example, often have diverse risks and complex processes which combine to create a planning conundrum for BC professionals. Just as we plan for recovery and continuity from natural and man-made disasters such as fires, floods, earthquakes, tornadoes, hurricanes and power outages, these facilities also must deal with exposure to hazardous materials, storage rack collapse, a clean room environment penetrated, vehicular impact, vandalism, malicious mischief and supply chain or labour interruptions.

Damage Assessment and Need with Media

Good pre-planning will only take you so far in speeding up a damage assessment. The real key is how well you mobilize after the disaster. Here, we outline the elements of a damage assessment.

1. *Examine Equipment and Electronics:* Identify items that require lab packing (containing and removing hazard classes of material such as flammable liquids and corrosives). You will also need to profile and dispose of those materials.

   Carefully examine electronics and, if necessary, have experienced technicians test them to ensure they meet the manufacturer's operating and performance specifications. For example, if electronic equipment has suffered thermal damage or been exposed to excessive heat, it's unlikely you can restore it. If equipment was exposed to just smoke for a short time, however, there may be very little damage.

   A moist, humid environment can severely corrode equipment within 48 to 72 hours. Ideally, you would be able to clean all of the equipment and remove the contaminants at the same time, but the volume of equipment, restoration versus replacement decisions, insurance coverage issues and re-certification requirements can delay the process.

You should also have pre-qualified specialists do the proper testing as quickly as possible to determine the quantitative and qualitative corrosivity. Emergency mitigation procedures, such as removing surface contamination and applying corrosion inhibitors, can buy you the time you need to make the necessary replaceor-restore decisions.

2. *Perform a Structural Damage Assessment:* Have a state-licensed structural engineer (or a professional engineer who specializes in structural integrity) perform a thorough investigation of the structure as quickly as possible. Be sure the engineer complies with your state requirements.

   After a fire, the engineer needs to look at structural conditions, including: distortions in structural columns, beams and slabs, fracturing of connections, spalling of concrete members and cracking of concrete members. "If these conditions exist extensively, perform material tests to determine if the strength of the structural materials has been affected by the fire," recommends Ian R. Chin, SE, AIA of the Chicago, Illinois firm Wiss, Janney, Elstner Associates, Inc. "Perform surveys of columns and beams to determine the extent of their distortions and to evaluate the affect of the distortion on the load carrying capacity of the structural members."

3. *Test for Hazardous Material Contamination:* OSHA requires every individual who enters the building to wear protective clothing and have special training, depending on the type and level of non-routine contamination experts find or suspect at the facility (including PCBs, asbestos, lead, cadmium, mercury, etc.).

   An internal or external certified industrial hygienist must test for any health, safety and environmental concerns that may exist. Once the hygienist performs an in-depth site assessment and analyzes samples, your pre-qualified hazardous material decontamination specialists can identify and perform the proper cleaning and decontamination protocols.

4. *Perform a Fire Damage Assessment* : Determine if any routine contamination exists, such as the by-products of a fire. In the event of fire, you may assume some areas of the building are unaffected. They can still suffer heatand soot-related damage, however. The initial damage assessment should always address both indirect as well as direct fire-damaged areas. Contamination, such as fire combus-tion by-products, may lie hidden behind the obvious physical damage.

   Other building materials can form sulfates and nitrates. Since each fire leaves its own unique chemical fingerprint in the soot, what burns in what quantities under what conditions will determine the chemical components.

5. *Check Water for Residual Chemical Damage:* Water from either floods or fire suppression can also carry contaminants. That water can deposit inorganic salts from building materials and atmospheric particulate matter on exposed circuit boards. Also, chilledwater systems often contain glycol, which can adversely affect certain types of paper and magnetic media. You should always analyze the water's ionic content, acidity, suspended solids and organic content.

6. *Inspect for Mold and Mildew:* You need to be concerned about the growth of mold and mildew spores anywhere there was standing water or moist, humid conditions for more than 48 hours. Mold affects not only the structure, HVAC systems and critical documents and magnetic media, but can produce "sick building syndrome" as well.

   Have a certified industrial hygienist conduct a thorough damage assessment and decontamination of the HVAC systems. With today's technology, it is unlikely you will need to replace the ductwork. Instead, you can apply the proper EPA-recognized biocide through various fogging and cleaning applications. In compliance with your local and state regulations, it will be necessary to do follow-up clearance sampling as the final step in returning the facility to a safe and healthful condition.

7. *Care for Wet Vital Records* : With major water damage, you can lose vital records very quickly. In dealing with paper in moist, humid conditions, you have about 48 hours before damaging mold and mildew grow.

Reduce high temperatures and vent the areas as soon as the water has receded or been pumped out. Keep water-soaked materials as cool as possible by good air circulation until you can stabilize them.

You should also complete certain procedures such as washing away accumulated mud, sewage and dirt prior to freezing the documents. When removing wet documents from file cabinets or shelving, do not attempt to pull them apart while wet. Remove all documents in blocks, if possible, so you do not increase deterioration. Leave a space about the size of your fist in the packing box for proper air circulation.

Once the documents are frozen and/or in cold storage, choose the proper drying method. Freeze-drying, a process involving freezing the documents immediately and then sublimating them, is the most effective way to restore water-soaked documents.

If the documents are not soaking wet, you can also air dry them through dehumidification. In this process, you introduce dry air (by using either desiccant or refrigeration dehumidification equipment) into the moist environment which absorbs the water vapor.

Successfully recovering vital records on magnetic media requires many of the same considerations as hard copy documents. Water can erode through the substrate, destroying data in the process. To be effective, you must employ proper recovery procedures, such as restoring a relative humidity below 50° Fahrenheit and use proper drying and cleaning protocols within 72 to 96 hours of damage.

The cleaning and drying methods you use will also depend on the type or degree of damage. You usually open and dry water-damaged floppy diskettes, for example, using isopropyl alcohol, then inserting them into empty jackets and copied onto new media. Depending on the situation, you can either freeze-dry or machine-dry magnetic tapes. While you must freeze-dry cartridge tapes, you can dry open-reel tapes on tape cleaning machines. You can then use tape drives with recovery software to copy the information onto new media, however you need to ensure the tapes are dry and clean before you make any attempt to copy the data.

You can lose data on wet microfilm through improper handling, such as allowing it to dry on its spool. In most cases, it is best to leave the microfilm in water until you can properly pack it and send it to the appropriate recovery location.

Flood waters can contain hazardous materials and therefore you must perform the proper health and safety procedures during retrieval and recovery of your vital records.

Being knowledgeable in what is required in a thorough damage assessment, utilizing personnel who are trained in this field and executing this part of the plan in a timely manner allows senior management to gain the critical initial damage information they require to make executive recovery decisions.

Need with Media

Many business continuity planners don't completely understand what damage assessment entails. You can't assume you'll get your building back the minute the fire is out, or the water is contained.

Until your local health department declares your building "safe for re-occupancy," you should not operate your business there.

Do you know what your organization's responsibilities are versus those of the municipal authorities and first responders? Who is responsible for performing a damage assessment and mitigating the loss? Where does your organization's responsibility for cleanup begin?

The Basics of Damage Assessment

Good pre-planning will only take you so far in speeding up a damage assessment. The real key is how well you mobilize after the disaster. Here, we outline the elements of a damage assessment.

1. *Examine Equipment and Electronics*: Identify items that require lab packing (containing and removing hazard classes of material such as flammable liquids and corrosives). You will also need to profile and dispose of those materials.

   Carefully examine electronics and, if necessary, have experienced technicians test them to ensure they meet the manufacturer's operating and performance specifications. For example, if electronic equipment has suffered thermal damage or been exposed to excessive heat, it's unlikely you can restore it. If equipment was exposed to just smoke for a short time, however, there may be very little damage.

   A moist, humid environment can severely corrode equipment within 48 to 72 hours. Ideally, you would be able to clean all of the equipment and remove the contaminants at the same time, but the volume of equipment, restoration versus replacement decisions, insurance coverage issues and re-certification requirements can delay the process.

   You should also have pre-qualified specialists do the proper testing as quickly as possible to determine the quantitative and qualitative corrosivity. Emergency mitigation procedures, such as removing surface contamination and applying corrosion inhibitors, can buy you the time you need to make the necessary replaceor-restore decisions.

2. *Perform a Structural Damage Assessment*: Have a state-licensed structural engineer (or a professional engineer who specializes in structural integrity) perform a thorough investigation of the structure as quickly as possible. Be sure the engineer complies with your state requirements.

After a fire, the engineer needs to look at structural conditions, including: distortions in structural columns, beams and slabs, fracturing of connections, spalling of concrete members and cracking of concrete members.

"If these conditions exist extensively, perform material tests to determine if the strength of the structural materials has been affected by the fire," recommends Ian R. Chin, SE, AIA of the Chicago, Illinois firm Wiss, Janney, Elstner Associates, Inc. "Perform surveys of columns and beams to determine the extent of their distortions and to evaluate the affect of the distortion on the load carrying capacity of the structural members."

3. *Test for Hazardous Material Contamination*: OSHA requires every individual who enters the building to wear protective clothing and have special training, depending on the type and level of non-routine contamination experts find or suspect at the facility (including PCBs, asbestos, lead, cadmium, mercury, etc.).

   An internal or external certified industrial hygienist must test for any health, safety and environmental concerns that may exist. Once the hygienist performs an in-depth site assessment and analyzes samples, your pre-qualified hazardous material decontamination specialists can identify and perform the proper cleaning and decontamination protocols.

4. *Perform a fire Damage Assessment*: Determine if any routine contamination exists, such as the by-products of a fire. In the event of fire, you may assume some areas of the building are unaffected. They can still suffer heatand soot-related damage, however. The initial damage assessment should always address both indirect as well as direct fire-damaged areas. Contamination, such as fire combus-tion by-products, may lie hidden behind the obvious physical damage.

   Other building materials can form sulfates and nitrates. Since each fire leaves its own unique chemical fingerprint in the soot, what burns in what quantities under what conditions will determine the chemical components.

5. *Check Water for Residual Chemical Damage*: Water from either floods or fire suppression can also carry contaminants. That water can deposit inorganic salts from building materials and atmospheric particulate matter on exposed circuit boards. Also, chilledwater systems often contain glycol, which can adversely affect certain types of paper and magnetic media. You should always analyze the water's ionic content, acidity, suspended solids and organic content.
6. *Inspect for Mold and Mildew*: You need to be concerned about the growth of mold and mildew spores anywhere there was standing water or moist, humid conditions for more than 48 hours. Mold affects not only the structure, HVAC systems and critical documents and magnetic media, but can produce "sick building syndrome" as well.

   Have a certified industrial hygienist conduct a thorough damage assessment and decontamination of the HVAC systems. With today's technology, it is unlikely you will need to replace the ductwork. Instead, you can apply the proper EPA-recognized biocide through various fogging and cleaning applications. In compliance with your local and state regulations, it will be necessary to do follow-up clearance sampling as the final step in returning the facility to a safe and healthful condition.
7. *Care for Wet Vital Records*: With major water damage, you can lose vital records very quickly. In dealing with paper in moist, humid conditions, you have about 48 hours before damaging mold and mildew grow.

   Reduce high temperatures and vent the areas as soon as the water has receded or been pumped out. Keep water-soaked materials as cool as possible by good air circulation until you can stabilize them.

You should also complete certain procedures such as washing away accumulated mud, sewage and dirt prior to freezing the documents. When removing wet documents from file cabinets or shelving, do not attempt to pull them apart while wet. Remove all documents in blocks, if possible, so you do not increase deterioration. Leave a space about the size of your fist in the packing box for proper air circulation.

Once the documents are frozen and/or in cold storage, choose the proper drying method. Freeze-drying, a process involving freezing the documents immediately and then sublimating them, is the most effective way to restore water-soaked documents.

If the documents are not soaking wet, you can also air dry them through dehumidification. In this process, you introduce dry air (by using either desiccant or refrigeration dehumidification equipment) into the moist environment which absorbs the water vapor. Successfully recovering vital records on magnetic media requires many of the same considerations as hard copy documents. Water can erode through the substrate, destroying data in the process. To be effective, you must employ proper recovery procedures, such as restoring a relative humidity below 50° Fahrenheit and use proper drying and cleaning protocols within 72 to 96 hours of damage.

The cleaning and drying methods you use will also depend on the type or degree of damage. You usually open and dry water-damaged floppy diskettes, for example, using isopropyl alcohol, then inserting them into empty jackets and copied onto new media. Depending on the situation, you can either freeze-dry or machine-dry magnetic tapes. While you must freeze-dry cartridge tapes, you can dry open-reel tapes on tape cleaning machines. You can then use tape drives with recovery software to copy the information onto new media, however you need to ensure the tapes are dry and clean before you make any attempt to copy the data. You can lose data on wet microfilm through improper handling, such as allowing it to dry on its spool. In most cases, it is best to leave the microfilm in water until you can properly pack it and send it to the appropriate recovery location.

Flood waters can contain hazardous materials and therefore you must perform the proper health and safety procedures during retrieval and recovery of your vital records.

Being knowledgeable in what is required in a thorough damage assessment, utilizing personnel who are trained in this field and executing this part of the plan in a timely manner allows senior management to gain the critical initial damage information they require to make executive recovery decisions.

Evacuation and Camp Management

Prescriptive codes address capacity and design measures,but how people actually behave is a key issue. Following 11 September,the ways in which people are likely to react to an alarm or emergency are even more unpredictable. Management, training and information systems should be able to deal with extreme events as well as more ' conventional ' emergencies. Decisions have to be made quickly,with awareness of the whole building and not just the fire floor.

The most important issues to consider are the management of an evacuation, and the training and selection of staff to carry out a vital task in stressful conditions. Formerly,most high-rise and large-plan buildings operated a phased evacuation regime, but 11 September showed the need for a more sophisticated management regime, should people have to be evacuated in an extreme or imminent catastrophic event. An evacuation strategy is needed that can deal with a range of threats and be able to communicate instructions clearly to occupants. Evacuation and safety management is a partnership between tenants and the building operator. A co-ordinated approach throughout the building is vital,as inconsistent actions by some tenants can threaten the safety of the whole building. A licensing regime for building operators of tall and large buildings along the lines of that applied to sports stadia has been suggested to regulatory authorities. Arup can develop a management strategy for building owners/occupiers for various emergency scenarios to develop a practical approach to imminent catastrophic events, fire emergency and other scenarios developed during a Risk Assessment process.

Camp Ellis-Ferry Beach-Bay View Evacuation Plan

The purpose of this plan is to establish procedures for the orderly movement of people from endangered or stricken areas to facilities in areas generally unaffected by the disaster or potentially safer from an impending emergency situation.

The major evacuation routes for Camp Ellis, Bay View and Ferry Beach will be:

A. All parties on the southerly side of Pond Avenue will evacuate by way of Ferry Road to Bay View Evacuation Dispatch Center (Camp Ellis Fire Station).

B. All parties on the northerly side of Pond Avenue will evacuate by way of Bay View to Bay View Evacuation Dispatch Center (Camp Ellis Fire Station).

C. When arriving at Bay View Evacuation Dispatch Center, all parties from the southerly side of Pond Avenue will be checked in and directed or transported to the Saco Community Center, 75 Franklin St.

D. When arriving at Bay View Evacuation Dispatch Center, all parties from the northerly side of Pond Avenue will be checked in and directed or transported to the Saco Community Center, 75 Franklin St.

Any inquiries can be made by contacting one of the following:

Saco Fire Department 282-3244 or 283-3661

Saco Police Department 284-4535

Saco Public Works 284-6641

Emergency Management Director 282-8201

NOTE: *Please follow the evacuation directional signs.*

This evacuation plan was made possible by a grant received from the Federal Emergency Management Agency in cooperation with Maine Emergency Management Agency and York County Emergency Management Agency. The National Hurricane Grant received in 1995-96 totaled $4,254, not including in-kind services provided by Public Works and the Fire Department.

Camp Management

Whilst camps do not provide durable solutions to situations of displacement, caused by conflict or natural disaster, they are often the only refuge for communities who have been forced to flee their homes and are seeking safety, shelter and material assistance.

It is estimated that around a quarter of all displaced communities live in camps or camp-like settings. With millions of refugees worldwide, and an escalating number of internally displaced people, there is a need for the effective management of camps, as part of an effective humanitarian relief response.

With a wide range of stakeholders and service providers involved in the life of a camp, camp management focuses on developing effective coordination mechanisms that support the provision of assistance and protection.

Camp management aims to ensure that gaps in services are identified, duplications are avoided, and the fundamental human right to life with dignity, is upheld for the camp community.

The Norwegian Refugee Council offers camp management expertise and capacity in three key ways:

as a camp management agency in the direct management of camps;

through the provision of camp management training and coaching;

through camp monitoring.

UNIT-VII

Prevention/Mitigation

Framework for Prevention and Mitigation

Professionals working to prevent child abuse and neglect have borrowed from other disciplines, including public health, education, and mental health, to influence and guide practice. However, public health has had the greatest influence in organizing a framework of prevention services. That framework consists of three levels of services: *primary* prevention programmes, directed at the general population (universal); *secondary* prevention programmes, targeted to individuals or families in which maltreatment is more likely (high risk); and *tertiary* prevention programmes, targeted toward families in which abuse has already occurred (indicated).

Distinctions among primary, secondary, and tertiary prevention do not necessarily reflect the way prevention-related services are actually organized and provided. Rather than sorting prevention initiatives into mutually exclusive categories, prevention is increasingly recognized as occurring along a continuum. A comprehensive system of care for improving outcomes for children and families needs to include strategies that coordinate resources across the entire continuum, from primary to secondary to tertiary prevention.

- Primary prevention
- Secondary prevention
- Tertiary prevention
- Ecological framework for prevention

Primary Prevention

Primary prevention activities are directed at the general population and attempt to stop maltreatment before it occurs. All members of the community have access to and may benefit from these services. Primary prevention activities with a universal focus seek to raise the awareness of the general public, service providers, and decision-makers about the scope and problems associated with child maltreatment. Universal approaches to primary prevention might include:

- Public service announcements that encourage positive parenting
- Parent education programmes and support groups that focus on child development, age-appropriate expectations, and the roles and responsibilities of parenting
- Family support and family strengthening programmes that enhance the ability of families to access existing services, and resources to support positive interactions among family members
- Public awareness campaigns that provide information on how and where to report suspected child abuse and neglect

Secondary Prevention

Secondary prevention activities with a high-risk focus are offered to populations that have one or more risk factors associated with child maltreatment, such as poverty, parental substance abuse, young parental age, parental mental health concerns, and parental or child disabilities. Programmes may target services for communities or neighborhoods that have a high incidence of any or all of these risk factors. Approaches to prevention programmes that focus on high-risk populations might include:

- Parent education programmes located in high schools, focusing on teen parents, or those within substance abuse treatment programmes for mothers and families with young children

- Parent support groups that help parents deal with their everyday stresses and meet the challenges and responsibilities of parenting
- Home visiting programmes that provide support and assistance to expecting and new mothers in their homes
- Respite care for families that have children with special needs
- Family resource centers that offer information and referral services to families living in low-income neighborhoods

Tertiary Prevention

Tertiary prevention activities focus on families where maltreatment has already occurred (indicated) and seek to reduce the negative consequences of the maltreatment and to prevent its recurrence. These prevention programmes may include services such as:

- Intensive family preservation services with trained mental health counselors that are available to families 24 hours per day for a short period of time (e.g., 6 to 8 weeks)
- Parent mentor programmes with stable, nonabusive families acting as "role models" and providing support to families in crisis
- Parent support groups that help parents transform negative practices and beliefs into positive parenting behaviors and attitudes
- Mental health services for children and families affected by maltreatment to improve family communication and functioning

Ecological Framework for Prevention

An ecological framework for prevention is based on the following assumptions:

- Children and families exist as part of an ecological system. This means that prevention strategies must target interventions at multiple levels: the individual, the family, the community, and society.

- Primary responsibility for the development and well-being of children lies within the family, and all segments of society must support families as they raise their children.
- Assuring the well-being of all families is the cornerstone of a healthy society and requires universal access to support programmes and services.

Hazard Mitigation Planning

To be effective, hazard vulnerability reduction activities must be designed and implemented in an integrated development framework. A comprehensive government policy in support of hazard vulnerability reduction, combined with an appropriate implementation plan, can provide this framework. A comprehensive hazard mitigation policy provides the context, direction and mandate for developing and implementing a coordinated risk reduction programme. Developing a viable implementation plan for such a policy requires a full understanding of the prevalent hazards, the existing and potential vulnerabilities and the context for response, all of which can be developed through a coordinated hazard mitigation planning process.

Hazard mitigation planning provides a comprehensive framework for understanding both the character and effects of hazards in an area and the context for responding to those hazards. It can encompass a wide range of hazards and involve representatives of a broad spectrum of disciplines and interests. A well-developed hazard mitigation plan charts a way forward for long-term hazard vulnerability reduction across all sectors of the economy and provides a framework for prioritizing mitigation interventions, which is critical in a time of tight budgets and high demands on governments and the private sector.

As a long-term, multi-sectoral activity, natural hazard loss reduction programmes require a strong commitment and coordination across sectors, many of which have not traditionally been involved directly in disaster management activities. Development and adoption of a national mitigation policy at the outset provides a critical framework and direction for any coordinated vulnerability reduction programme, including hazard mitigation planning.

To support the practice of mitigation planning in the Caribbean region, a hazard mitigation planning methodology was developed under the USAID/OAS Caribbean Disaster Mitigation Project (CDMP), in coordination with CDERA. Steps in this process include: 1) hazard assessment and mapping, 2) vulnerability assessment, 3) institutional capability assessment, 4) development of hazard mitigation goals and objectives and 5) implementation of a mitigation response. This approach is described in the document Planning to Mitigate the Impacts of Natural Hazards in the Caribbean.

Structural Mitigation

Checklist

The following are suggested checklists (list is not all inclusive) of recommended structural and nonstructural mitigation actions:

Structural Mitigation

Structural mitigation is reinforcing, bracing, anchoring, bolting, strengthening or replacing any portion of the building that may become damaged and cause injury such as:

- exterior walls – (e.g., use a wind resistant design for tornados or windstorms)
- exterior doors – (e.g., non-combustible materials for wildfires or urban fires)
- exterior windows – (e.g., use shutters on windows for tornados or windstorms)
- foundation – (e.g., brace, anchor or bolt the facility for earthquakes)
- exterior columns/pilasters/corbels – (e.g., steel or concrete columns)
- roof – (e.g., use non-combustible materials for wildfires or urban fires)

Structural

- *Earthquakes* – anchor/brace or bolt the facility to its foundation and reinforce any portion of the exterior of the facility that may cause injury.
- *Floods and flashfloods* – elevate and reinforce the facility but ultimately avoid a floodplain location.
- *Landslide and mudflow* – build retaining walls on slopes. Build masonry walls to direct the mudflow around the facility. Bolt the foundation and reinforce the walls of the facility.
- *Tsunami* – elevate at-risk coastal facilities. Even the strongest building can be damaged by a powerful tsunami.
- *Wildfire and urban fire* – use fire resistant materials (e.g., non-combustible roofing material) on the exterior of the facility.
- *Tornado* – follow local building codes to use a wind resistant design for your facility.
- *Dam failure* – reinforce and flood-proof the facility.

Structural Mitigation Strategies

ARA develops strategies for renovation and retrofit of existing buildings and designs new structures to resist potential terrorist attacks. We also develop new innovative protective methods and perform testing of protection products.

Our designs consider the full spectrum of blast, chemical, biological, and radiological threats. We develop mitigation strategies for military and civilian facilities including military bases, federal buildings (offices, courthouses, embassies, etc.), airports, and industrial facilities. Our mitigation strategies are designed to minimize facility damage and maximize occupant safety.

Community Based Disaster Management (CBDM)

Most of disaster response can be characterized as command and control structure one that is top down and with logistic centre approach. Because of this, we observe, lack of community participation that results into failures in meeting the appropriate and vital humanitarian needs, unnecessary increase in requirement for external resources, and general dissatisfaction over performance despite the use of exceptional management measures.

Recognizing these limitations, the Community Based Disaster Management (CBDM) approach promotes a bottom-up approach working in harmony with the top-down approach, to address the challenges and difficulties. To be effective, local communities must be supported into analyzinge their hazardous conditions, their vulnerabilities and capacities as they see themselves.

In case of disasters, the people at the community level have more to lose because they are the ones directly hit by disasters, whether major or minor. They are the first ones to become vulnerable to the effects of such hazardous events. On the other hand, they have the most to gain if they can reduce the impact of disasters on their community. This concept gave rise to the idea of community-based disaster management where communities are put at the forefront. Through the CBDM, the people's capacity to respond to emergencies is increased by providing them with more access and control over resources and basic social services. Using a community-based approach to managing disasters certainly has its advantages. Through CBDM, it is hoped that communities will be strengthened to enable them undertake any programmes of development including disaster preparedness and mitigation.

The CBDM approach provides opportunities for the local community to evaluate their own situation based on their own experiences initially. Under this approach, the local community not only becomes part of creating plans and decisions, but also becomes a major player in its implementation. Although the community is given greater roles in the decision-making and implementation processes, CBDM does not ignore the importance of scientific and objective risk assessment and planning. The CBDM approach acknowledges that as many stakeholders as needed should be involved in the process, with the end goal of achieving capacities and transferring of resources atto the community, which level who would assume the biggest responsibility inover disaster reduction.

Institutional and Legal Mechanisms

Center for International Environmental Law (CIEL)

The CDM of the Kyoto Protocol is designed to allow developed countries to sponsor projects in developing countries designed to reduce atmospheric concentrations of greenhouse gases. For example, such projects may be designed to reduce the carbon emissions by improving the efficiency of the energy sector or to increase carbon "sinks" by preserving or expanding forests. The Protocol provides limited detail as to how the CDM should operate. Consequently, many operational details remain to be clarified by the Parties.

This chapter summarizes the recommendations for a legal and institutional framework for the CDM contained in a report, Carbon Conservation: Climate Change, Forests and the Clean Development Mechanism, presented by the Center for International Environmental Law at the meeting of the UNFCCC subsidiary bodies in June 1998. The report, identifies problems and solutions emerging from experience with activities implemented jointly (AIJ) forestry projects in Costa Rica, and discusses their significance to the design of the Clean Development Mechanism (CDM) established by the 1997 Kyoto Protocol. It also addresses many of the concerns of project developers, environmentalists, and Parties as they grapple with defining the CDM and the role of forest management in climate change mitigation.

The report concludes that a legal and institutional framework must be in place before project crediting can begin. If this framework is not in place and project credits are accepted, investors and host countries will create a de facto framework through their actions. This could lead to serious imbalances and flaws in the framework, threatening the integrity and legitimacy of the CDM. Article 12 of the Protocol lays out the beginnings of an institutional framework. The CDM is to be subject to the authority and guidance of the Conference of the

Parties/Meeting of the Parties (COP/MOP), which must: elaborate modalities and procedures with the objective of ensuring transparency, efficiency, and accountability through independent auditing and verification; ensure that a share of the proceeds from certified project activities will cover administrative expenses and assist in meeting the costs of adaptation for particularly vulnerable developing country Parties; determine what "part" of Annex I Parties' quantified emissions limitation and reduction commitments may be met with certified emission reductions (CERs). establish an executive board to supervise the CDM; and designate operational entities to certify emissions reductions resulting from project activities.

Based on this skeletal framework and the results of CIEL's review of existing JI forest projects, we make the following recommendations for the legal and institutional framework of the Clean Development Mechanism.

Recommendations for a Legal and Institutional Framework

The Executive Board: The structure and composition of the executive board must reflect a careful balance between developed and developing country interests. The executive board should coordinate its activities with the Council of the Global Environment Facility (GEF) to ensure that the work of the two institutions is complementary and not competitive or redundant. There is a natural divide between GEF and CDM projects. The GEF could finance cutting edge projects utilizing technology that might be deemed inappropriate for CDM projects. It also could fund infrastructure development and capacity building to support CDM activities. The GEF even has a mandate to assist vulnerable developing country Parties with adaptation. As reflected in Article 12, the executive board should provide "guidance" for both public and private projects.

Operational Entities: Operational entities should be independent auditors performing third party certifications. To avoid conflict of interest, operational entities should not be organizations that are themselves helping to finance projects, such as multilateral development banks. If institutions such as the World Bank are designated as operational entities, however, certification should be contingent upon a third party verification of the certification.

Criteria for Certification: For CDM project activities to be certified, climate benefits must be real, measurable, and long-term; and the resulting emissions reductions must be additional to any that would occur in the absence of the certified project. Consequently:

- additionality should be based on objective, clear criteria;
- these criteria should be established by technical advisory panels of experts acting in their own capacity;
- where uncertainty exists, estimates of benefits must be conservative, and CERs must be discounted for that uncertainty;
- emission reductions may be certified only after they have accrued and been verified by an independent audit; and
- the temporal dimension of greenhouse gas emissions must be fully accounted for on a ton-year basis.

Contributing to Sustainable Development

One of the primary purposes of the CDM set forth in Article 12 is to assist developing countries to achieve sustainable development. In light of this:

activities must not harm forest ecosystems, biodiversity, or other environmental assets;

environmental assessments should be conducted to identify both positive and negative environmental impacts;

where opportunities are identified to provide ancillary benefits, though at a higher cost, co-financing arrangements should be made available;

the CDM should require that project benefits be shared with local communities and, in the case of forest projects, with long-term forest dwellers;

the CDM must promote the development of domestic institutional capacities to allow host countries to evaluate proposed CDM projects and monitor their outputs;

the CDM must promote the development and transfer of technology that provides maximum environmental benefit while complementing the social, economic and technical settings of host countries; and

the CDM should maintain a balance between forest and energy projects to ensure that the CDM promotes sustainable development in both these key sectors.

Ensuring Transparency and Public Accountability

Article 12 requires the CDM to be transparent, efficient, and accountable. Consistent with these criteria:

independent auditing and verification must be required and all complete audits be made available to the public;

the COP/MOP must also develop clear, detailed modalities for independent auditing and verification, so as not to exacerbate existing problems of incomplete data and lack of comparability between reported information;

all affected constituencies must receive early notice about which areas and resources are being considered for inclusion in CDM activities. These constituencies must have a meaningful opportunity to participate in project design, implementation, and monitoring;

in particular, long-term occupants directly dependent on forest resources being considered for inclusion in a CDM project must be asked for approval and invited to recommend modifications or alternatives and to share in the benefits of the project; and

projects should not be planned on indigenous people's lands without their prior consultation and approval. Involuntary resettlement of long-term residents is not an option.

Ensuring that CER Prices Are Sufficient

Given the potential for different marginal costs of reductions in Annex I and non-Annex I countries, an unregulated market could result in prices for CERs from some CDM projects being bid down to very low levels. In order to ensure that developing countries are able to benefit from CDM projects, that sufficient resources are available to ensure environmental and social co-benefits, and to prevent the CDM from being skewed in favour of any particular type of project, mechanisms should be put in place to prevent the price of CERs from dropping too low. Potential options include:

Setting price floors for CERs;
Limiting the amount of CERs that may be used in a particular period;
Auctioning of available CERs by the CDM and;
Enhancing the value of CERs by reducing risk through market-based approaches (e.g. portfolios, insurance, escrows or guarantees).

Covering Administrative Expenses and Assisting in Adaptation

The CDM will need to raise sufficient funds to cover the cost of administrative expenses and assisting in adaptation. Hence:

proceeds from the sale of CERs should be used to assist in arranging funding of certified project activities (as required by Article 12.6), covering administrative expenses, and meeting a portion of adaptation costs.
alternatively, the CDM could acquire the necessary funds by retaining a certain share of CERs generated by projects.
the cost of CERs should be linked to the cost of adaptation to climate change; the greater the need for countries to adapt, the higher should be the price of CERs.

An Interim CDM Phase

Initially, the CDM, and all of its institutional parts, should operate an interim phase. This phase could culminate once the total CERs generated reaches some fixed percentage of combined Annex I assigned amounts. Other similar financing mechanisms, including the GEF, the Montreal Protocol Multilateral Fund, and activities implemented jointly (AIJ) under the FCCC, have gone through interim phases. While they experienced varying degrees of success, all of these mechanisms were either improved during their interim phase or, in the case of AIJ, replaced by a different and hopefully better mechanism. An interim phase would give the Parties an opportunity to experiment with and evaluate the mechanism, and make mid-course corrections where needed.

Determining What Part of Annex I Commitments May Be Met with CERs

Article 12.3(b) directs that Annex I Parties may use the CDM to achieve "part of" their emission limitation and reduction commitments under the Protocol. The COP/MOP is charged with determining how this limitation will be applied. There is currently no consensus as to how this limitation should be interpreted and applied. As suggested above, the CDM should start small and grow as it learns; with an automatic review triggered once the use of the CDM reaches some level (e.g., one or two percent of total Annex I assigned amounts). In addition, an overall limit on the use of the CDM should be imposed. Rather than imposing a per country limitation, the limit should again be based on an overall percentage of Annex I assigned amounts. Since Annex I countries presumably could purchase CERs from each other (or an equivalent part of their assigned amount), no obvious purpose would be served by limiting the portion of the total that could be purchased by any of them. The COP/MOP may decide to set a conservative initial limit on the use of the CDM, then if the automatic review proves that the CDM is functioning effectively, the limit may be further increased.

Financial Additionality

Financial additionality requirements should be mandated as well. Government funds to the CDM must be additional to GEF, Overseas Development Assistance (ODA) and other existing development assistance. This is very important because donor countries may have more incentive to finance the CDM than other development assistance institutions. For example, Annex I Parties, faced with the choice of financing the GEF and receiving global benefits, or financing the CDM and receiving CERs, will be tempted to put all their money in the CDM.

Increasing Non-Annex I Participation in the Protocol

After the interim phase, the CDM should review the need for conditioning the participation of non-Annex I Parties in the CDM on their agreement to increase their level of participation in the CDM and the rest of the Protocol regime, including developing sectoral or national baselines below business as usual, adopting full inventory and reporting requirements, and perhaps establishing national emission limitation and reduction commitments.

Consistency with International Norms

Project activities should not undermine other international environmental and human rights norms. Consequently:

the CDM should require that projects be consistent with the requirements of other international environmental agreements and international human rights norms;

countries should only be allowed to participate in the CDM to the extent they are in substantial compliance with other major environmental agreements and international human rights norms to which they are parties; and

CDM project activities should not be allowed on indigenous lands or territory without their informed consent and participation in the design and implementation of the project.

Vintaging of CERs

The location, date and project resulting in certified emission reductions must be identified on each CER. Tracking of CERs through this type of vintaging is essential for maintaining the integrity of the CDM. Identification of the project also allows buyers to choose the projects in which they want to invest, based on type of activity, integrity of project infrastructure and likelihood of project success.

Early Start for the CDM

Article 12.10 permits emissions reductions obtained between 2000 and 2008 to be used during the first commitment period provided that they have been certified by operational entities. These entities are to be selected by the COP/MOP, however, which means they are unlikely to be operational by 2000, or perhaps even much before the start of the commitment period, since the Protocol must enter into force before the COP/MOP may be constituted. Consequently, any projects that begin before that date do so at their own risk. This suggests that the COP, prior to the first meeting of the Protocol Parties, should provide guidance regarding what types of projects will be eligible for certification, possibly including retroactive certification.

Independent Evaluation of AIJ and Interim Phase of the CDM

The CDM should be informed by experience of the JI pilot phase (AIJ). Much work has already been done on methodological issues, such as additionality, baselines, leakage, project duration, monitoring, and verification. This information should be considered in the design of a set of standard methodologies for CDM projects. This could be accomplished as part of an independent evaluation of existing AIJ projects. In addition, any CDM interim phase should be subject to an independent review and evaluation.

Conclusion

A full range of climate mitigation and other environmental and social strategies should be linked through the CDM, not only because this approach can work, but because any other approach will fail. If the legal and institutional framework for the CDM is not carefully designed, with both climate and other environmental and social impacts considered, the resulting investments and incentives could undermine national and international goals beyond the climate change regime. The CDM should require that all projects internalize all social and environmental costs, over the long-term. Furthermore, the CDM must provide socio-economic benefits for recipient countries, and especially for local communities. Otherwise, long-term support for CDM projects cannot be guaranteed, and projects may not last. Given the right legal and institutional framework, the CDM can be a potent tool in achieving both global climate and sustainable development benefits.

Role of Public Awareness

Several different and sometimes conflicting constituencies have an interest in the development of biotechnology. In the broader sense, though, this session focuses on the proper relationship between the biotechnology community and the media. In democratic societies, the public has an obligation and a right to shape the developments of technology. The media is key to providing information on biotechnology to the public. The relationship between the media, the scientist and the biotechnology community in general will determine both the quality and quantity of information that is provided to the public.

Recommendations

ABSF proposes that a Data Base be developed to:

- Establish a more detailed breakdown of target audiences in national, Regional and international public opinion research, employing common methodology.
- Conduct internationally comparable, systematic analysis of media coverage to identify technology presentation and give direction; compare with public opinion.
- Determine the level of public interest in science and its change over time.
- Assess credibility of scientists with the news media and the general public identifying national differences in opinion.
- Encourage two-way communications and be aware that concerns expressed in questions reflect public attitudes.
- Increase the biotechnology community's awareness of the importance of cooperating with the media.
- Improve understanding of how the media functions on a daily basis, including the need to meet rigid deadlines.
- Sensitize scientists to how they are perceived by the media.
- Encourage scientists to enroll in media training exercises.

- Encourage institutions to explore internships and other cross fertilization programmes between educational institutions and the media.

Working with the Media

- Scientists and biotechnology institutions should develop an active approach to the media.
- Help create a variety of background materials, briefing documents, etc., useful to various media.
- Participate in on-going dialogue with select key journalists, including but by no means limited to science reporters.
- Be aware of opportunities to present information in a variety of non obvious media segments.
- Encourage professional scientific organizations to discuss communications issues, and involve the media where appropriate.
- Give media calls a high priority.
- Encourage development of a Crisis Communications Management Plan (e.g., pre-identified media spokesperson). Anticipate negative issues and address them in advance.
- Track issues in the popular press.

Key Audiences and Information Vehicles

ABSF/ABNETA believes that messages must be adapted to successfully communicate with the broad variety of audiences and appropriate vehicles:

Audiences:

- Agricultural groups
- News media
- Men's and women's organizations Scientists Citizen groups
- Teachers
- Youth
- Families

Vehicles:

- Traditional news media vehicles other media vehicles
- Science festivals
- Science fairs
- Lectures
- School speakers
- Open houses
- Demonstration projects

Preparation of Mitigation Strategies

For purposes of this discussion, development planning is considered the process by which governments produce plans to guide economic, social, and spatial development over a period of time. The hazard management process consists of a number of activities carried out before, during, and after a hazardous event in order to reduce loss of life and destruction of property. Natural hazard management has often been conducted independently of development planning. A distinctive feature of OAS technical assistance is the integration of the two processes.

The natural hazard management process can be divided into pre-event measures, actions during and immediately following an event, and post-disaster measures. In approximate chronological order, these are as follows:

1. Pre-event Measures:
   a. Mitigation of Natural Hazards:
      - Data Collection and Analysis
      - Vulnerability Reduction

   b. Preparation for Natural Disasters:
      - Prediction
      - Emergency preparedness (including monitoring, alert, evacuation)
      - Education and Training
2. Measures During and Immediately after Natural Disasters:

   a. Rescue
   b. Relief
3. Post-disaster Measures
   a. Rehabilitation
   b. Reconstruction

Of these, the mitigation mechanisms are most cost effective in reducing loss of life and property and most compatible with the development planning process. The data collection effort refers to data on the hazards themselves, vulnerability, and risk. The mitigation mechanisms are described briefly below.

Natural Hazard Assessments

Studies that assess hazards provide information on the probable location and severity of dangerous natural phenomena and the likelihood of their occurring within a specific time period in a given area. These studies rely heavily on available scientific information, including geologic, geomorphic, and soil maps; climate and hydrological data; and topographic maps, aerial photographs, and satellite imagery. Historical information, both written reports and oral accounts from long-term residents, also helps characterize potential hazardous events. Ideally, a natural hazard assessment promotes an awareness of the issue in a developing region, evaluates the threat of natural hazards, identifies the additional information needed for a definitive evaluation, and recommends appropriate means of obtaining it.

Vulnerability Assessments

Vulnerability studies estimate the degree of loss or damage that would result from the occurrence of a natural phenomenon of given severity. The elements analyzed include human populations; capital facilities and resources such as settlements, lifelines, production facilities, public assembly facilities, and cultural patrimony; and economic activities and the normal functioning of settlements. Vulnerability can be estimated for selected geographic areas, e.g., areas with the greatest development potential or already developed areas in hazardous zones. The techniques employed include lifeline (or critical facilities) mapping and sectoral vulnerability analyses for sectors such as energy, transport, agriculture, tourism, and housing. In Latin America and the Caribbean vulnerability to natural hazards is rarely considered in evaluating an investment even though vulnerability to other risks, such as fluctuating market prices and raw-material costs, is taken into account as standard practice.

Risk Assessments

Information from the analysis of an area's hazards and its vulnerability to them is integrated in an analysis of risk, which is an estimate of the probability of expected loss for a given hazardous event. Formal risk analyses are time-consuming and costly, but shortcut methods are available which give adequate results for project evaluation. Once risks are assessed, planners have the basis for incorporating mitigation measures into the design of investment projects and for comparing project versus no-project costs and benefits.

Vulnerability Reduction

Risk from natural hazards can be substantially reduced by the introduction of mitigation measures, both structural and non-structural. Mitigation measures are discussed in detail in the section Hazard Mitigation Strategies for Project Preparation.

Incorporating Mitigation Measures into an Integrated Development Planning Study: Integrated development planning is a multidisciplinary, multisectoral approach to planning. Issues in the relevant economic and social sectors are brought together and analyzed vis-a-vis the needs of the population and the problems and opportunities of the associated natural resource base. A key element of this process is the generation of investment projects, defined as an investment of capital to create assets capable of generating a stream of benefits over time. A project may be independent or part of a package of projects comprising an integrated development effort. The process of generating projects is called the project cycle. This process proceeds from the establishment of development policies and strategies, the identification of project ideas, and the preparation of project profiles through prefeasibility and feasibility analyses (and, for large projects, design studies) to final project approval, financing, implementation, and operation.

While the process is more or less standardized, each agency develops its own version. The development planning process evolved by the OAS Department of Regional Development consists of four stages: Preliminary Mission, Phase I (development diagnosis), Phase II (project formulation and preparation of an action plan), and implementation. Because the process is cyclical, activities relating to more than one stage can take place at the same time. The main elements ofthe process are a synthesis of the activities and products of each stage. A comprehensive set of guidelines for executing a study following this process is given in Regional Development Planning: Guidelines and Case Studies from OAS Experience.

This presentation of the procedures of an integrated study features the incorporation of hazard management considerations at each stage. The relationships of the integrated development planning process, the hazard management process, and the project cycle are summarized. Generally, planners depend on the science and engineering community to provide the required information for natural hazard assessments. If the information available is adequate, the planner may decide to make an assessment. If it is not adequate, the planner usually decides that the time and cost of generating more would be excessive, and the assessment is not made. While the information available on hurricanes and geologic hazards is often adequate for a preliminary evaluation, the information on desertification, flooding, and landslide hazards rarely is. The OAS has developed fast, low-cost methodologies that make these evaluations possible in the context of a development study. The differences in treating the various hazards in each stage of the process are highlighted in the following discussion.

Preliminary Mission: Designing the Study

The first step in the process of technical assistance for an integrated development planning study is to send a "preliminary mission" to consult with officials in the interested country. Experience has shown that this joint effort of OAS staff and local planners and decision-makers is frequently the most critical event in the entire study. They take action to:

- Determine whether the study area is affected by one or more natural hazards. For example, the National Environmental Study of Uruguay conducted by the OAS with financial support from the Inter-American Development Bank determined in the preliminary mission that natural hazards were an important environmental problem, and consequently an assessment of all significant hazards, to be conducted by reviewing existing information, was programmed for Phase I.
- Identify the information available for judging the threat posed by those hazards in the study area: history of hazardous events; disaster and damage reports; assessments of hazards, vulnerability, risk; maps and reports on natural resources and hazards; topographic maps, aerial photographs, satellite imagery.
- Determine whether the available data are sufficient to evaluate the threat of hazards. If they are not, determine what additional data collection, hazard assessment, remote sensing, or specialized equipment will be needed for the next stage of the study. For example, in preliminary missions in Dominica, Saint Lucia, and St. Vincent and the Grenadines, landslides were determined to be a serious problem, and landslide assessments were included in the work plan for Phase I.
- Determine whether the studies required would serve more than one sector or project. If so, establish coordination.
- Establish coordination with the national institution responsible for disaster planning.
- Prepare an integrated work plan for Phase I that specifies the hazard work to be done, the expertise needed, and the time and cost requirements.

UNIT-VIII

Mitigation Models

Disaster Mitigation Models

The geographic scope of most natural and man-made disasters in the United States is regional rather than local or national. This is not to diminish the individual suffering or the national concern. It stems from the fact that even local impacts ripple spatially to the boundaries of larger economic trading areas. It also stems from the vast size of the U.S. and the limits of man-made and even natural forces.

Thus the appropriate geographic area for analysis is often the county or county group, though not necessarily within the boundaries of a single state. A factor that extends disaster losses beyond the area of the initial stimulus is the interdependence of the economy. One view of interdependence is the production pyramid, which characterizes the economy as consisting of layers of building blocks. Primary commodities, such as minerals, agricultural crops, and forest products, are at the foundation of this economic edifice because they are at the starting point of the production process. But intertwined with all layers are roads, utilities, and communication networks that provide the lifelines of logistic support for even the most basic economic activity.

Thus, all goods and services in the economy are interdependent, but infrastructure may be the most critical. But infrastructure is not necessarily best characterized by the rigidity of road, pipeline, or transmission networks. Instead, it possesses features of resilience, or flexibility and the ability to rebound. The purpose of this paper is to share some insights into infrastructure interdependence and resilience through models of economic interaction and responsiveness. The emphasis will be on input-output (I-O) analysis, still the most widely used tool of regional economic impact analysis, and computable general equilibrium (CGE) analysis, a state of the art approach that captures most of the advantageous features of I-O and overcomes many of its limitations. The focus will be on business interruption (BI) stemming from damaged infrastructure, as opposed to the property damage itself.

Infrastructure is rather unique in that relatively small scale components (e.g., a single bridge, transformer, or pipe) can bring an entire economic system to a halt. A recent study of the U.S. Federal Emergency Management Agency hazard mitigation grant programmes by Rose et al. (2006) found that the highest benefit-cost ratios were those associated with mitigation projects for public utilities.

For example, base isolation of sub-station equipment or burying power lines underground often cost less than a few million dollars, but can prevent large portions of a region's economy from shutting down. The paper will also address infrastructure resilience, with an emphasis on customer response. This focuses on ways to reduce the consequences of infrastructure failure through inherent and adaptive measures by individuals (both businesses and households), markets, and the regional economy as a whole.

Economic Interdependence

One way economists illustrate interdependence is through the simple circular flow diagram. In factor markets, households offer labour and capital to businesses in exchange for income payments. Businesses then use these factors to produce goods and services to sell to households.

This simple version of the economy, however, is not adequate to reflect the critical role of infrastructure, but it can be made effective by providing. At the far left of this figure, we first acknowledge that businesses do not just use labour and capital to produce goods and services, but also need various types of raw and processed materials, as well as various services, referred to as "Intermediate Goods." Infrastructure falls into this category of intermediate goods and in a fundamental way, since it is essentially required by all businesses. Purchase of infrastructure services by households would be part of the "Business Production of Final Goods and Services," though this implicitly includes government production of priced infrastructure services as well.

A large amount of infrastructure, especially roads, bridges, and in some cases airports and waterports, are not provided through the market or through direct user fees by government. These would be part of the box in the lower right hand corner. Note that one of the advantages of CGE models to be discussed below is the ability to calculate efficient prices for these infrastructure services under normal and hazard-event circumstances.

An extension of the activities of households to include ways that they can combine market goods and services with time and household resources to yield "household production," such as cooked meals, recreation, etc. This enables us to estimate the value of infrastructure service to households, especially those not transmitted through the market.

This is important in that households typically purchase between thirty and forty percent of water and electricity. If they need to cope with a disruption through the substitution of other inputs, use of their leisure time, or if they suffer inconvenience, these responses are not normally reflected in formal economic (income and product) accounts. -

However, this reflection of market failure (or the absence of markets in the first place) should not be construed as lack of value for infrastructure services, but rather failures and biases in the way most informal economic activities are evaluated. Again, this extended formulation enables us to find implicit prices for infrastructure services and to measure a reduction in their service flows as a type of household economic interruption, in addition to the lost wages/salaries, dividends, rents, and royalties that can be omputed with most existing models.

Economic Models of Interdependence

In this section, we summarize the two major modeling approaches to regional economic impact analysis. We focus on insights they yield on infrastructure interdependence.

A. Input-Output Analysis

Input-output can be defined as a static, linear model of all purchases and sales between sectors of an economy, based on the technological relationships of production (see, e.g., Rose and Miernyk, 1989). Essentially, this is a detailed, comprehensive, double-entry bookkeeping record of all production activity.

Flat Source Model

Herbsleb looked at cases where many developers around the world would successfully collaborate on one piece of software. He also examined why this distributed development model hasn't thrived in industry. In fact, Herbsleb said he found that it takes companies more than twice as long to develop software in disparate locations than in one location.

One of the reasons why free and open-source software development has been successful over disparate locations is that the work has been done by the users, and these developer-users determine the functionality, Herbsleb said.

"Because work is done by the users, they're more likely to get the functionality right, so a major class of errors is eliminated," he noted, adding that developers of commercial software are rarely users of the software, and the functionality is determined by project managers.

"Project managers tend to understand purchasing designs — why companies buy software—so they'll build a project that plays into those hands," Herbsleb explained. This means that commercial software can be created without fully meeting user requirements. Because free and open-source software developers are its users, they create the functions they specifically need.

But one of the drawbacks to the open-source software development model is that mainstream users often get left behind because the really technical people create the software design functionality for themselves, not for the average user. The geek creed — "If you can't install it, you don't deserve to use it" — is still alive in many open-source projects, said Nancy Frishberg who works on user-centered software design in the software division at Sun Microsystems Inc.

As a result, "it is sometimes said [that lack of] usability is the Achilles' heel of open source," said Steve Easterbrook, associate professor in the department of computer science and associate director of the Knowledge and Media Institute at the University of Toronto.

Sun's Frishberg added that the open-source mantra that "everyone can contribute" is actually misleading because adding to an open-source project is basically limited to code, bugs and patches.

She said even developers have to be assertive to get themselves into an open-source software development community, and even though it's a meritocracy, who you know can often help you get your foot in the door. Also, "everyone" tends to mean people who are technically proficient with computers, so creative individuals who aren't programming experts can't contribute to free and open-source software undertakings.

But when designing open-source software, developers get to choose their own work assignments, compared with a commercial project, where the managers assign the work. This means that open-source software developers are working in an area where they are experts and are motivated by their personal interests. In addition, the coordination of open-source software projects tends to emerge naturally from its workers sidestepping the bureaucratic clogs characteristic of commercial development, Herbsleb said. He added that free and open-source software projects tend to encourage open technical discussions, whereas commercial projects tend to close the door on participation by everyone.

IBM discovered this cultural rift between open-source software and commercial software-development environments when it open-sourced its Eclipse development platform in February 2004.

Paul Buck, IBM's director of Java Platform Strategy and Eclipse, said IBM's Eclipse developers had to adjust their frame of mind from a proprietary development strategy to an open-source software development strategy, facing the biggest change with code transparency.

Because users can see and manipulate Eclipse code, the developers received a lot of feedback. In the proprietary model, developers just keep their head down and don't have time to go around explaining things to users, Buck said. But when Eclipse went open, the developers were suddenly expected to adapt to the give-and-take element of open-source software creation. That is, they were expected to take time every day to peruse and contribute to newsgroups, offer explanations to users and conduct demonstrations. They also had to examine the user feedback, including feature requests and examine the submitted patches and enhancements.

Structured Source Model

The objective of earthquake engineering is to prevent or mitigate disasters, especially damage to structures, cause by earthquakes. Academic or practical methods of simulating or evaluating 1) design earthquake motion, 2) response, 3) seismic performance, 4) damage, or 5) risk, are developed and improved through observation, experiment, analysis, and theory, for application to seismic design, repair and strengthening of structures and ground.

Damageability of Strong Ground Motions

In order to mitigate earthquake disaster, we have to investigate damageability of strong ground motions in addition to investigation of strong ground motions and structures. Damageability of strong ground motions, i.e., structural damage, is determined by the relationship between intensity of strong ground motions and strength of structures, therefore, we have to grasp characteristics of both strong ground motions and structures. The result of the investigation leads to index of representing damageability of strong ground motions, such as J.M.A. (Japan Meteorological Agency) seismic intensity. Such index is essential to grasp actual structural damage rapidly and accurately for quick post-disaster response. Slow post-disaster response enlarged human damage in the 1995 Hyogoken-Nanbu Earthquake. However, many strong ground motions records are need to be obtained under the same structural condition for such investigation.

In the 1999 Chi-Chi earthquake, Taiwan, many strong ground motions records were obtained under the same structural condition. This made it possible to investigate index of representing damageability of strong ground motions from actual structural damage for the first time. The relationship between often used index and proposed index (elastic response with a 5% damping factor around 1.0 sec) and actual damage (area damage level, respectively. Almost no correlation was found for PGA and a weak correlation for PGV, SI and JMA intensity whereas, there is good correlation for proposed index with area damage level.

Strong Motion Seismology

A quantitative prediction of strong ground motion is the most fundamental and inevitable subject for preventing and reducing earthquake damage. Along this subject, we have studied following items.

1) Study on source spectral characteristics based on strong motion observations near a fault: We focus to identify generations of high frequency motions on a fault and to increase an accuracy of strong motion predictions.
2) Strong ground motion simulations mainly using the empirical Green's function method: Examples are estimations of source parameters and strong ground motions of the 1855 Ansei-Edo earthquake and assessments of strong ground motion near the surface fault during the 1999 Turkey earthquake.
3) Effects of sites on strong motion and their relation to structural damage: We have faced that no or light damage near a fault and heavy damage to buildings,

on the contrary, were found at relatively long distance (>100km) from the source. This is mainly due to properties of surface sediments at sites and we are practically studying based on the data from the 1999 Turkey earthquake.

4) Determination of S-wave velocity structure for assessing site characteristics: The spatial auto-correlation method applied to array data of microtremors. The method has been confirmed by the comparisons of S-wave velocity structure with those by the other methods. The method is especially superior in determining velocity model at deep sediment sites with low cost

5) *Strong Motion Database:* Strong motion data are most invaluable for confirming a seismic safety of buildings and man-made structures. We have started to construct a user-friendly database.

Applied Seismology

Seismologists are responsible for mitigating earthquake disasters, so precisely estimating seismic ground motions is one of our most important tasks. We are working on any problems related to this task, and our recent research subjects are as follows:

1) Modeling earthquake faults and their rupture processes as sources of seismic ground motions (e.g. Rupture process of the 1995 Kobe earthquake).
2) Exploring detailed images of underground structures, which should influence seismic ground motions (e.g. three-dimensional ray tracing in a subduction zone and tomographic analysis of explosion data).
3) Numerical simulation of seismic ground motion caused by fault rupture in a three dimensional heterogeneous structure (e.g. simulation of strong ground motion caused by the 1995 Kobe earthquake).

Strong Motion Simulation

The dense networks of strong ground motion instruments in Japan (K-NET and KiK-net) make it possible to directly visualize regional wave propagation during large earthquakes. For the 2000 Tottori-ken Seibu earthquake (Mw 6.6) in western Japan, snapshots of ground motion, derived directly from interpolation of a large number of array observations, demonstrate clearly the nature of the source radiation pattern and the character of the seismic wavefield propagating to regional distances (Fig.9-right). During the earthquake of shallow thrust faulting, the favefield is dominated in longer-period (T =10 s) fundamental-mode Love waves on displacement records.

The observation is then comparing with results from a 3-D numerical simulation. A realistic model of the source process for the earthquake and 3-D subsurface structural model of western Japan are included in the simulation model. The computation is conducted by using a cluster of 8 PCs. There is good agreement in the dominant features of the regional wavefield propagating through the complex structure.For example, the amplification effects in the highly populated sedimentary basins can be observed. The simulation model is, therefore, suitable for estimating the main pattern of ground motion expected for future earthquake scenarios.

Hub

A common connection point for devices in a network. Hubs are commonly used to connect segments of a LAN. A hub contains multiple ports. When a packet arrives at one port, it is copied to the other ports so that all segments of the LAN can see all packets.

A passive hub serves simply as a conduit for the data, enabling it to go from one device (or segment) to another. So-called intelligent hubs include additional features that enables an administrator to monitor the traffic passing through the hub and to configure each port in the hub. Intelligent hubs are also called manageable hubs.

A third type of hub, called a switching hub, actually reads the destination address of each packet and then forwards the packet to the correct port.

Less Model

While all the attention has been focused on a paper by Warren Washington and colleagues that has just been accepted by the scientific journal *Geophysical Research Letters* (GRL), whose conclusions can perhaps best be summarized by "Yes, Virginia, there is something you (acting together with 7 billion of your closest friends) can do to lessen climate change," another paper has been published by *GRL* that seems to argue that if climate models had a better handle on the true behavior of clouds, that they may project less warming than they do now.

So, perhaps Virginia, if you wait for the scientists to get things right, there may be less that you actually have to do in the first place (which is a good thing, because according to the Washington et al. results, you are way behind already).

Researcher Kevin Trenberth and John Fasullo examined how climate models actually calculate why the earth warms as greenhouse gases increase (and aerosol emissions decrease). They found that initially, the enhanced greenhouse gas concentrations (and the accompanying positive feedback from water vapor increases) warm the planet. But then, as the planet warms, it emits more radiation to space, and that at some point in the second half of this century, the extra radiation emitted to space by a warmer planet about equals the radiation that is trapped by the enhancing greenhouse effect and so the two effectively cancel each other out. Still though, the planet continues to warm. Why? Because of the way climate models handle clouds.

All models, by and large, have the total cloud amount of the earth (or at least between the latitudes 60ºS and 60ºN) decreasing as greenhouse gases build-up. This allows more direct solar radiation to reach the earth's surface and thus things continue to warm up.

However, there is some indication, that this is not quite correct. Instead of a decreasing cloud cover in the future, some processes may serve to increase cloud cover, at least in the lower levels of the atmosphere. And, low level clouds turn out to be particularly good at reflecting away incoming solar radiation—that is, they act to cool the earth's surface.

In one climate model (the NCAR model) that actually has a different cloud parameterization scheme than most of the other climate models, total cloud cover actually increases a bit as the greenhouse effect enhances. And, it turns out, that the temperature rise (and climate sensitivity) produced by the NCAR model is less than the overall average of all models—although, admittedly, not all that much less.

Trenberth and Fasullo describe this result:

A key question is how large the role of changing cloud is in the overall climate change? The NCAR model is the only one with increasing cloud between 60°N and 60°S, but has a climate sensitivity of 2.7 K for doubling of carbon dioxide, only slightly lower than the overall mean of all models which average 3.2 ± 0.7 K. The transient climate response at time of doubling of carbon dioxide of 1.6 K is typical of many models which average 1.7 ± 0.4 K. Hence without the change in model clouds, warming would still occur and, while it may not be quite as large, it would be manifested somewhat differently owing to the change in solar radiation at the surface.

The biggest point that Trenberth and Fasullo make is to reaffirm the fact that clouds play an important role in climate and climate change, and that climate models are still all over the place when it comes in how they simulate them. And, for the most part, the models don't even include some cloud-influencing processes that are likely very important in developing an accurate overall picture of cloud and cloud changes in the future.

Disaster Coordination Centre

The Gold Coast City Council maintains a Disaster Coordination Centre, to be activated in the event of a disaster affecting Gold Coast City. Council staff are responsible for coordinating the response in conjunction with representatives of the lead responding agencies.

The $1.5 million, purpose-built Disaster Co-ordination Centre is believed to be the only stand-alone council facility of its type in the nation. The new centre, adjacent to Council's SES headquarters in Queen Street, Southport, opened in May 2006.

Fully equipped and designed to operate around the clock, in times of emergency it accommodates Council's disaster management team and personnel from the Local District Management Group.

This centre highlights the importance Gold Coast City Council places on emergency response and disaster management.

As an adjunct to our state-of-the-art 'nerve centre', six community centres and 49 other facilities have been identified across the city as evacuation centres in times of emergency.

During a disaster, the public can seek assistance by telephoning the Centre on 1800 606 000.

Coastal Hazards

Causes and Effects of Different Coastal Hazards

(i) *Storm Surges:* Storms form over warm seas (sea surface temperature should exceed ~ 28 ° C in the Indian Ocean) (*Gadgil et al.* 1984). The frequency of storms is highest in the Bay of Bengal (Fig. 3). Though storms are tracked better today owing to satellite remote sensing, there is need for improvement in modelling of storm track and intensity because this is today one of the weakest links in storm-surge prediction. The impact of a storm as it crosses a coast is caused by the surge due to strong winds and low atmospheric pressure, and the high waves riding over the surge.

(ii) *Tsunami:* Tsunami is caused by vertical displacement of the water column owing to earthquakes, volcanic eruptions, and submarine mudslides. Though they are almost undetectable in the open sea owing to their low amplitude, the tsunami waves can reach heights exceeding 10 m in the vicinity of a coast. The high impact they have on a coast is due to high water velocity

and wave height. Tsunami is not as frequent as storm surges along the Indian coast (Table 2).

Percentage of tsunami worldwide (Table 1.1 in Bryant 2001)

Location	%
Atlantic East Coast	1.6%
Mediterranean	10.1%
Bay of Bengal	0.8%
East Indies	20.3%
Pacific Ocean	25.4%
Japan and Russia	18.6%
Pacific east Coast	8.9%
Caribbean	13.8%
Atlantic West Coast	0.4%

(iii) *Pollution Due to Industrial and Domestic Effluents:* The coastal area of the country has several major cities, with the consequent high concentration of industrial and domestic effluents. About 80% of municipal wastewater and industrial effluents that contain heavy metals or persistent organic pollutants are discharged into the coastal seas; they are dispersed in the near-coastal seas by tidal currents. Pollution has an impact on the marine food chain, and eventually through seafood on human health.

(iv) *Coastal Erosion:* Coasts are subject to almost continuous change, and can either erode (retreat) or build seawards (accrete). Erosion is a natural phenomenon, but it can also be caused and exacerbated by anthropogenic activities. It is affected by several factors that can be site-specific: near-shore topography and geomorphology, drainage patterns of local streams, etc. Erosion poses a threat to any activity, especially construction, in the coastal zone.

(v) *Oil Spills:* These are caused by accidents involving tankers, barges, pipelines, refineries, and storage facilities; this usually happens while the oil is being transported. The oil usually spreads out rapidly across the water surface to form a thin layer that we call "oil spill". Depending on the circumstances, oil spills can harm marine birds and mammals, and can also harm fish and shellfish. As with pollution, the effect can cascade up the food chain to human beings.

(vi) *Harmful Algal Blooms (HAB):* Eutrophication of waters caused by excessive nutrients, especially nitrogen, leads to potentially harmful algal blooms (HAB). They result in rapid growth of an algal species that contains toxins or causes a negative impact on natural resources or human beings; HABs can occur naturally, but are exacerbated by pollution. HABs are a serious coastal problem, affecting the coastal ecosystem and, through the food-chain cascade, eventually human health; apart from the impact on tourism and recreation through their impact on health, they also affect this industry through visual pollution of the coastal waters.

(vii) *Submarine Mudslides:* As on land, mudslides can occur on the continental slopes; apart from the obvious risk they pose to offshore platforms, they can also trigger tsunami.

(viii) *Hazards Related to Global Climate Change:* Anthropogenic impact on climate is more certain now owing to increasing confidence in observations and models. There have been suggestions that the frequency of storms in the Bay of Bengal might increase (*http://ipcc-wg1.ucar.edu/*). Since surges due to storms already pose a considerable threat to the region (Fig. 3), any increase in the intensity and frequency owing to global changes in climate will exacerbate the hazard.

Magnitude of Impact of Different Coastal Hazards

Each of the hazards mentioned above has its own unique features in terms of the duration of an event and its impact on life and property. The schematic in Fig. 4 gives an idea of each hazard in terms of these two variables. Some hazards like tsunami and storm surges are short-lived, i.e. they are events, but each event has a high impact per unit time.

They cause considerable damage in a short time and therefore are more easily embedded in our conscious mind. If their frequency of occurrence, however, happens to be low, as in the case of tsunami along the Indian coast, they disappear from our conscious mind after a while. Other hazards like coastal pollution occur over a long duration, i.e. they are not events but *processes,* and have a small impact per unit time. Any damage they cause occurs gradually and in an incremental fashion.

Hence, these long-duration, low-impact hazards are less easily recognized and do not register as strongly in our consciousness as the short-duration, high-impact events. That they act more persistently, however, implies that the cumulative effect of these processes over some time usually will exceed that of the high-impact events.

Some hazards like HABs may not cause loss of life, but can lead to outbreak of disease, thereby affecting normal life and the economy, if they find their way up the food chain to human beings. Some hazards like secular sea-level rise may not cause fatalities, but have the potential for disrupting life if it becomes necessary to abandon flourishing coastal towns and cities. Likewise, coastal erosion has a serious impact on coastal settlements and the infrastructure along the coastline. Submarine mudslides too, though not affecting life directly, have the potential to disrupt economy on a large scale because they directly affect the basis for modern industrial civilisation: fossil fuels.

It is necessary to quantify these hazards to determine our vulnerability to each of them. Information is needed on the frequency of their occurrence, on their spatial distribution, and on the magnitudes of the extremes associated with them. This is essential if their economic impact is to be assessed; insurance premium calculations, for example, require an estimate of the potential risk. Since these hazards do not affect all coastal regions uniformly, it is essential to map them quantitatively. Table provides a summary of our knowledge about different coastal hazards.

Summary of coastal hazards and our current knowledge of these hazards with respect to India.

Hazard	*Region most affected*	*Frequency of occurrence*	*Magnitude of impact*	*Remarks*
Storm surges	Bay of Bengal.	See Fig. 3.	Biggest killer in this part of the world.	Impact event by event is not easily available, but it should be possible to assemble for the last century at least based on instrumental records. Research is needed to extend the record back in time.
Tsunami	Needs further study.	Sporadic, not known	Highly damaging.	Need to document occurrence in the past and evaluate the impact (if possible).
Coastal pollution	All major coastal industrial areas, ports, major cities and towns on the coastline.	Persistent, but sporadic bursts of heavy pollution may occur.	Affects biodiversity & tourism industry, and human health through the marine food chain.	Impact needs to be monitored on continuous basis. Need to generate data base of the major pollution constituents and their effects on ecology. Not well documented or quantified in spite of several EIA studies. Need to integrate the results of disparate EIA studies to form a coherent picture.
Coastal erosion	Not fully known.	Persistent hazard, but exacerbated by other hazards like cyclones and storms, floods, tsunami, etc., and by anthropogenic activity.	Variable, but can be disruptive.	As with pollution, there is a need to integrate the results of several small-scale, disparate studies.
Oil spills	Usually along shipping routes and around harbours, but, in the event of an accident, almost anywhere.	Variable.	Harmful effect on the coastal or marine ecosystem.	Need to understand how a potential spill will spread, and for studies related to new methodology to reduce effect of harmful toxins.
Harmful algal blooms (HABs)	Mostly off the southwest coast of India, but also occur at other places.	Annual event (may be more), but of short duration.	Variable; affects sea-food chain, tourism; human health hazard.	Need to understand causative effects and spatio-temporal spread; satellite remote sensing is a promising tool.
Submarine mudslides	Not predictable as this depends on soil/sediment structure & texture.	Not known.	Can have serious impact on offshore structures, and result in huge loss for the oil sector.	Need for a detailed study of past events using paleontological methods, and sediment stratification classification.
Impact of global change	Global, but projections suggest an increase in the already high frequency of storms in the Bay of Bengal.	Projected increase in the frequency of storms in the Bay of Bengal	Not known, subject to uncertainty inherent in global climate models.	Needs to be taken seriously because an already stressed and fragile coastal zone may be subject to more intense and frequent hazards.

Coastal Hazard Preparedness

Having examined the vulnerability to coastal hazards along the Indian coast, the following elements need to be considered for our preparedness for such hazards:

(i) *awareness* of (a) evolution of a hazard based on past experience and its frequency of occurrence, and

(b) distribution of the magnitude of past hazardous events;

(ii) *appreciation* (quantitative as far as possible) of vulnerability to a hazard;

(iii) *ability to predict* either deterministically or stochastically;

(iv) *response readiness* before and after the hazard(ous) event; and

(v) *education at all levels.*

Current Conditions

A Rural Perspective on Land Use

The Rural-Urban Connections Strategy was initiated by the SACOG Board in January, 2008 to identify ways to help the rural areas of the 6-county SACOG region to have healthy economies. The project is developing knowledge about the economic realities of rural county and rural city local governments and property owners who are trying to earn a living for the uses of their rural lands. Through the Blueprint and Metropolitan Transportation Plan projects over the last six years, SACOG has developed data, analysis and plans that illustrate that the success of our region's urban and rural areas are inextricably linked – one can not succeed over the long-term without the other succeeding as well.

The Land Use topic focuses on the current land use policies and plans that guide the use of rural lands. Whether for agricultural, habitat or conservation, rural home sites, urban development, recreation or open space, the use of land has implications for the viability of rural communities, agricultural operations, and natural habitats, as well as the provision of public services and the creation and maintenance of physical infrastructure. Taken together, these various uses of land determine the long-term economic and environmental sustainability of rural areas and are an important part of achieving similar objectives for the entire region. This paper summarizes current policies that affect rural land use in the Sacramento Region and begins to explore how these policies and development standards encourage or discourage agricultural uses, urbanization, rural home sites, or habitat conservation. Many counties are updating their general plans and new policies being drafted in those processes will be examined in the "innovations" phase of this study.

The opportunities and challenges in rural parts of our region are directly affected by the Sacramento region's strong population growth and commensurate development pressure, particularly over the last ten years. From 1988 to 2005, the region grew by approximately 657,000 people. In that same time, approximately 200,000 acres of farmland were lost to urban and rural development. That is over 5% of the total farmland acres existing in the region much of which is higher quality farmland and in unincorporated areas. The six counties in the SACOG region, although unique in many ways, face similar challenges when it comes to policy making for their rural lands. Policy makers are often confronted with the competing demands of maintaining agricultural and open space, funding infrastructure and public services, economic development, growth pressures and land rights.

Development of the Rural Land Use Policies Current Conditions Inventory

An inventory of current rural general plan land use policies was developed in cooperation with the six counties in the SACOG region. SACOG staff summarized general plan polices and zoning ordinances and then met with staffs from each county to vet the findings of the inventory. This research helps SACOG staff and planning staff across the region understand generally and specifically what policies are being used in each county to guide the use of land. The inventory is intended to provide a starting foundation for a regional discussion and inquiry into key questions for the Land Use Working Group, including:

- What are the goals of land use policies and standards in rural areas of the region?
- Are recent land use trends consistent with the goals?
- What is unique and what is common about land use goals and trends in the rural areas of our region?

Policy makers for a long time have searched for effective means for transitioning between urban and rural uses, contemplating what types of agricultural uses work most harmoniously near urban uses and vice versa. Rural residential, homes on parcels typically ranging from 1 to 10 acres in size, has long been seen as a possible answer to this "edge" question. As such, rural residential uses are an important focus area for the Land Use Working Group and this introductory paper.

- What are the various approaches to rural residential zoning in the region?
- Are some rural residential policies and codes more effective than others at providing an effective transition, or buffer zone between development and agriculture or open space uses?
- What are the relevant trends for rural residential development in the six counties?

Ten topics were reviewed as part of the inventory. These include:

- Spheres of Influence/City Limits defining the urban/rural edge
- Rural Land Use Designations
- Conflicts between land uses
- Development Mitigation
- Agriculture Conservation Easements
- Williamson Act programme
- Flood Control
- Farm worker housing in rural areas
- Jobs-housing ratio standards
- Economic development or agri-tourism policies and plans

Spheres of Influence/City Limits Defining the Urban/Rural Edge

All six counties have general plan policies that direct or limit urban growth to urban areas, community areas, or spheres of influences of cities. These policies aim to preserve agricultural and natural resource lands and also promote orderly growth. Yolo and Sutter Counties have policies that are somewhat more restrictive than the others, directing urban development to existing cities and/or their spheres of influence and to existing unincorporated communities. In Sutter County, land use planning for the spheres of influences of Yuba City and Live Oak are the responsibility of those cities, subject to county approval (General Plan Policy 1.B-1). Similarly, Yolo County requires urban uses to be placed within incorporated cities or within the urban service areas of unincorporated urban areas (General Plan Policy ADM 15). In its policy to restrict urban growth to urban areas, Yolo County as a matter of policy responds negatively to proposals to extend existing service facilities outside of urban areas. Additionally, Yolo County has a "Pass Through Agreement" with the cities of Davis and Woodland to further restrict urban development in the unincporated area between the two cities.

In addition to spheres of influence, El Dorado, Placer, Sacramento, and Yuba counties direct urban growth into community area boundaries in unincorporated parts of the counties. In El Dorado County, it is Rural Centers and Community Regions, and in Yuba County and Placer County, it is community boundaries. In Sacramento County, land expected to receive urban levels of public infrastructure and services within the planning period of the General Plan is defined by the Urban Policy Area (UPA). The County's Urban Services Boundary (USB) indicates the ultimate boundary of the urban area in the unincorporated County. These boundaries establish infrastructure extension limitations; therefore these are currently the limitations of urban expansion into rural areas.

In addition to city and county policies, Local Agency Formation Commissions (LAFCOs) are governed in their review and approval of spheres of influence and city boundary changes by the Cortese-Knox-Hertzberg Local Government Reorganization Act of 2000. As a protection for lands under Williamson Act contract, the CKH Act prohibits LAFCos from including such lands in a sphere adjustment or city annexation without first making certain findings and/or the Williamson Act contract meeting certain provisions. Additionally, the Yolo County LAFCO has adopted an agricultural mitigation policy that is required as part of annexations, if the jurisdiction doesn't have a formal agricultural mitigation policy adopted.

Rural Land Use Designations

Across the region, rural uses are generally categorized as agricultural (intensive and extensive agriculture), open space, recreation, forest (or timber) and rural or agricultural residential. Development standards typically require minimum lot sizes of 10 or 20 acres for agricultural and forested lands and 1 or 5 acres in the case of rural residential lands. Hence, by policy, agriculture generally starts at parcel sizes of 10 acres, with the exception of Placer County where its "Farm" zone has a minimum lot size of 4.6 acres and some parcels area as small as one acre.

With the exception of some protected open space designations, most rural land use designations (agricultural, timber, and open space) allow for the development of at least one home site, but are intended mainly for agriculture production. Conversely, rural residential designations allow for at least limited agricultural use where ample water supply and suitable soils are available, but are intended primarily for residential use that supports the rural and agricultural character of these areas.

Conflicts Between Land Uses

One consequence of development in the rural areas is sometimes a conflict between agriculture and non-agricultural uses. Mainly as a result of increasing complaints from residents near farmland (regarding noise, dust, sprays, smells, etc), all six counties have adopted Right-to-Farm ordinances. The Right-to-Farm Ordinance requires a real estate disclosure be given to all new property owners in the counties explaining the farmer's right to farm and that sounds, smells, etc. are part of a normal farming practice and shall not be considered a nuisance. However, the agricultural department in each county reported that they still receive complaints on a regular basis.

Placer and El Dorado Counties also receive complaints related to agricultural tourism, specifically wineries where tasting is allowed or special events are permitted. These complaints are generally targeted towards the traffic and noise associated with events and safety on the rural roads. As a result, Placer and El Dorado Counties have developed Winery Ordinances, which provide wineries with specific regulations and regulate associated uses like wine tasting and promotional events. Placer County's Winery Ordinance was adopted at the end of August 2008, while El Dorado County continues to refine their current ordinance.

Additionally, non-agricultural lands in the region are subject to buffer requirements to help minimize the conflict between agricultural and non-agricultural uses. Sutter and Placer Counties' agricultural buffers range from 100-800 feet depending on crop type, Yuba and Yolo Counties require a minimum 100-300 foot buffer, Sacramento County ranges from 300-500 feet, and El Dorado County requires 200 foot buffer that may be administratively reduced if certain Board adopted criteria are met. El Dorado County also has minimum lot size requirement of 10 acres for rural parcels adjacent to urban areas.

Development Mitigation

Many areas across the rural landscape in this region provide habitat for threatened and endangered species. All of the counties' general plan policies have mitigation requirements generally stating that habitat land lost due to development shall be mitigated for. To that end, each county is also working on a Habitat Conservation Plan or some form of conservation strategy to identify areas that are important for species protection and areas where development may occur. Some of these efforts are building on existing conservation plans such as Placer County's Placer Legacy or El Dorado County's Oak Woodland Management Plan. The only completed HCP in the region covers lands in the Natomas basin.

There can be conflict between habitat conservation and agricultural land. Parts of the region are experiencing a conversion of agricultural land to habitat preservation for development mitigation purposes, which has the effect of removing land from agricultural use (and into habitat conservation) and sometimes creates difficulties for adjacent agricultural lands with the invasion of weeds, rodents, birds, and waterfowl.

However, there can also be "working" relationships between the two land uses in which both needs can be met: rice fields have become part of the Pacific Flyway, alfalfa is great foraging habitat for Swainson's Hawk, grazing helps keep non-native grasses in check and helps vernal pools function. Yolo, Sacramento, and Placer Counties are addressing this and planning for these working relationships in their HCPs. Sutter and Yuba counties have begun developing a joint HCP that will also address these issues. Yolo and Sacramento County staff indicate that some components of their HCP will be dependent on agricultural land preservation for implementation; in Sacramento County as much as 90% is dependent on agriculture.

In addition to mitigation requirements for habitat lands, Yolo, El Dorado, and Sacramento Counties have mitigation policies specifically for loss of agricultural land. For example, Yolo County adopted an Agricultural Mitigation Ordinance which requires all projects that result in a permanent loss of either farmland and/or habitat to mitigate an equal amount of land. Agricultural and habitat easements may not be "stacked" within the same property, and must be mitigated separately. The ordinance requires agricultural conservation easements be located within two miles of the development that is being mitigated. The purpose of this is to give first protection priority to lands close to urban areas which in Yolo County are viewed as higher risk for conversion to urban uses. Within Yolo County, the cities of Woodland and Davis also have agricultural mitigation requirements. The Yolo County LAFCO has also requires agricultural mitigation when agricultural land is lost as a result of annexation.

Agriculture Conservation Easements

Another way agricultural land is being preserved in the region is through conservation easements. Conservation easements require the transfer of development rights to ensure the parcel is preserved.

Yuba County encourages the voluntary donation of conservation easements to preserve agricultural or timber use (General Plan Policies 38 and 44-LUP). Similarly Placer County supports conservation easements as a tool for private conservation organizations to preserve agriculture (General Plan Policy 7.A.11). Sacramento County's general plan policy AG-5 encourages mitigation of projects on prime, statewide, unique, and locally important farmlands to provide in-kind protection (must be of equal or higher farmland category). Sutter County has an agricultural preserve zoning district, which requires the development rights on the remainder of a parcel that has been allowed to develop a residence be transferred to the county. El Dorado has a similar requirement in its agricultural preservation zones. Yolo County has an Agricultural Mitigation Ordinance requiring agricultural easements at a 1:1 ratio for projects that result in a loss of farmland.

Williamson Act Programme

The California Land Conservation Act, better known as the Williamson Act, was enacted by the California State Legislature in 1965 to encourage the preservation of agricultural lands. The Williamson Act programme permits property tax adjustments for landowners who contract with a city or county to keep their land in agricultural production or approved open space uses for at least 10 years. Lands covered by Williamson Act contracts are assessed on the basis of their agricultural value instead of their potential market value under nonagricultural uses. In return for the preferential tax rate, the landowner is required to contractually agree to keep their land in agricultural production or approved open space uses for a period of at least 10 years.

El Dorado, Placer, Sacramento, Sutter, and Yolo Counties all participate in the Williamson Act programme and have general plan policies encouraging enrollment and/or discouraging non-renewal. Yolo also participates in the

Farmland Security Zone (Super Williamson Act) programme, which extends the contract period to 20 years and reduces the tax burden even further; Sacramento County also supports this programme. Approximately 87,000 acres of farmland in the SACOG region reported a non-renewal of their Williamson Act contract between 2004 and 2006 (about 6% of the lands in contract).

Flood Control

Four counties, Sutter, Yuba, Yolo, and Sacramento, have large floodplains along the Sacramento, Yuba, Feather, and American Rivers and their tributaries. Flood control projects – dams and levees – have made it possible to develop urban areas in these floodplains. However, recent state legislation imposing a higher level of protection (200-year v. 100-year) for urban areas (defined as 10,000 people or more) and changing Army Corps of Engineers levee standards are making it more difficult and expensive to protect areas already fortified with urban levees, let alone areas that might want to urbanize outside of these urban levees. To date, there are no plans to build new urban levees; jurisdictions are simply focused on improving the urban levees they already have. This may have implications for limiting the spread of development beyond those areas currently planned for urbanization in the floodplain.

As well, some flood control plans include setting aside farmland to reduce the amount of land needing an urban level of protection in the future and thereby minimizing overall flood risk. In some cases, levee improvements may impact agricultural lands within the basin being protected. In Yuba County, for example, setback levees will be built over as much as 1,500 acres of farmland and will bisect orchards and other farmland in areas with high quality soils. In southern Sutter County and northern Sacramento County, levees improvements in the Natomas basin are estimated to impact more than 1,600 acres of farmland that also serves as habitat for the Giant Garter Snake and Swainson's Hawk. Additionally, up to 700 acres of farmland will be converted to habitat for required mitigation. Similar impacts may be seen for other levee improvement projects in the region. The Delta Protection Commission is considering the use of "ring levees" around legacy Delta communities. Other small towns, such as Knights Landing in Yolo, are considering the development of new levees to provide100-year flood protection.

Science & Technology

Science and technology has been in the forefront of transforming the Indian economic structure helping India evolve as a globally competitive economic powerhouse. With the available scientific manpower—which is third largest in the world— the Indian science and technology has been growing well above world average.

While the Indian output of science, as measured by the quality and quantity of Science Citation Index (SCI) papers, has been growing at a CAGR of 8 per cent in the past three years, the world average was only 4 per cent. Also, the number of technical workforce is also increasing at a rapid clip and is set to cross the 2 million mark, with the march from one million to two million happening in just about three years.

A number of world-class institutions have instrumental in this: 162 universities award 4,000 doctorates and 35,000 postgraduate degrees and the Council of Scientific and Industrial Research runs 40 research laboratories that have made some significant achievements.

Space Technology

India is one of the few countries with expertise to conceptualise, design and manufacture satellites and the capability to launch them into space. In fact, it has the largest constellation of remote sensing satellites in the world. Also, the Indian Space Research Organisation (ISRO) is the world's third non-US supplier of 1-metre imageries and holds nearly 25 per cent of the US$ 120-million global free-play imageries market.

The year 2007 saw several major accomplishments being made in the Indian space programme: successful orbiting and recovery of a space capsule (which is a prelude to the development of space recovery capsule), launch of Cartosat-2 (a remote sensing satellite with a resolution capacity below 1 metre) and successfully testing indigenously developed cryogenic upper stage among others.

India has also lined up some interesting projects for the future: a lunar mission, a project for manned space outing around 2015, development of space recovery capsule (which would lay the foundation for future returning missions) and establishing indigenous regional GPS by 2012 among others.

Renewable Energy

India has been tapping energy from renewable sources to meet its growing energy demands. This also helps in diversifying its sources of energy. Some notable achievements in this field are:

- India has the largest number of biomass gasifier systems in the world.
- India is the third largest producer of solar photovoltaic cells in the world
- India is the world's fourth largest wind power user.
- India has the ninth largest solar thermal power generation in terms of million units per square meter.

Even after these achievements there is considerable scope for growth as there is a huge gap between potential and achievement in various sectors.

Oceanography

India was the first country to be accorded the status of a Pioneer Investor and was allocated an exclusive area in the central Indian Ocean by the UN for exploration and utilisation of resources. India has already sent 13 scientific research expeditions to Antarctica and has two permanent stations in Antarctica. In May 2007, India got approval from the Antarctic Treaty Consultative Committee (ATCM) to construct its third station at Larsemann Hills in Antartica.

India has also set up the Tsunami Early Warning Centre to predict the likelihood of tsunami within 30 minutes after a quake in Indian Ocean system. Further, it plans to become the first country in the world to acquire capabilities in predicting the likelihood of a tsunami in seven minutes after any major earthquake in Indian Ocean.

Nanotechnology

India plans to become the global hub for nano science and nanotechnology. To this end, the government has started a five-year nano science and technology mission (NSTM) spearheaded by the Department of Science and Technology (DST) with the aim to create nano clusters in the country. The government has planned an investment of US$ 254 million.

This has resulted in the initiation of over 100 R&D projects, establishment of 12 centres of excellence in nano science and 7 centres in nano technology and 4 centres of excellence in public private partnership.

In this endeavor India is favorably placed as it would have the youngest scientific talent pool in the world by 2020. Already, many countries have entered in to bilateral cooperation with India in this field which includes countries like USA, UK, Canada, European Union, Germany and Italy among others.

Biotechnology

Biotechnology seems to be the next big thing in India after information technology. With a year on year growth of 35 per cent, the biotechnology industry has touched the US$ 2-billion mark in revenues in 2006-07 from US$ 1 billion in 2004-05. The industry is on the track to meet its target of US$ 5 billion by 2010.

Already the biggest two of the top ten global biotech companies have already set up wholly owned subsidiaries in India. The rest of them have made their presence through marketing partnerships and have exploring larger business opportunities in the country.

The Indian biotechnology sector offers a wide variety of products and services including affordable vaccines, non-vaccine therapeutics, innovative product development and contract services. In its latest global biotech survey, Ernst & Young ranked India number three after Japan and Korea in the Asia-Pacific region.

The Government has also approved the National Biotechnology Development Strategy to fully utilize the current opportunities and lay a strong foundation for discovery and innovation.

Intellectual Property

The number of patent applications has increased from about 13,000 in 2003-04 to around 29,000 in 2006-07. Significantly, the number of patents granted rose by almost four-fold from 1911 in 2004-05 to 7539 in 2006-07.Also, over the same period, the industry's expenditure on R&D has gone up from US$ 989.36 million to US$ 1.48 billion, with 50 per cent of the in-house R&D units registered with the Department for Scientific & Industrial Research (DSIR) having an R&D intensity of over 1 per cent. Simultaneously, the number of trademarks registered rose to a record level of about 326,000 during 2004-07 from around 167,000 during all the previous years, showing a marked acceleration of activity in this segment.

The prominence of India in the Intellectual Property Regime can also be seen in the Indian Patent Office being granted the prestigious status of "International Searching Authority" (ISA) by the World Intellectual Property Organisation (WIPO). This puts India in to the 14 member exclusive group of countries who are recognized as world leaders in the field of IPRs.

Also, there has been increase in the number of patents filed by Indian centres of multinationals. A government report of US has pointed out that patent applications from top five emerging markets (which includes India) rose by 759 per cent, much higher than the 116 per cent growth rate of US. In fact there has been increasing reliance on Indian R&D centres and over 300 multinationals have already established their R&D centres in India.

Government Initiatives

With a view to attract and motivate students to take up science education and research, the Department of Science and Technology (DST), Government of India, has taken many initiatives:

- Scholarships for 10,000 standard XII students across the country interested in pursuing a five-year integrated Masters in Science (M.Sc) programme.
- Organising an interactive meet with Noble Laureates and Icons of Indian Science.
- Instituting a new scheme to attract brilliant Scientists and Technologists of Indian Origin (STIO) abroad to work on collaborative R&D projects.

India has also entered into many bilateral and multilateral framework agreements at the international level in the field of science and technology. In fact, in recognition of India's capability in science and technology, it has been invited to participate in many mega science projects at the global level, which includes Facility for Anti-proton & Ion Research (FAIR), International Rice Genome Sequencing Consortium, International Consortium on Lepidopteron genomics and International Thermonuclear Experimental Reactor (ITER) project among others.

Different Application Level—Local, Regional and National

With most businesses today dependent on multiple key applications, IT managers continually juggle resources to deliver required service levels while remaining efficient. Users continue to need more and more data, while management continues to seek cost reductions. Balancing a business™s resource and cost requirements is particularly difficult because of the impact of data growth on IT functions"backups exceed assigned backup windows, restores cannot be accomplished quickly enough, and IT tasks take up nights and weekends. All of these challenges mean more work for IT managers"and higher cost.

Consolidation

One strategy for improving operations and reducing costs is to consolidate storage in a SAN. Like server consolidation, storage consolidation can result in many benefits " not only less equipment to maintain and manage, but also reduced floor space and environmental costs, better utilization rates (e.g., doing more with less hardware), lower licensing costs, and fewer points of management. In a consolidated environment storage administrators manage a single pool of storage (comprised of one or many arrays) while applications share all available capacity and system resources.

In this environment, operational improvements are the result of adding advanced features and flexibility that are impossible with direct attached storage"many SANs provide better redundancy, data sharing across servers, faster backup and restore, disaster protection, and rapid deployment. And, the more automation, the better"for IT and financial managers"since automatic functions simplify operations. For example, in an EqualLogic PS Series SAN, multiple storage systems join together in a single pool, and as new arrays are added they are automatically assimilated into the configuration. In addition, automatic and transparent balancing of workloads across disks and arrays delivers optimum performance at all times. Because the single pool can be managed as a single system, even as it grows, management functions remain simple while operations are optimized.

Tiered Storage for Workload Variations

For many, consolidation alone solves most problems"well-implemented SANs with advanced, automated features improve reliability, utilization rates, and management. But in some environments, workloads have different levels of importance and performance requirements. In a consolidated environment, how does an administrator manage different application service level requirements? If your Oracle and SQL Server databases require fast performance but backup and file and print applications do not, can you still consolidate your storage and reap those benefits?

One answer is to prioritize applications and place them on separate hardware resources, each optimally configured for the required service level. By creating different storage tiers, you can optimize your production environment for whatever feature is most important for each application. For instance, for applications that need fast performance, you optimize for speed;

for those that don, you can optimize for maximum capacity and utilization. By tiering applications and using multiple storage pools you can ensure that service levels are met and often avoid unnecessary storage purchases. A tiered-storage strategy can be implemented using different disk technologies, speeds, and RAID levels, enabling you to more efficiently manage costs and service levels in today™s varied application environment.

SAN within a SAN

A built-in tiering capability allows administrators to configure separate storage pools within a single SAN to build the most efficient, flexible, easy-to-manage environment. By isolating storage resources in a SAN, administrators can control service levels, costs, and utilization rates online. This œSAN within a SAN offers the advantages of both consolidation and greater control, enabling administrators to easily separate workloads to support any business need: by application, by service level, by department, etc. Want to separate production databases from DR data? Keep your messaging data isolated from other applications, but still manage storage from a central point? Isolate engineering data from the marketing department? Multiple storage tiers within a SAN will handle all these requirements. For example, some organizations assign mission-critical applications to their own storage tier that utilizes 15,000 RPM, 146 GB SAS drives configured with RAID 10"this ensures fast, consistent performance and the best IOPS per dollar. They place disaster recovery replicas, backups, and archive data on less expensive, 7.2K RPM SATA drives that maximize capacity and provide the lowest cost per terabyte.

SAN within a SAN: Tiering applications can help you better manage service levels and storage costs, while retaining the benefits of storage consolidation. Production data can be placed in a high-performance tier utilizing 15,000 rpm SAS drives, while data that is not accessed as often can reside on high-capacity SATA drives.

A key feature of this environment is that all this data is in the same SAN. Ideally, these various applications and business operations would continue uninterrupted even during tiering or re-tiering, and load-balancing would be automatic for consistently optimal performance. A system with these features allows administrators to move data to different storage tiers online to optimize service levels without downtime or after-hours maintenance. This kind of system offers the most cost-efficient, simple-to-manage environment, delivering the optimum requirements of each application or service level.

What about Management?

Creating storage tiers does add a little complexity"instead of just combining all the data in the SAN, the administrator can actually improve the SAN. It™s like driving an automatic vs. a standard transmission"both cars get you where youare going, but the gear shift gives you more control if your willing to accept a little more complexity. The additional management is minimal"when you create a volume, you need to identify the applications priority to determine what tier to place it in, and that means a little more planning for the administrator.

Local Mitigation Strategy

A Local Mitigation Strategy (LMS) is a local government plan in the United States, typically at county level, that is designed to reduce or eliminate risks to people and property from natural and man-made hazards. Mitigation strategies are supported by state government and federal programmes, in line with the Disaster Mitigation Act.

The need for hazard mitigation has become more recognized over the past few years due to the large number of natural hazards which have occurred in the U.S and the increase in the costs to achieve post disaster recovery. Money spent prior to a hazardous event to reduce the impacts of a disaster can result in substantial savings in life and property following the event. The benefits of implementing a mitigation programme usually far outweigh the costs. Because of this, the Federal Emergency Management Agency (FEMA) and the states have developed national and state Mitigation Strategies and funding is becoming increasingly more available to support hazard mitigation efforts.

The advantages of developing a local LMS programme are numerous including guidance in developing pre and post mitigation plans; identifying priority projects and programmes for funding; and increasing the likelihood of State and Federal funding for pre-and post-hazard mitigation projects.

The mitigation initiatives that a community develops must have their basis in the community's guiding principles on hazard mitigation. The initiatives must also actively reduce a community's vulnerability to hazards. This can be justified through the vulnerability assessment section of the strategy. Finally, mitigation initiatives must accurately reflect the community's needs. The working group assigned to develop the strategy can help assure that local needs are incorporated in the mitigation initiatives. These steps prevent a projects that have no basis in a community's overall vision of hazard mitigation, or in its vulnerability to hazards on the vulnerability assessment, from being proposed.

Regional Mitigation Plan

Regional Southside Hampton Roads Hazard Mitigation Plan: The Cities of Virginia Beach, Norfolk, Portsmouth, Suffolk, and Isle of Wight County worked together to develop a Regional Hazard Mitigation Plan, with FEMA funding, as part of a mitigation planning requirement of the Disaster Mitigation Act of 2000 (DMA 2000). The DMA 2000 charged localities with the responsibility of identifying, assessing, and mitigating the risks within their communities to ensure that critical services would continue to function if a natural disaster were to occur.

The Hazard Mitigation Plan was approved by the Virginia Department of Emergency Management (VDEM) and the Federal Emergency Management Agency, and adopted by City Council. It is important to note that once the plan is approved, the city will be eligible for future mitigation function, if available, to implement pre-and post-disaster projects.

The Hazard Mitigation Plan PowerPoint presentation introduces the mitigation planning process and the Hazard Mitigation Plan Abstract provides a brief overview of the plan's contents and includes the city's hazards and mitigation strategies. The plan and the abstract are located in the Related Information portion of the Emergency Management homepage.

National Cyclone Risk Mitigation Project (NCRMP)

1. Hazard risk mitigation is key to sustainable development and this has been the policy of Government of India, which lays greater emphasis on prevention, preparedness and mitigation.
2. In line with the present policy, the Ministry of Home Affairs, entrusted with the mandate of disaster management, have launched multifaceted initiatives and projects aiming at mitigating hazard risks in the country and enhancing capabilities at various levels to effectively respond to emergencies. Three major projects have been drawn up namely National Cyclpne Risk Mitigation Project. National Earthquake Risk Mitigation Project and Strengthening Fire and Emergency Services so as to address multiple hazard risks in the country. The Planning Commission has appraised these projects and accorded in-principle clearance.
3. The World Bank has offered to support the National Cyclone Risk Mitigation Project covering all 13 cyclone prone coastal and island States/UTs. These States and UTs are *Andhra Pradesh, Gujarat, Orissa, West Bengal, Maharashtra, Karnataka, Kerala, Tamil Nadu, Goa, Daman & Diu, Pond / cherry, Lakshadeep and Andaman & Nicobar Islands.*
4. On receipt of formal communication from DEA, a four member Mission Team from the World Bank visited India in the last fortnight of September 2004. During their visit the Mission had elaborate discussions with various stake holders whose involvement is envisaged under the project such as Indian Meteorological Department (IMD), National Centre for Medium Range Weather Forecasting (NCMRWF), Ministry of Environment and Forests (MoEF), Central Water Commission (CWC), National Institute for Disaster

Management (NIDM), IITs etc. The Mission held extensive discussions with officers of NDM Division on the scope of the project and methodologies for implementation. A one-day brainstorming session was also held with representatives of States/UTs (proposed to be covered under the project) where the Mission Team discussed in detail the programme implementation/management modalities. It is noted that the Project was developed in a consultative manner based on the deliberations made in a two-day workshop held in February, 2003 at Kolkata and attended by States/UTs prone to cyclones and other relevant Central Ministries/ Departments and Agencies.

5. The World Bank Mission has estimated the overall cost of the proposed National Cyclone Risk Mitigation Project at around Rs. 1642.50 crore1 (US $ 365 million)2. World Bank/IDA funding is proposed at Rs. 1350 crore (US $ 300 million). Four identified key components that are to be supported under the project are indicated below;
   - o Component A-Upgradation of the Cyclone Forecasting, tracking and warning system
   - o Component B-Cyclone Risk Mitigation Investments
   - o Component C-Technical Assistance for Hazard Risk Management Capacity Building
   - o Component D-Project Management and Monitoring
   - o Total-Rs. 1350 crore (US $ 300 million)

   MHA will decide on allocation of resources among four broad components of the project mentioned above.

6. Areas of support and expected outputs under these four components are given below:
   a. *Component A:* Upgradation of the Cyclone Forecasting, tracking and warning system-The activities that are to be supported under this component envisage upgrading the cyclone modeling, forecasting, tracking, and warning system. Under this component Indian

Meteorological Department (IMD) will be strengthened by installation of Doppler Radars using digital processing for weather and cyclone forecasting. In addition, the sensor infrastructure will be upgraded where required. The computer processing capabilities of National Centre for Medium Range

Weather Forecasting (NCMRWF) will be improved and the concerned staff members will be trained in the use of the new infrastructure and state-of the art cyclone forecasting models. The expected outcome will be putting in place a modern system of cyclone warning with longer lead time in warning potentially affected people in the coastline to move to shelters and place cattle and other animals in areas where losses could be minimized. In addition fishermen will be equipped with communication devices to better prepare themselves in case of cyclone track changes. b. Component B: Cyclone Risk Mitigation Investments in States/UTs-Cyclone Risk Mitigation Investments in States/UTs is the major component of the project which includes identification and implementation of high priority activities for cyclone risk mitigation (i.e., construction of cyclone shelters, shelterbelt plantation, mangrove regeneration, construction of embankments to stop sea water inundation etc.) in the project States/UTs and commissioning ' This includes 25% contribution from States towards Component B. 75% resources will be provided from this project to the State Govts.

-1 USD= INR 45.00 of technical assistance/studies to sustain these initiatives. It is envisaged that the project States/UTs will draw up proposals as per their local needs by identifying priority areas where interventions are most crucial for effective mitigation of cyclone risks in line with the State/UT Disaster Management Policy. This would ensure that proposals/schemes firmed up by states/UTs are need based and specifically address the cyclone risk mitigation aspects. Detailed sets of guidelines will be prepared by MHA to help States/UTs in formulating comprehensive project proposals as per the World Bank norms.

Considering the occurrence of cyclones, size of population and the existing institutional mechanisms for disaster management the States/UTs can be categorized into two categories:

Category-I: higher vulnerability (Andhra Pradesh, Gujarat, Orissa and West Bengal) and

Category-II: lower vulnerability (Maharashtra, Goa, Karnataka, Kerala, Tamil Nadu, Daman & Diu, Pondicherry, Lakshadweep and Andaman & Nicobar Islands). Category-II States/UTs can be further divided into two sub-categories i.e.,

Category-II (A) and Category-II (B) considering their geographical size.

i. Taking into account the vulnerability of States/UTs to cyclones, and size of population and availability of financial resources, it is proposed that the allocation of cyclone mitigation investments in States/UTs should be pre-determined.

The table below shows the categorization of States/UTs and the resource allocation to each State/UT as per their categorization

UNIT-IX

Implementation

Change Management

Managing the Change

Preparation for Change:

- Environmental analysis.
- Set out the strengths and weaknesses of the organisation
  - Current provisions
  - Resources
  - Roles and responsibilities
- Identify the change required
- Determine the major issues
- Identify and assess the key stakeholders
- Win the support of key individuals
- Identify the obstacles
- Determine the degree of risk and the cost of change
- Understand why change is resisted
- Recognize the need for change, identify current position, devise a suitable method

Building the vision:

- Develop a clear vision
- Make it people clear about what a change involves and how they are involved in it
- What is involved
- What is the proposed change

- Why should we do it
- What the major effects will be
- How we can manage the change

Plan the change:

- Devise appropriate strategies to introduce change
- Design the change
- Identify the significant steps in the change process
- Discuss the need for change and the full details of what is involved
- Allow people to participate in planning change
- Communicate the plan to all concerned
- Produce a policy statement
- Devise a sensible time scale
- Produce action plans for monitoring the change
- Allow people to participate in planning change
- Get all parties involved in and committed to the change
- Inspire confidence by forestalling problems and communicating regularly
- Devise a sensible time scale for implementation of change
- Anticipate the problems of implementation
- Understand why change is resisted

Implementing the Change:

- Check on and record progress
- Make sure that change is permanent
- Evaluate the change
- Improve on any weak areas
- Overcome resistance
- Involve all personnel affected
- Keep everyone informed
- Devise an appropriate reward system
- Be willing to compromise on detail
- Ensure that strategies are adaptable

- Select people to champion change
- Provide support and training
- Monitor and review

Two Types of Change:

(1) *Step change*

- Dramatic or radical change in one fell swoop
- Radical alternation in the organisation
- Gets it over with quickly
- May require some coercion

(2) *Incremental change*

- Ongoing piecemeal change which takes place as part of an organisation's evolution and development
- Tends to more inclusive

Step vs Incremental Change

Techniques to help implement change

Teams building across units

Internal communication

Negotiation

Action planning

Change agents or champions of change

And a certain amount of compulsion manipulation and coercion

Change Agents

Managers should be able to act as change agents:

- To identify need for change
- Be open to goods ideas for change
- To able to successfully implement change

Advantages of Using a Change Agent:

- Forces trough change
- Becomes the personification of the process
- Responsibility for change is delegated thus freeing up senior managers to focus on future strategy

Helping People to Accept Change:

- Consider how they will be affected
- Involve them in the change
- Consult and inform frequently
- Be firm but flexible
- Make controversial change as gradually as possible
- Monitor the change
- Develop a change philosophy

Six Ways of Overcoming Resistance to Change

(1) Education and communication-if people understand the needs for change and what is involved they are more likely to co-operate.

(2) Participation and involvement-to encourage people to feel ownership of the change.

(3) Facilitation and support-listening to the real concerns of people affected.

(4) Negotiation and agreement-agreement and compromise if necessary.

(5) Manipulation-e.g. "buying off" leaders of resistance.

(6) Explicit and implicit coercion-threats where necessary but this is a high risk strategy.

(source: Kotter and Schlesinger In HBR 1979) Monitor and review

- Adapt as necessary
- Recording and monitor the changes
- Measure progress against targets
- Have the desired results been achieved?
- Has the process been successful?
- How do those affected feel about the new situation?
- What might have been done differently?
- How can those not responding well to the change be helped?
- Sustain the change.-prevent any back sliding

Kotter's change phases model:

- Establish a sense of urgency
- Create a coalition
- Develop a clear vision
- Share the vision
- Empower people to clear obstacles
- Secure short term wins
- Consolidate and keep moving
- Anchor the change

Change Management Failures

What not to do

Ways to increase resistance to change:

Managers can increase resistance by:

- Failing to specific about a change
- Failing to explain why change is needed
- Not consulting
- Keeping people in the dark
- Creating excess work pressure
- Expecting immediate results
- Not dealing with fears and anxieties
- Ignoring resistance

Reasons why change can fail:

- Employees do not understand the purpose or even the need for change
- Lack of planning and preparation
- Poor communication
- Employees lack the necessary skills and/ or there is insufficient training and development offered
- Lack of necessary resources
- Inadequate/inappropriate rewards

Eight common reasons for failure of change management:

- Allowing too much complexity
- Failing to build a substantial coalition

- Failing to understand the need for a clear vision
- Failure to clearly communicate that vision
- Permitting roadblocks against that vision
- Not planning for short term results and not realising them
- Declaring victory too soon
- Failure to anchor changes in corporate culture

Accountability in Disaster Risk Management

The Department's approach to performance management integrates planning, accountability, reporting and evaluation activity. The approach links individual performance with corporate goals, and includes a system of performance review at several levels-from individual staff members through to broad organisational elements. The Department's budgeting, accountability and reporting mechanisms are aligned to the Government's accrual-based budgeting outcomes and outputs framework. The Executive and managers are supported by financial and human resource management systems and Ministerial and Parliamentary support systems.

Strategic Planning

As part of the integrated performance management approach, the Executive's role is to set the broad strategic direction for the Department. This broad strategic direction is supported by business/operational plans for each organisational element within the Department that detail activities and associated resource and performance information. All activities are related to an output within the outcomes and outputs framework. Area work plans are developed as appropriate, in line with the business/operational plans.

Links to Individual Performance

Individual performance agreements are linked to the business/operational plan or area work plan performance targets. Individual performance is reviewed twice a year against the performance agreement as part of the Programme for Performance Improvement.

Executive Performance Reviews

The departmental Executive conducts performance reviews of organisational elements twice a year. These reviews focus on organisational performance against business/operational plan performance measures or, in relation to routine activities, departmental performance standards.

Performance Information and Reporting

The strategic direction is reflected in the Department's entry in the Portfolio Budget Statements (PBS) that follows the accrual-based budgeting outcomes and outputs framework.

In addition to detailing appropriations, the PBS contains performance information for each item of administered expenditure and each output within the framework. The annual report outlines performance against measures contained in the PBS. The departmental annual report complies with the *Requirements for Annual Reports for Departments, Executive Agencies and FMA Act Bodies* issued by the Department of the Prime Minister and Cabinet and approved by the Joint Committee of Public Accounts and Audit. A separate compliance index identifies the location in this report of the information specified in the Requirements (see page 260 of print version).

Review of Corporate Performance Management Framework

During the reporting period the Department completed a review of its corporate performance management framework. The review identified a need for more consistent planning approaches across the Department. It recommended developing a performance management framework and process that would:

- clearly articulate strategic vision
- establish work priorities to enable effective allocation of resources
- more clearly define accountabilities, and
- introduce more effective monitoring.

As a result, the Department's Executive endorsed a trial of a revised planning process in the Corporate Services Group (CSG). The trial has two purposes:

- to establish a clear business plan for all the business units in CSG, and
- to model business planning processes that may be used throughout the Department.

By the end of the reporting period a CSG business plan was developed and communicated to staff in the group.

The next stages, to be undertaken later in 2004, include the development of branch plans and section/team plans, and the alignment of individual performance agreements to those plans. An evaluation of the trial will be conducted to assess the suitability of using the business planning framework and process throughout the Department.

Conduct and Ethics

The Australian Public Service (APS) Values and Code of Conduct contained in the *Public Service Act 1999* and Public Service Commissioner's Directions made under the Act apply to all employees of the Attorney-General's Department.

The Department's Certified Agreement and Australian Workplace Agreements contain a commitment from employees to uphold the APS Values and to comply with the Code of Conduct.

All people who are to become employees of the Department are provided with a copy of the APS Values and Code of Conduct and elements of the *Crimes Act 1914*. They are required to sign a statement that they have read and understood these provisions before beginning employment with the Department.

The APS Values, Code of Conduct, Chief Executive's Instructions and other material relevant to ethical conduct are incorporated, as appropriate, into relevant departmental policies, guidelines and instructions.

All Senior Executive Service (SES) employees are provided with a copy of the APS Commission publications *APS Values and Code of Conduct in practice: a guide to official conduct for APS employees and agency heads and Embedding the APS Values*.

Monitoring and Evaluation

Monitoring and evaluation (M&E) of development projects are increasingly recognized as indispensable management functions. For many years, M&E of development projects in Palestine have been given little attention. Some of the main constraints and problems that hampered M&E in development project include: weak interest and commitment to the evaluation function by both donors and Palestinian civil society organizations, weak culture of carrying out, sharing, discussing and using the results of evaluation activities among Palestinian NGOs and donors, a relative shortage of professional evaluation experts (in comparison with researchers, trainers, etc.), insufficient technical resources, limited monitory allocation to M&E work by donors, limited training opportunities in evaluation, shortage of trained staff, etc.

The last few years have witnessed an increased interest in strengthening project M&E by donors and Palestinian civil society organizations. More Palestinian nonprofit and civil society organizations are interested in strengthening their M&E capacity. This document reviews the nature of programme M&E, presents basic concepts, principles, tools and methods of M&E, reviews the process of planning and implementing effective M&E processes for nonprofit programmes, and suggests ways for using M&E results. Many of the principles presented in this document are also applicable for "for-profit" organizations.

There are many reasons why development project staff and managers of civil society organizations should know about M&E. *First*, knowledge about M&E helps project staff to improve their ability to effectively monitor and evaluate their projects, and therefore, strengthen the performance of their projects. We should remember that project staff need not be evaluation experts in order to monitor their projects; with basic orientation and training, project staff can implement appropriate techniques to carry out a useful evaluation. *Second*, programme evaluations, carried out by inexperienced persons, might be time-consuming, costly and could generate impractical or irrelevant information. *Third*, if development organizations are to recruit an external evaluation expert they should be smart consumers aware of standards, and know what to look for and require in this service.

The Need for Monitoring and Evaluation

There are many reasons for carrying out project M&E.

- Project managers and other stakeholders (including donors) need to know the extent to which their projects are meeting their objectives and leading to their desired effects.
- M&E build greater transparency and accountability in terms of use of project resources.
- Information generated through M&E provide project staff with a clearer basis for decision-making.
- Future project planning and development is improved when guided by lessons learned from project experience.

Project Monitoring

Monitoring represents an on-going activity to track project progress against planned tasks. It aims at providing regular oversight of the implementation of an activity in terms of input delivery, work schedules, targeted outputs, etc. Through such routine data gathering, analysis and reporting, programme/ project monitoring aims at:

1) Providing project management, staff and other stakeholders with information on whether progress is being made towards achieving project objectives. In this regard, monitoring represents a continuous assessment of project implementation in relation to project plans, resources, infrastructure, and use of services by project beneficiaries.
2) Providing regular feedback to enhance the ongoing learning experience and to improve the planning process and effectiveness of interventions.
3) Increasing project accountability with donors and other stakeholders.
4) Enabling managers and staff to identify and reinforce initial positive project results, strengths and successes.

As well, monitoring alerts managers to actual and potential project weaknesses, problems and shortcomings before it is too late. This would provide managers with the opportunity to make timely adjustments and corrective actions to improve the programme/project design, work plan and implementation strategies.

5) Checking on conditions or situations of a target group, and changes brought about by project activities. In this regard, monitoring assists project management to check whether the project continues to be relevant to the target group and/or geographical area, and whether project assumptions are still valid.

Monitoring actions must be undertaken throughout the lifetime of the project. Ad hoc evaluation research might be needed when unexpected problems arise for which planned monitoring activities cannot generate sufficient information, or when socio economic or environmental conditions change drastically in the target area.

Effective monitoring needs adequate planning, baseline data, indicators of performance, and results and practical implementation mechanisms that include actions such as field visits, stakeholder meetings, documentation of project activities, regular reporting, etc. Project monitoring is normally carried out by project management, staff and other stakeholders.

Project Evaluation

Programme/project evaluation represents a systematic and objective assessment of ongoing or completed projects or programmes in terms of their design, implementation and results. In addition, evaluations usually deal with strategic issues such as programme/project relevance, effectiveness, efficiency (expected and unexpected), in the light of specified objectives, as well as programme/project impact and sustainability. Those terms are described in detail in the following sections and in the glossary.

Periodic evaluations of ongoing projects are conducted to review implementation progress, predict project's likely effects and highlight necessary adjustments in project design. Terminal evaluations (or final evaluations) are evaluations carried out at the end of a project to provide an overall assessment of project performance and effects/impact, as well as to assess the extent to which the project has succeeded in meeting their objectives and their potential sustainability.

There are many reasons for conducting an evaluation, including:

1) *Providing managers with information regarding project performance. Project* plans might change during the implementation process. Evaluations can verify if the programme is really running as originally planned. *In addition, they provide* signs of project strengths and weaknesses, and therefore, enable managers *to improve future planning, delivery of services and decision-making.*
2) Assisting project managers, staff and other stakeholders to determine in a systematic and objective manner the relevance, effectiveness, and efficiency of activities (expected and unexpected) in light of specified objectives.
3) Mid-term evaluations may serve as a means of validating the results of initial assessments obtained from project monitoring activities.
4) If conducted after the termination of a programme/ project, an evaluation determines the extent to which the interventions are successful in terms of their impact and sustainability of results.
5) Assisting managers to carry out a thorough review and re-thinking about their projects in terms of their goals and objectives, and means to achieve them.
6) Generating detailed information about project implementation process and results. Such information can be used for public relations, fundraising, promotion of services in the community, as well as identifying possibilities for project replication.
7) Improving the learning process. *Evaluations often document and explain the causes as to why activities*

succeeded or failed. Such documentation can help in making future activities more relevant and effective.

As in monitoring, evaluation activities must be planned at the programme/ project level. Baseline data and appropriate indicators of performance and results must be established.

Evaluation goals and objectives should be determined by project management and staff. Many organizations do not have the resources to carry out the ideal evaluation. Therefore, it is preferred that they recruit an external evaluation consultant to lead the evaluation process. This would increase the objectivity of the evaluation. Project strengths and weaknesses might not be interpreted fairly when data and results are analyzed by project staff members that are responsible for ensuring that the programme is successful.

In case the organization does not have the technical expertise to carry out the evaluation and can not afford outside help, or prefers to carry out the evaluation using its own resources, it is recommended to engage an experienced evaluation expert to advise on developing the evaluation plan, selecting evaluation methods, and analyzing and reporting results.

Relationship between Monitoring and Evaluation

Monitoring and evaluation are two different management tools that are closely related, interactive and mutually supportive. Through routine tracking of project progress, monitoring can provide quantitative and qualitative data useful for designing and implementing project evaluation exercises. On the other hand, evaluations support project monitoring. Through the results of periodic evaluations, monitoring tools and strategies can be refined and further developed.

Some might argue that good monitoring substitutes project evaluations. This might be true in small-scale or short-term projects, or when the main objective on M&E is to obtain information to improve the process on implementation of an ongoing project. However, when a final judgment regarding project results, impact, sustainability, and future development are needed, an evaluation must be conducted.

Development of Personal Action Plan

A Surefire Roadmap to Success

Everyone has the ability to become abundantly successful. Some of the most successful people in the world attribute their success to writing personal action plans in one form or another. Personal action plans are potential roadmaps to achieving success. As with all roadmaps, sometimes there are detours, U-turns or unexpected road construction, but ultimately, they lead to the charted destination.

Creating a personal action plan is not difficult. It takes a little time, thought and planning. Here's one of the many ways to go about creating a personal action plan:

1. *Define the Goal:* With any roadmap there is a beginning point and an endpoint. The endpoint in a personal action plan is the goal. The goal can be anything from losing weight for an important event or saving money to go on vacation. The destination is something that is important and personal to the goal setter.
2. *Chart the Route:* It is important to plan a direct route from beginning to end. Expect a few detours along the way, but do not intentionally build detours into the personal action plan. For example, if the goal is to lose weight, do not build in a detour if it is taking longer than expected. Building a Twinkie pit stop on the roadmap is an intentional detour..
3. Define every step it will take to attain the goal and keep track of it. If the goal is to lose weight by Aunt Mary's wedding, the obvious steps to reaching the personal action plan goal will be to exercise, modify food intake, and drink more water. Personal action plans need more than the obvious steps to be successful. They need steps that can be quantified. Exercising for 45 minutes 4 times a week is better than the obvious goal to simply exercise. Drinking eight 8-oz glasses of water daily is more detailed than the goal of drinking more water.Track your progress with a personal goal log.

4. Modify the personal action plan as necessary. The great thing about action plans is that they can be modified. An unexpected detour and/or road construction is cause to modify the personal action plan. For example, an athlete's goal of running 5 miles in the park daily hits a detour upon hearing the forecast of a severe snowstorm. Instead of running in the park, the athlete will have to use a less desirable means of exercise, the stationary bike. The athlete is still headed in the right direction, but has had to take a temporary side road to reach the goal.
5. *Review the Action Plan:* The best personal action plan in the world is useless if it's not reviewed. Review the personal action plan as often as necessary in order to reach the desired goal.

Remember, a personal action plan is a map to attain a personal goal. It is a life enhancement tool. As with life, detours happen. When the detours and road construction occur, be flexible, embrace them and move on.

Development Action Plans for Employee Development Through Behavior Changes and Skill Improvement

Development Action Plans can be one of the most important tools in employee development. Successful realization of behavior changes or skill improvement requires not only solid coaching and communication, but a clear plan to make the necessary behavior changes or skill improvement come to fruition.

The plan should be used in the 'W' phase of the IGROW Model as well as a tool implemented after coaching has occurred to plan the next steps that will be taken. Keep in mind Development Action Plans are only meant for use in coaching scenarios. If you are working with a counseling scenario, a Development Action Plan will not be your best resource as the employee is not working to make a behavior change or skill improvement but is making a choice not to perform. You can learn more about the difference between Coaching and Counseling in an additional article.

While often times, managers and coaches look at planning for development as associated only with opportunities, the Development Action Plan is best utilized as a more proactive tool. Since employee development should be occurring continuously, instituting a Development Action Plan to improve upon strengths will only increase its value when a need arises to use it for opportunities as well. Take a minute to consider how having even your top performers spend time focusing on skill improvement could have a positive impact on their individual performance and the overall team's performance.

A Development Action Plan can be formal or informal, but it is always recommended to be in a documented format. This ensures that while focusing on employee development, both the coach and the employee have a reference tool and a guide to improvement. We will focus on the more formal approach and will leave it up to you to tailor this tool to your needs.

An important factor to keep in mind is to ensure that the employee, rather than the manager or coach is the one to develop the plan. Having the employee take ownership in crafting and documenting their Development Action Plan will ensure that they are engaged and are willing to put in the effort to make a skill improvement or behavior change. This does not mean that the manager or coach should not collaborate with the employee as they are crafting their Development Action Plan, as the coach's feedback will be crucial in the 'O' phase of the IGROW Model that provides an input to the plan.

To provide an example to work from we will use the scenario of Brian, a people manager in a manufacturing company. Brian has been struggling with his communication skills as evidenced by feedback from his direct reports and peers. During an *employee development coaching session*, Brian and his manager discuss using a Development Action Plan to focus on the needed behavior change.

Now, let's get started!

Each Development Action Plan should begin with an objective statement. This statement should fully encompass the result that is expected upon completion of the plan, referencing the desired skill improvement or the behavior change that is expected. A good example of an objective statement for Brian might be "Improve communication skills through applying direct communication, active listening, and responsive body language." This objective statement is not only clear in the overall goal of improving his communication, but it also outlines some of the *behaviors* that contribute to his opportunity as identified in the 'R' phase of the IGROW Model.

Next Brian and his manager identify the behaviors or skills Brian will be working to change. You want to outline these in a clear and visual way so that it becomes apparent what the *end result* will be. A best practice to identify these behaviors or skills, is to ask the employee to picture someone that exemplifies the skills they wish to master. Ask the employee how that person demonstrates the skill. What does it look like? The better they can describe the behavior or skill the better directed their action steps will be. In Brian's case, the behaviors and skills are documented as "1. Communicate in a manner that gets to the point and provides clear behavioral examples 2. Demonstrate active listening by asking clarifying questions and restating key points to ensure understanding 3. Focus on leaning in to show interest, keeping body language open (no crossed arms), and facially displaying interest." In this example, the behavior changes Brian is focused on are clear and specific allowing him to better plan his next step, the actions he will take to improve.

Now that we have determined the focus of our Development Action Plan, we must outline the actions we will take to achieve our objectives. The action portion of our plan encapsulates the steps that the employee will take while developing their new skill or behavior. This section should be broken into 3 distinct areas: Learn, Practice, Feedback.

In the *Learn* section, the employee should outline the steps and resources they will use to learn the new behavior. Since the Development Action Plan is being used to improve upon a strength or to develop an opportunity, it is key that the employee use resources and tools outside themselves. In Brian's case, he chooses to use a number of tools to learn to improve his communication skills. Earlier when he was asked to picture another person that embodied the communication skills he wished to attain, he was given the idea of spending some time peering with this person to observe their behaviors in various types of interactions. Another resource Brian chose to use was a book that many of his colleagues had recommended but he had yet found the time to read. While Brian chose only two resources, in many cases, employee development will require a number of tools in the learning phase of the plan. Since the Development Action Plan is a road map to employee development, like any good plan a timeline to accomplish each step should be documented. This will give Brian a deadline to focus on and his coach will know when to follow up on his progress.

In the next step of the action phase, Brian will have the ability to *practice* the new behaviors and skills he has learned. This is a time to focus on applying the skills and behaviors without the pressure of being perfect but in a way that allows for continuous learning. Brian chooses to conduct some role play sessions with both his mentor and his manager, allowing him to practice his new skills prior to applying them with his team. He also chooses to act as a note keeper for his manager's team meeting. This activity allowed him the opportunity to ask clarifying questions and to ensure that he was on the same page with the rest of his peers in the meeting regarding what was discussed or communicated.

The last step in the action phase is one of the most important: *feedback*. Now that Brian has had the opportunity to learn and practice the new skills and behaviors, he needs to receive feedback on how he is progressing in making a behavior change and overall skill improvement. Without this constant feedback loop, Brian would not know if he was truly improving or what areas he still needs to focus on. Documenting some avenues for feedback up front will establish how the employee wishes to receive feedback and will also ensure that they are seeking it out. Brian plans to solicit feedback from his mentor and manager during their role playing sessions. This will allow him to make immediate behavior changes and to repeat the practice step. Keep in mind that immediate feedback is crucial to consistent behavior changes.

Now that we have discussed how to set up the action portion of our *Development Action Plan*, we need to discuss how we will measure success. This step is imperative to establish up front so that both the coach and the employee have a clear target they are working toward. In production environments this is often an easy step to document, but when the strength or opportunity being addressed is more focused on a *soft skill*, coaches and employees can often struggle with determining how to measure the improvement. For Brian, he does not have a hard metric to apply as a success measure such as dollars collected, percent to goal, quality scores, etc. Brian instead must focus on more creative ways to measure his behavior changes and skill improvement. Some examples of how Brian could implement a measurement would be by conducting a pre and post team survey on his communication skills, improved competency or review ratings from his manager, or increased productivity from his team based on his more direct approach in delivering feedback.

Once the success measures have been identified you have a Development Action Plan lan that fully outlines the challenge or opportunity, the path the employee will take to accomplish their goal, and the way in which success will be measured. This should provide a clear *road map* for increased performance and employee development.

UNIT-X

Use of Technologies

Geographic Information System (GIS)

A geographic information system (GIS), or geographical information system, captures, stores, analyzes, manages, and presents data that is linked to location.

In the strictest sense, the term describes any information system that integrates, stores, edits, analyzes, shares, and displays geographic information. In a more generic sense, GIS applications are tools that allow users to create interactive queries (user created searches), analyze spatial information, edit data, maps, and present the results of all these operations. Geographic Information Science is the science underlying the geographic concepts, applications and systems, taught in degree and GIS Certificate programmes at many universities.

Applications

GIS technology can be used for scientific investigations, resource management, asset management, archaeology, environmental impact assessment, urban planning, cartography, criminology, geographic history, marketing, logistics, Prospectivity Mapping, and other purposes.

For example, GIS might allow emergency planners to easily calculate emergency response times in the event of a natural disaster, GIS might be used to find wetlands that need protection from pollution, or GIS can be used by a company to site a new business location to take advantage of a previously under-served market.

History of Development

About 15,500 years ago, on the walls of caves near Lascaux, France, Cro-Magnon hunters drew pictures of the animals they hunted. Associated with the animal drawings are track lines and tallies thought to depict migration routes. While simplistic in comparison to modern technologies, these early records mimic the two-element structure of modern GIS, an image associated with attribute information.

In 1854, John Snow depicted a cholera outbreak in London using points to represent the locations of some individual cases, possibly the earliest use of the geographic method. His study of the distribution of cholera led to the source of the disease, a contaminated water pump (the Broad Street Pump, whose handle he disconnected terminating the outbreak) within the heart of the cholera outbreak.

While the basic elements of topography and theme existed previously in cartography, the John Snow map was unique, using cartographic methods not only to depict but also to analyze clusters of geographically dependent phenomena for the first time. The early 20th century saw the development of "photo lithography" where maps were separated into layers. Computer hardware development spurred by nuclear weapon research would lead to general purpose computer "mapping" applications by the early 1960s.

The year 1962 saw the development of the world's first true operational GIS in Ottawa, Ontario, Canada by the federal Department of Forestry and Rural Development. Developed by Dr. Roger Tomlinson, it was called the "Canada Geographic Information System" (CGIS) and was used to store, analyze, and manipulate data collected for the Canada Land Inventory (CLI)—an initiative to determine the land capability for rural Canada by mapping information about soils, agriculture, recreation, wildlife, waterfowl, forestry, and land use at a scale of 1:50,000. A rating classification factor was also added to permit analysis.

CGIS was the world's first "system" and was an improvement over "mapping" applications as it provided capabilities for overlay, measurement, and digitizing/scanning. It supported a national coordinate system that spanned the continent, coded lines as "arcs" having a true embedded topology, and it stored the attribute and locational information in separate files. As a result of this, Tomlinson has become known as the "father of GIS," particularly for his use of overlays in promoting the spatial analysis of convergent geographic data. CGIS lasted into the 1990s and built the largest digital land resource database in Canada. It was developed as a mainframe based system in support of federal and provincial resource planning and management. Its strength was continent-wide analysis of complex datasets. The CGIS was never available in a commercial form.

In 1964, Howard T Fisher formed the Laboratory for Computer Graphics and Spatial Analysis at the Harvard Graduate School of Design (LCGSA 1965-1991), where a number of important theoretical concepts in spatial data handling were developed, and which by the 1970s had distributed seminal software code and systems, such as 'SYMAP', 'GRID', and 'ODYSSEY' — which served as literal and inspirational sources for subsequent commercial development — to universities, research centers, and corporations worldwide.

By the early 1980s, M&S Computing (later Intergraph), Environmental Systems Research Institute (ESRI) and CARIS (Computer Aided Resource Information System) emerged as commercial vendors of GIS software, successfully incorporating many of the CGIS features, combining the first generation approach to separation of spatial and attribute information with a second generation approach to organizing attribute data into database structures. In parallel, the development of two public domain systems began in the late 1970s and early 1980s. MOSS, the Map Overlay and Statistical System project started in 1977 in Fort Collins, Colorado under the auspices of the Western Energy and Land Use Team (WELUT) and the US Fish and Wildlife Service. GRASS GIS was begun in 1982 by the U.S. Army Corps of Engineering Research Laboratory (USA-CERL) in Champaign, Illinois, a branch of the U.S. Army Corps of Engineers to meet the need of the United States military for software for land management and environmental planning. The later 1980s and 1990s industry growth were spurred on by the growing use of GIS on Unix workstations and the personal computer.

By the end of the 20th century, the rapid growth in various systems had been consolidated and standardized on relatively few platforms and users were beginning to export the concept of viewing GIS data over the Internet, requiring data format and transfer standards. More recently, there are a growing number of free, open source GIS packages which run on a range of operating systems and can be customized to perform specific tasks.

GIS Software

Geographic information can be accessed, transferred, transformed, overlaid, processed and displayed using numerous software applications. Within industry, commercial offerings from companies such as Autodesk, Bentley Systems, ESRI, Intergraph, Manifold System, Mapinfo and Smallworld dominate, offering an entire suite of tools. Government and military departments often use custom software, open source products such as GRASS or uDig, or more specialized products that meet a well defined need. Although free tools exist to view GIS datasets, public access to geographic information is dominated by online resources such as Google Earth and interactive web mapping.

Background

Originally up to the late 1990s, when GIS data was mostly based on large computers and used to maintain internal records, software was a stand-alone product. However with increased access to the internet and networks and demand for distributed geographic data grew, GIS software gradually changed its entire outlook to the delivery of data over a network. GIS software is now usually marketed as combination of various interoperable applications and APIs. And functionalities on an existing system to suit the requirements of a customer. It helps to automate many complex processes without worrying about underlying algorithms and processing steps in conventional GIS software.

Modern GIS technologies use digital information, for which various digitized data creation methods are used. The most common method of data creation is digitization, where a hard copy map or survey plan is transferred into a digital medium through the use of a computer-aided design (CAD) programme, and geo-referencing capabilities. With the wide availability of ortho-rectified imagery (both from satellite and aerial sources), heads-up digitizing is becoming the main avenue through which geographic data is extracted. Heads-up digitizing involves the tracing of geographic data directly on top of the aerial imagery instead of by the traditional method of tracing the geographic form on a separate digitizing tablet (heads-down digitizing).

Relating Information from Different Sources

You might be able to tell which wetlands dry up at certain times of the year. Using information from many different sources in many different forms, GIS can help with such analysis. The primary requirement for the source data consists of knowing the locations for the variables. Location may be annotated by x, y, and z coordinates of longitude, latitude, and elevation, or by other geocode systems like ZIP Codes or by highway mile markers. Any variable that can be located spatially can be fed into a GIS. Several computer databases that can be directly entered into a GIS are being produced by government agencies and non-government organizations. Different kinds of data in map form can be entered into a GIS.

A GIS can also convert existing digital information, which may not yet be in map form, into forms it can recognize and use. For example, digital satellite images generated through remote sensing can be analyzed to produce a map-like layer of digital information about vegetative covers. Another fairly recently developed resource for naming GIS objects is the Getty Thesaurus of Geographic Names (GTGN), which is a structured vocabulary containing around 1,000,000 names and other information about places.

Likewise, census or hydrological tabular data can be converted to map-like form, serving as layers of thematic information in a GIS.

Data Representation

GIS data represents real world objects (roads, land use, elevation) with digital data. Real world objects can be divided into two abstractions: discrete objects (a house) and continuous fields (rain fall amount or elevation). There are two broad methods used to store data in a GIS for both abstractions: Raster and Vector.

Raster

A raster data type is, in essence, any type of digital image represented in grids. Anyone who is familiar with digital photography will recognize the pixel as the smallest individual unit of an image. A combination of these pixels will create an image, distinct from the commonly used scalable vector graphics which are the basis of the vector model. While a digital image is concerned with the output as representation of reality, in a photograph or art transferred to computer, the raster data type will reflect an abstraction of reality. Aerial photos are one commonly used form of raster data, with only one purpose, to display a detailed image on a map or for the purposes of digitization. Other raster data sets will contain information regarding elevation, a DEM, or reflectance of a particular wavelength of light, LANDSAT.

Raster data type consists of rows and columns of cells, with each cell storing a single value. Raster data can be images (raster images) with each pixel (or cell) containing a colour value. Additional values recorded for each cell may be a discrete value, such as land use, a continuous value, such as temperature, or a null value if no data is available. While a raster cell stores a single value, it can be extended by using raster bands to represent RGB (red, green, blue) colours, colormaps (a mapping between a thematic code and RGB value), or an extended attribute table with one row for each unique cell value. The resolution of the raster data set is its cell width in ground units.

Raster data is stored in various formats; from a standard file-based structure of TIF, JPEG, etc. to binary large object (BLOB) data stored directly in a relational database management system (RDBMS) similar to other vector-based feature classes. Database storage, when properly indexed, typically allows for quicker retrieval of the raster data but can require storage of millions of significantly-sized records.

Vector

In a GIS, geographical features are often expressed as vectors, by considering those features as geometrical shapes. Different geographical features are expressed by different types of geometry:

- *Points:* Zero-dimensional points are used for geographical features that can best be expressed by a single point reference; in other words, simple location. For example, the locations of wells, peak elevations, features of interest or trailheads. Points convey the least amount of information of these file types. Points can also be used to represent areas when displayed at a small scale. For example, cities on a map of the world would be represented by points rather than polygons. No measurements are possible with point features.
- *Lines or Polylines:* One-dimensional lines or polylines are used for linear features such as rivers, roads, railroads, trails, and topographic lines. Again, as with point features, linear features displayed at a small scale will be represented as linear features rather than as a polygon. Line features can measure distance.
- *Polygons:* Two-dimensional polygons are used for geographical features that cover a particular area of the earth's surface. Such features may include lakes, park boundaries, buildings, city boundaries, or land uses. Polygons convey the most amount of information of the file types. Polygon features can measure perimeter and area.

Each of these geometries is linked to a row in a database that describes their attributes. For example, a database that describes lakes may contain a lake's depth, water quality, pollution level. This information can be used to make a map to describe a particular attribute of the dataset. For example, lakes could be coloured depending on level of pollution. Different geometries can also be compared. For example, the GIS could be used to identify all wells (point geometry) that are within 1-mile (1.6 km) of a lake (polygon geometry) that has a high level of pollution.

Vector features can be made to respect spatial integrity through the application of topology rules such as 'polygons must not overlap'. Vector data can also be used to represent continuously varying phenomena. Contour lines and triangulated irregular networks (TIN) are used to represent elevation or other continuously changing values. TINs record values at point locations, which are connected by lines to form an irregular mesh of triangles. The face of the triangles represent the terrain surface.

Advantages and Disadvantages

There are advantages and disadvantages to using a raster or vector data model to represent reality. Raster datasets record a value for all points in the area covered which may require more storage space than representing data in a vector format that can store data only where needed. Raster data also allows easy implementation of overlay operations, which are more difficult with vector data. Vector data can be displayed as vector graphics used on traditional maps, whereas raster data will appear as an image that, depending on the resolution of the raster file, may have a blocky appearance for object boundaries. Vector data can be easier to register, scale, and re-project. This can simplify combining vector layers from different sources. Vector data is more compatible with relational database environments. They can be part of a relational table as a normal column and processed using a multitude of operators.

The file size for vector data is usually much smaller for storage and sharing than raster data. Image or raster data can be 10 to 100 times larger than vector data depending on the resolution. Another advantage of vector data is that it is easy to update and maintain. For example, a new highway is added. The raster image will have to be completely reproduced, but the vector data, "roads," can be easily updated by adding the missing road segment. In addition, vector data allows much more analysis capability, especially for "networks" such as roads, power, rail, telecommunications, etc. For example, with vector data attributed with the characteristics of roads, ports, and airfields, allows the analyst to query for the best route or method of transportation. In the vector data, the analyst can query the data for the largest port with an airfield within 60 miles and a connecting road that is at least two lane highway. Raster data will not have all the characteristics of the features it displays.

Non-spatial Data

Additional non-spatial data can also be stored along with the spatial data represented by the coordinates of a vector geometry or the position of a raster cell. In vector data, the additional data contains attributes of the feature. For example, a forest inventory polygon may also have an identifier value and information about tree species. In raster data the cell value can store attribute information, but it can also be used as an identifier that can relate to records in another table.

There is also software being developed to support spatial and non-spatial decision-making. In this software, the solutions to spatial problems are integrated with solutions to non-spatial problems. The end result it is hoped with these Flexible Spatial Decision-Making Support Systems (FSDSS) will be that non experts can use GIS and spatial criteria with their other non spatial criteria to view solutions to multi-criteria problems that will support decision making.

Data Capture

Data capture—entering information into the system—consumes much of the time of GIS practitioners. There are a variety of methods used to enter data into a GIS where it is stored in a digital format.

Existing data printed on paper or PET film maps can be digitized or scanned to produce digital data. A digitizer produces vector data as an operator traces points, lines, and polygon boundaries from a map. Scanning a map results in raster data that could be further processed to produce vector data.

Survey data can be directly entered into a GIS from digital data collection systems on survey instruments using a technique called Coordinate Geometry (COGO). Positions from a Global Navigation Satellite System (GNSS) like Global Positioning System (GPS), another survey tool, can also be directly entered into a GIS.

Remotely sensed data also plays an important role in data collection and consist of sensors attached to a platform. Sensors include cameras, digital scanners and LIDAR, while platforms usually consist of aircraft and satellites.

The majority of digital data currently comes from photo interpretation of aerial photographs. Soft copy workstations are used to digitize features directly from stereo pairs of digital photographs. These systems allow data to be captured in two and three dimensions, with elevations measured directly from a stereo pair using principles of photogrammetry. Currently, analog aerial photos are scanned before being entered into a soft copy system, but as high quality digital cameras become cheaper this step will be skipped.

Satellite remote sensing provides another important source of spatial data. Here satellites use different sensor packages to passively measure the reflectance from parts of the electromagnetic spectrum or radio waves that were sent out from an active sensor such as radar. Remote sensing collects raster data that can be further processed using different bands to identify objects and classes of interest, such as land cover.

When data is captured, the user should consider if the data should be captured with either a relative accuracy or absolute accuracy, since this could not only influence how information will be interpreted but also the cost of data capture.

In addition to collecting and entering spatial data, attribute data is also entered into a GIS. For vector data, this includes additional information about the objects represented in the system.

After entering data into a GIS, the data usually requires editing, to remove errors, or further processing. For vector data it must be made "topologically correct" before it can be used for some advanced analysis. For example, in a road network, lines must connect with nodes at an intersection. Errors such as undershoots and overshoots must also be removed. For scanned maps, blemishes on the source map may need to be removed from the resulting raster. For example, a fleck of dirt might connect two lines that should not be connected.

Raster-to-vector Translation

Data restructuring can be performed by a GIS to convert data into different formats. For example, a GIS may be used to convert a satellite image map to a vector structure by generating lines around all cells with the same classification, while determining the cell spatial relationships, such as adjacency or inclusion.

More advanced data processing can occur with image processing, a technique developed in the late 1960s by NASA and the private sector to provide contrast enhancement, false colour rendering and a variety of other techniques including use of two dimensional Fourier transforms.

Since digital data is collected and stored in various ways, the two data sources may not be entirely compatible. So a GIS must be able to convert geographic data from one structure to another.

Projections, Coordinate Systems and Registration

A property ownership map and a soils map might show data at different scales. Map information in a GIS must be manipulated so that it registers, or fits, with information gathered from other maps. Before the digital data can be analyzed, they may have to undergo other manipulations—projection and coordinate conversions, for example—that integrate them into a GIS.

The earth can be represented by various models, each of which may provide a different set of coordinates (e.g., latitude, longitude, elevation) for any given point on the earth's surface. The simplest model is to assume the earth is a perfect sphere. As more measurements of the earth have accumulated, the models of the earth have become more sophisticated and more accurate. In fact, there are models that apply to different areas of the earth to provide increased accuracy (e.g., North American Datum, 1927-NAD27-works well in North America, but not in Europe). See datum (geodesy) for more information.

Projection is a fundamental component of map making. A projection is a mathematical means of transferring information from a model of the Earth, which represents a three-dimensional curved surface, to a two-dimensional medium—paper or a computer screen.

Different projections are used for different types of maps because each projection particularly suits certain uses. For example, a projection that accurately represents the shapes of the continents will distort their relative sizes.

Since much of the information in a GIS comes from existing maps, a GIS uses the processing power of the computer to transform digital information, gathered from sources with different projections and/or different coordinate systems, to a common projection and coordinate system. For images, this process is called rectification.

Today, even laypeople are aware of GPS used for locating in terms of latitude, longitude and height. Many people are aware of Google Earth and even GIS. In this scenario, however, majority of us misunderstands latitude and longitude. Authalic coordinates are what generally conceived as latitude and longitude, in which the Earth is assumed as spherical in shape. In day-to-day life, the coordinates we see on maps such as those from GPS are geodetic latitude and longitude. It is also imperative to know the datum of the map in use; and if the datum is changed, any selected location can have different geodetic coordinates.

Spatial Analysis with GIS

Given the vast range of spatial analysis techniques that have been developed over the past half century, any summary or review can only cover the subject to a limited depth. This is a rapidly changing field, and GIS packages are increasingly including analytical tools as standard built-in facilities or as optional toolsets, add-ins or 'analysts'. In many instances such facilities are provided by the original software suppliers (commercial vendors or collaborative non commercial development teams), whilst in other cases facilities have been developed and are provided by third parties. Furthermore, many products offer software development kits (SDKs), programming languages and language support, scripting facilities and/or special interfaces for developing one's own analytical tools or variants. The website Geospatial Analysis and associated book/ebook attempt to provide a reasonably comprehensive guide to the subject. The impact of these myriad paths to perform spatial analysis create a new dimension to business intelligence termed "spatial intelligence" which, when delivered via intranet, democratizes access to operational sorts not usually privy to this type of information.

Data Modeling

It is difficult to relate wetlands maps to rainfall amounts recorded at different points such as airports, television stations, and high schools. A GIS, however, can be used to depict two- and three-dimensional characteristics of the Earth's surface, subsurface, and atmosphere from information points. For example, a GIS can quickly generate a map with isopleth or contour lines that indicate differing amounts of rainfall.

Such a map can be thought of as a rainfall contour map. Many sophisticated methods can estimate the characteristics of surfaces from a limited number of point measurements. A two-dimensional contour map created from the surface modeling of rainfall point measurements may be overlaid and analyzed with any other map in a GIS covering the same area.

Additionally, from a series of three-dimensional points, or digital elevation model, isopleth lines representing elevation contours can be generated, along with slope analysis, shaded relief, and other elevation products. Watersheds can be easily defined for any given reach, by computing all of the areas contiguous and uphill from any given point of interest. Similarly, an expected thalweg of where surface water would want to travel in intermittent and permanent streams can be computed from elevation data in the GIS.

Topological Modeling

In recent years, has there been any gas stations or factories operating next to a swamp? Any within two miles (3 km) and uphill from a swamp? A GIS can recognize and analyze the spatial relationships that exist within digitally stored spatial data. These topological relationships allow complex spatial modelling and analysis to be performed. Topological relationships between geometric entities traditionally include adjacency (what adjoins what), containment (what encloses what), and proximity (how close something is to something else).

Networks

If all the factories near a wetland were accidentally to release chemicals into the river at the same time, how long would it take for a damaging amount of pollutant to enter the wetland reserve? A GIS can simulate the routing of materials along a linear network. Values such as slope, speed limit, or pipe diameter can be incorporated into network modeling in order to represent the flow of the phenomenon more accurately. Network modelling is commonly employed in transportation planning, hydrology modeling, and infrastructure modeling.

Cartographic Modeling

An example of use of layers in a GIS application. In this example, the forest cover layer (light green) is at the bottom, with the topographic layer over it. Next up is the stream layer, then the boundary layer, then the road layer. The order is very important in order to properly display the final result. Note that the pond layer was located just below the stream layer, so that a stream line can be seen overlying one of the ponds.

The term "cartographic modeling" was (probably) coined by Dana Tomlin in his PhD dissertation and later in his book which has the term in the title. Cartographic modeling refers to a process where several thematic layers of the same area are produced, processed, and analyzed. Tomlin used raster layers, but the overlay method (see below) can be used more generally. Operations on map layers can be combined into algorithms, and eventually into simulation or optimization models.

Map Overlay

The combination of several spatial datasets (points, lines or polygons) creates a new output vector dataset, visually similar to stacking several maps of the same region. These overlays are similar to mathematical Venn diagram overlays. A union overlay combines the geographic features and attribute tables of both inputs into a single new output. An intersect overlay defines the area where both inputs overlap and retains a set of attribute fields for each. A symmetric difference overlay defines an output area that includes the total area of both inputs except for the overlapping area.

Data extraction is a GIS process similar to vector overlay, though it can be used in either vector or raster data analysis. Rather than combining the properties and features of both datasets, data extraction involves using a "clip" or "mask" to extract the features of one data set that fall within the spatial extent of another dataset.

In raster data analysis, the overlay of datasets is accomplished through a process known as "local operation on multiple rasters" or "map algebra," through a function that combines the values of each raster's matrix. This function may weigh some inputs more than others through use of an "index model" that reflects the influence of various factors upon a geographic phenomenon.

Automated Cartography

Digital cartography and GIS both encode spatial relationships in structured formal representations. GIS is used in digital cartography modeling as a (semi)automated process of making maps, so called Automated Cartography. In practice, it can be a subset of a GIS, within which it is equivalent to the stage of visualization, since in most cases not all of the GIS functionality is used. Cartographic products can be either in a digital or in a hardcopy format. Powerful analysis techniques with different data representation can produce high-quality maps within a short time period. The main problem in Automated Cartography is to use a single set of data to produce multiple products at a variety of scales, a technique known as Generalization.

Geostatistics

Geostatistics is a point-pattern analysis that produces field predictions from data points. It is a way of looking at the statistical properties of those special data. It is different from general applications of statistics because it employs the use of graph theory and matrix algebra to reduce the number of parameters in the data. Only the second-order properties of the GIS data are analyzed. When phenomena are measured, the observation methods dictate the accuracy of any subsequent analysis. Due to the nature of the data (e.g. traffic patterns in an urban environment; weather patterns over the Pacific Ocean), a constant or dynamic degree of precision is always lost in the measurement. This loss of precision is determined from the scale and distribution of the data collection.

To determine the statistical relevance of the analysis, an average is determined so that points (gradients) outside of any immediate measurement can be included to determine their predicted behavior. This is due to the limitations of the applied statistic and data collection methods, and interpolation is required in order to predict the behavior of particles, points, and locations that are not directly measurable.

Interpolation is the process by which a surface is created, usually a raster dataset, through the input of data collected at a number of sample points. There are several forms of interpolation, each which treats the data differently, depending on the properties of the data set. In comparing interpolation methods, the first consideration should be whether or not the source data will change (exact or approximate). Next is whether the method is subjective, a human interpretation, or objective. Then there is the nature of transitions between points: are they abrupt or gradual. Finally, there is whether a method is global (it uses the entire data set to form the model), or local where an algorithm is repeated for a small section of terrain. Interpolation is a justified measurement because of a Spatial

Autocorrelation Principle that recognizes that data collected at any position will have a great similarity to, or influence of those locations within its immediate vicinity.

Digital elevation models (DEM), triangulated irregular networks (TIN), Edge finding algorithms, Theissen Polygons, Fourier analysis, Weighted moving averages, Inverse Distance Weighted, Moving averages, Kriging, Spline, and Trend surface analysis are all mathematical methods to produce interpolative data.

Address Geocoding

Geocoding is interpolating spatial locations (X,Y coordinates) from street addresses or any other spatially referenced data such as ZIP Codes, parcel lots and address locations. A reference theme is required to geocode individual addresses, such as a road centerline file with address ranges. The individual address locations are interpolated, or estimated, by examining address ranges along a road segment. These are usually provided in the form of a table or database. The GIS will then place a dot approximately where that address belongs along the segment of centerline. For example, an address point of 500 will be at the midpoint of a line segment that starts with address 1 and ends with address 1000. Geocoding can also be applied against actual parcel data, typically from municipal tax maps. In this case, the result of the geocoding will be an actually positioned space as opposed to an interpolated point.

It should be noted that there are several (potentially dangerous) caveats that are often overlooked when using interpolation. See the full entry for Geocoding for more information.

Various algorithms are used to help with address matching when the spellings of addresses differ. Address information that a particular entity or organization has data on, such as the post office, may not entirely match the reference theme. There could be variations in street name spelling, community name, etc. Consequently, the user generally has the ability to make matching criteria more stringent, or to relax those parameters so that more addresses will be mapped. Care must be taken to review the results so as not to map addresses incorrectly due to overzealous matching parameters.

Reverse Geocoding

Reverse geocoding is the process of returning an estimated street address number as it relates to a given coordinate. For example, a user can click on a road centerline theme (thus providing a coordinate) and have information returned that reflects the estimated house number. This house number is interpolated from a range assigned to that road segment. If the user clicks at the midpoint of a segment that starts with address 1 and ends with 100, the returned value will be somewhere near 50. Note that reverse geocoding does not return actual addresses, only estimates of what should be there based on the predetermined range.

Data Output and Cartography

Cartography is the design and production of maps, or visual representations of spatial data. The vast majority of modern cartography is done with the help of computers, usually using a GIS but production quality cartography is also achieved by importing layers into a design programme to refine it. Most GIS software gives the user substantial control over the appearance of the data.

Cartographic work serves two major functions:

First, it produces graphics on the screen or on paper that convey the results of analysis to the people who make decisions about resources. Wall maps and other graphics can be generated, allowing the viewer to visualize and thereby understand the results of analyses or simulations of potential events. Web Map Servers facilitate distribution of generated maps through web browsers using various implementations of web-based application programming interfaces (AJAX, Java, Flash, etc).

Second, other database information can be generated for further analysis or use. An example would be a list of all addresses within one mile (1.6 km) of a toxic spill.

Graphic Display Techniques

Traditional maps are abstractions of the real world, a sampling of important elements portrayed on a sheet of paper with symbols to represent physical objects. People who use maps must interpret these symbols. Topographic maps show the shape of land surface with contour lines or with shaded relief.

Today, graphic display techniques such as shading based on altitude in a GIS can make relationships among map elements visible, heightening one's ability to extract and analyze information. For example, two types of data were combined in a GIS to produce a perspective view of a portion of San Mateo County, California.

- The digital elevation model, consisting of surface elevations recorded on a 30-meter horizontal grid, shows high elevations as white and low elevation as black.
- The accompanying Landsat Thematic Mapper image shows a false-colour infrared image looking down at the same area in 30-meter pixels, or picture elements, for the same coordinate points, pixel by pixel, as the elevation information.

A GIS was used to register and combine the two images to render the three-dimensional perspective view looking down the San Andreas Fault, using the Thematic Mapper image pixels, but shaded using the elevation of the landforms. The GIS display depends on the viewing point of the observer and time of day of the display, to properly render the shadows created by the sun's rays at that latitude, longitude, and time of day.

An archeochrome is a new way of displaying spatial data. It is a thematic on a 3D map that is applied to a specific building or a part of a building. It is suited to the visual display of heat loss data.

Spatial ETL

Spatial ETL tools provide the data processing functionality of traditional Extract, Transform, Load (ETL) software, but with a primary focus on the ability to manage spatial data. They provide GIS users with the ability to translate data between different standards and proprietary formats, whilst geometrically transforming the data en-route.

Future

Many disciplines can benefit from GIS technology. An active GIS market has resulted in lower costs and continual improvements in the hardware and software components of GIS. These developments will, in turn, result in a much wider use of the technology throughout science, government, business, and industry, with applications including real estate, public health, crime mapping, national defense, sustainable development, natural resources, landscape architecture, archaeology, regional and community planning, transportation and logistics. GIS is also diverging into location-based services (LBS). LBS allows GPS enabled mobile devices to display their location in relation to fixed assets (nearest restaurant, gas station, fire hydrant), mobile assets (friends, children, police car) or to relay their position back to a central server for display or other processing. These services continue to develop with the increased integration of GPS functionality with increasingly powerful mobile electronics (cell phones, PDAs, laptops).

Distributed GIS

Distributed GIS concerns itself with GIS that do not have all of the system components in the same physical location. This could be the processing, the database, the rendering or the user interface. Examples of distributed systems are web-based GIS, Mobile GIS, Corporate GIS and GRID management.

OGC Standards

The Open Geospatial Consortium (OGC) is an international industry consortium of 334 companies, government agencies and universities participating in a consensus process to develop publicly available geoprocessing specifications. Open interfaces and protocols defined by OpenGIS Specifications support interoperable solutions that "geo-enable" the Web, wireless and location-based services, and mainstream IT, and empower technology developers to make complex spatial information and services accessible and useful with all kinds of applications. Open Geospatial Consortium (OGC) protocols include Web Map Service (WMS) and Web Feature Service (WFS).

GIS products are broken down by the OGC into two categories, based on how completely and accurately the software follows the OGC specifications.

Compliant Products are software products that comply to OGC's OpenGIS Specifications. When a product has been tested and certified as compliant through the OGC Testing Programme, the product is automatically registered as "compliant" on this site.

Implementing Products are software products that implement OpenGIS Specifications but have not yet passed a compliance test. Compliance tests are not available for all specifications. Developers can register their products as implementing draft or approved specifications, though OGC reserves the right to review and verify each entry.

Web Mapping

In recent years there has been an explosion of mapping applications on the web such as Google Maps and Live Maps. These websites give the public access to huge amounts of geographic data. Some of them, like Google Maps and OpenLayers, expose an API that enable users to create custom applications. These toolkits commonly offer street maps, aerial/satellite imagery, geocoding, searches, and routing functionality.

Other applications for publishing geographic information on the web include MapInfo's MapXtreme or PlanAcess or Stratus Connect, Cadcorp's GeognoSIS, Intergraph's GeoMedia WebMap (TM), ESRI's ArcIMS, ArcGIS Server, Autodesk's Mapguide, SeaTrails' AtlasAlive, and the open source MapServer.

In recent years web mapping services have begun to adopt features more common in GIS. Services such as Google Maps and Live Maps allow users to annotate maps and share the maps with others.

Global Change, Climate History Programme and Prediction of its Impact

Maps have traditionally been used to explore the Earth and to exploit its resources. GIS technology, as an expansion of cartographic science, has enhanced the efficiency and analytic power of traditional mapping. Now, as the scientific community recognizes the environmental consequences of human activity, GIS technology is becoming an essential tool in the effort to understand the process of global change. Various map and satellite information sources can combine in modes that simulate the interactions of complex natural systems.

Through a function known as visualization, a GIS can be used to produce images-not just maps, but drawings, animations, and other cartographic products. These images allow researchers to view their subjects in ways that literally never have been seen before. The images are often invaluable for conveying the technical concepts of GIS study subjects to non-scientists.

Prediction of the impact of climate change inherently involves many uncertainties stemming from data and models. GIS incorporated with uncertainty theory has been used to model the coastal impact of climate change, including inundation due to sea-level rise and storm erosion.

Adding the Dimension of Time

The condition of the Earth's surface, atmosphere, and subsurface can be examined by feeding satellite data into a GIS. GIS technology gives researchers the ability to examine the variations in Earth processes over days, months, and years.

As an example, the changes in vegetation vigor through a growing season can be animated to determine when drought was most extensive in a particular region. The resulting graphic, known as a normalized vegetation index, represents a rough measure of plant health. Working with two variables over time would then allow researchers to detect regional differences in the lag between a decline in rainfall and its effect on vegetation.

GIS technology and the availability of digital data on regional and global scales enable such analyses. The satellite sensor output used to generate a vegetation graphic is produced for example by the Advanced Very High Resolution Radiometer (AVHRR). This sensor system detects the amounts of energy reflected from the Earth's surface across various bands of the spectrum for surface areas of about 1 square kilometer. The satellite sensor produces images of a particular location on the Earth twice a day. AVHRR and more recently the Moderate-Resolution Imaging Spectroradiometer (MODIS) are only two of many sensor systems used for Earth surface analysis. More sensors will follow, generating ever greater amounts of data.

GIS and related technology will help greatly in the management and analysis of these large volumes of data, allowing for better understanding of terrestrial processes and better management of human activities to maintain world economic vitality and environmental quality.

In addition to the integration of time in environmental studies, GIS is also being explored for its ability to track and model the progress of humans throughout their daily routines. A concrete example of progress in this area is the recent release of time-specific population data by the US Census. In this data set, the populations of cities are shown for daytime and evening hours highlighting the pattern of concentration and dispersion generated by North American commuting patterns. The manipulation and generation of data required to produce this data would not have been possible without GIS.

Using models to project the data held by a GIS forward in time have enabled planners to test policy decisions. These systems are known as Spatial Decision Support Systems.

Remote Sensing (RS)

Remote sensing is the small or large-scale acquisition of information of an object or phenomenon, by the use of either recording or real-time sensing device(s) that is not in physical or intimate contact with the object (such as by way of aircraft, spacecraft, satellite, buoy, or ship). In practice, remote sensing is the stand-off collection through the use of a variety of devices for gathering information on a given object or area. Thus,

Earth observation or weather satellite collection platforms, ocean and atmospheric observing weather buoy platforms, monitoring of a pregnancy via ultrasound, Magnetic Resonance Imaging (MRI), Positron Emission Tomography (PET), and space probes are all examples of remote sensing. In modern usage, the term generally refers to the use of imaging sensor technologies including but not limited to the use of instruments aboard aircraft and spacecraft, and is distinct from other imaging-related fields such as medical imaging.

There are two kinds of remote sensing. Passive sensors detect natural radiation that is emitted or reflected by the object or surrounding area being observed. Reflected sunlight is the most common source of radiation measured by passive sensors. Examples of passive remote sensors include film photography, infra-red, charge-coupled devices, and radiometers. Active collection, on the other hand, emits energy in order to scan objects and areas whereupon a passive sensor then detects and measures the radiation that is reflected or backscattered from the target. RADAR is an example of active remote sensing where the time delay between emission and return is measured, establishing the location, height, speed and direction of an object.

Remote sensing makes it possible to collect data on dangerous or inaccessible areas. Remote sensing applications include monitoring deforestation in areas such as the Amazon Basin, the effects of climate change on glaciers and Arctic and Antarctic regions, and depth sounding of coastal and ocean depths. Military collection during the cold war made use of stand-off collection of data about dangerous border areas. Remote sensing also replaces costly and slow data collection on the ground, ensuring in the process that areas or objects are not disturbed.

Orbital platforms collect and transmit data from different parts of the electromagnetic spectrum, which in conjunction with larger scale aerial or ground-based sensing and analysis, provides researchers with enough information to monitor trends such as El Niño and other natural long and short term phenomena. Other uses include different areas of the earth sciences such as natural resource management, agricultural fields such as land usage and conservation, and national security and overhead, ground-based and stand-off collection on border areas.

Data Acquisition Techniques

The basis for multi-spectral collection and analysis is that of examined areas or objects that reflect or emit radiation that stand out from surrounding areas.

Applications of Remote Sensing Data

- Radar Conventional radar is mostly associated with aerial traffic control, early warning, and certain large scale meteorological data. Doppler radar is used by local law enforcements' monitoring of speed limits and in enhanced meteorological collection such as wind speed and direction within weather systems. Other types of active collection includes plasmas in the ionosphere). Interferometric synthetic aperture radar is used to produce precise digital elevation models of large scale terrain (See RADARSAT, TerraSAR-X, Magellan).
- Laser and radar altimeters on satellites have provided a wide range of data. By measuring the bulges of water caused by gravity, they map features on the seafloor to a resolution of a mile or so. By measuring the height and wave-length of ocean waves, the altimeters measure wind speeds and direction, and surface ocean currents and directions.
- LIDAR Light Detection And Ranging-is well known in the examples of weapon ranging, laser illuminated homing of projectiles. LIDAR is used to detect and measure the concentration of various chemicals in the atmosphere, while airborne LIDAR can be used to measure heights of objects and features on the ground more accurately than with radar technology. Vegetation remote sensing is a principle application of LIDAR.
- Radiometers and photometers are the most common instrument in use, collecting reflected and emitted radiation in a wide range of frequencies. The most

common are visible and infrared sensors, followed by microwave, gamma ray and rarely, ultraviolet. They may also be used to detect the emission spectra of various chemicals, providing data on chemical concentrations in the atmosphere.

- Stereographic pairs of aerial photographs have often been used to make Topographic maps by Imagery Analysts, Terrain Analysts in trafficability and highway departments for potential routes.
- Simultaneous multi-spectral platforms such as Landsat have been in use since the 70's. These thematic mappers take images in multiple wavelengths of electro-magnetic radiation (multi-spectral) and are usually found on earth observation satellites, including (for example) the Landsat programme or the IKONOS satellite. Maps of land cover and land use from thematic mapping can be used to prospect for minerals, detect or monitor land usage, deforestation, and examine the health of indigenous plants and crops, including entire farming regions or forests.
- Within the scope of the combat against desertification, remote sensing allows to follow-up and monitor risk areas in the long term, to determine desertification factors, to support decision-makers in defining relevant measures of environmental management, and to assess their impacts.

Geodetic

- Overhead geodetic collection was first used in aerial submarine detection and gravitational data used in military maps. This data reveal minute perturbations in the Earth's gravitational field (geodesy) may be used to determine changes in the mass distribution of the Earth, which in turn may be used for geological or hydrological studies.

Acoustic and Near-acoustic

- Passive; Sonar is used for detecting, ranging and measurements of underwater objects and terrain.

- Seismograms taken at different locations can locate and measure earthquakes (after they occur) by comparing the relative intensity and precise timing.
- Active; pulses are used by geologists to detect oil fields.

To coordinate a series of large-scale observations, most sensing systems depend on the following; platform location, what time it is, and the rotation and orientation of the sensor. High-end instruments now often use positional information from satellite navigation systems. The rotation and orientation is often provided within a degree or two with electronic compasses. Compasses can measure not just azimuth (i.e. degrees to magnetic north), but also altitude (degrees above the horizon), since the magnetic field curves into the Earth at different angles at different latitudes. More exact orientations require gyroscopic-aided orientation, periodically realigned by different methods including navigation from stars or known benchmarks.

Resolution impacts collection and is best explained with the following relationship; less resolution=less detail & larger coverage, More resolution=more detail, less coverage. The skilled management of collection results in cost-effective collection and avoid situations such as the use of multiple high resolution data which tends to clog transmission and storage infrastructure.

Data Processing

Generally speaking, remote sensing works on the principle of the inverse problem. While the object or phenomenon of interest (the state) may not be directly measured, there exists some other variable that can be detected and measured (the observation), which may be related to the object of interest through the use of a data-derived computer model. The common analogy given to describe this is trying to determine the type of animal from its footprints. For example, while it is impossible to directly measure temperatures in the upper atmosphere, it is possible to measure the spectral emissions from a known chemical species (such as carbon dioxide) in that region. The frequency of the emission may then be related to the temperature in that region via various thermodynamic relations.

The quality of remote sensing data consists of its spatial, spectral, radiometric and temporal resolutions.

Spatial Resolution

The size of a pixel that is recorded in a raster image-typically pixels may correspond to square areas ranging in side length from 1 to 1,000 metres (3.3 to 3,280 ft).

Spectral Resolution

The number of different frequency bands recorded-usually, this is equivalent to the number of sensors carried by the platform(s). Current Landsat collection is that of seven bands, including several in the infra-red spectrum. The MODIS satellites are the highest resolving at 31 bands.

Radiometric Resolution

The number of different intensities of radiation the sensor is able to distinguish. Typically, this ranges from 8 to 14 bits, corresponding to 256 levels of the gray scale and up to 16,384 intensities or "shades" of colour, in each band.

Temporal Resolution

The frequency of flyovers by the satellite or plane, and is only relevant in time-series studies or those requiring an averaged or mosaic image as in deforesting monitoring. This was first used by the intelligence community where repeated coverage revealed changes in infrastructure, the deployment of units or the modification/introduction of equipment. Cloud cover over a given area or object makes it necessary to repeat the collection of said location.

In order to create sensor-based maps, most remote sensing systems expect to extrapolate sensor data in relation to a reference point including distances between known points on the ground. This depends on the type of sensor used. For example, in conventional photographs, distances are accurate in the center of the image, with the distortion of measurements increasing the farther you get from the center. Another factor is that of the platen against which the film is pressed can cause severe errors when photographs are used to measure ground distances. The step in which this problem is resolved is called georeferencing, and involves computer-aided matching up of points in the image (typically 30 or more points per image) which is extrapolated with the use of an established benchmark, "warping" the image to produce accurate spatial data. As of the early 1990s, most satellite images are sold fully georeferenced.

In addition, images may need to be radiometrically and atmospherically corrected.

Radiometric Correction

Gives a scale to the pixel values, e.g. the monochromatic scale of 0 to 255 will be converted to actual radiance values.

Atmospheric Correction

eliminates atmospheric haze by rescaling each frequency band so that its minimum value (usually realised in water bodies) corresponds to a pixel value of 0. The digitizing of data also make possible to manipulate the data by changing gray-scale values.

Interpretation is the critical process of making sense of the data. The first application was that of aerial photographic collection which used the following process; spatial measurement through the use of a light table in both conventional single or stereographic coverage, added skills such as the use of photogrammetry, the use of photomosaics, repeat coverage, Making use of objects' known dimensions in order to detect modifications. Image Analysis is the recently developed automated computer-aided application which is in increasing use.

Object-Based Image Analysis (OBIA) is a sub-discipline of GIScience devoted to partitioning remote sensing (RS) imagery into meaningful image-objects, and assessing their characteristics through spatial, spectral and temporal scale.

Old data from remote sensing is often valuable because it may provide the only long-term data for a large extent of geography. At the same time, the data is often complex to interpret, and bulky to store. Modern systems tend to store the data digitally, often with lossless compression. The difficulty with this approach is that the data is fragile, the format may be archaic, and the data may be easy to falsify. One of the best systems for archiving data series is as computer-generated machine-readable ultrafiche, usually in typefonts such as OCR-B, or as digitized half-tone images. Ultrafiches survive well in standard libraries, with lifetimes of several centuries. They can be created, copied, filed and retrieved by automated systems. They are about as compact as archival magnetic media, and yet can be read by human beings with minimal, standardized equipment.

History

Beyond the primitive methods of remote sensing our earliest ancestors used (ex.: standing on a high cliff or tree to view the landscape), the modern discipline arose with the development of flight. The balloonist G. Tournachon (alias Nadar) made photographs of Paris from his balloon in 1858. Messenger pigeons, kites, rockets and unmanned balloons were also used for early images. With the exception of balloons, these first, individual images were not particularly useful for map making or for scientific purposes.

Systematic aerial photography was developed for military surveillance and reconnaissance purposes beginning in World War I and reaching a climax during the Cold War with the use of modified combat aircraft such as the P-51, P-38, RB-66 and the F4-C, or specifically designed collection platforms such as the U2/TR-1, SR-71, A-5 and the OV-1 series both in overhead and stand-off collection. A more recent development is that of increasingly smaller sensor pods such as those used by law enforcement and the military, in both manned and unmanned platforms. The advantage of this approach is that this requires minimal modification to a given airframe. Later imaging technologies would include Infra-red, conventional, doppler and synthetic aperture radar.

The development of artificial satellites in the latter half of the 20th century allowed remote sensing to progress to a global scale as of the end of the cold war. Instrumentation aboard various Earth observing and weather satellites such as Landsat, the Nimbus and more recent missions such as RADARSAT and UARS provided global measurements of various data for civil, research, and military purposes. Space probes to other planets have also provided the opportunity to conduct remote sensing studies in extraterrestrial environments, synthetic aperture radar aboard the Magellan spacecraft provided detailed topographic maps of Venus, while instruments aboard SOHO allowed studies to be performed on the Sun and the solar wind, just to name a few examples.

Recent developments include, beginning in the 1960s and 1970s with the development of image processing of satellite imagery. Several research groups in Silicon Valley including NASA Ames Research Center, GTE and ESL Inc. developed Fourier transform techniques leading to the first notable enhancement of imagery data.

The introduction of online web services for easy access to remote sensing data in the 21st century (mainly low/medium-resolution images), like Google Earth, has made remote sensing more familiar to the big public and has popularized the science.

Remote Sensing Software

Remote Sensing data is processed and analyzed with computer software, known as a remote sensing application. A large number of commercial and open source applications exist to process remote sensing data. According to an NOAA Sponsored Research by Global Marketing Insights, Inc. the most used applications among Asian academic groups involved in remote sensing are as follows: ESRI 30%; ERDAS IMAGINE 25%; ITT Visual Information Solutions ENVI 17%; MapInfo 17%; ERMapper 11%. Among Western Academic respondents as follows: ESRI 39%, ERDAS IMAGINE 27%, MapInfo 9%, AutoDesk 7%, ITT Visual Information Solutions ENVI 17%.

Global Positioning System (GPS)

The Global Positioning System (GPS) is a global navigation satellite system (GNSS) developed by the United States Department of Defense and managed by the United States Air Force 50th Space Wing. It is the only fully functional GNSS in the world, can be used freely by anyone, anywhere, and is often used by civilians for navigation purposes. It uses a constellation of between 24 and 32 medium Earth orbit satellites that transmit precise radiowave signals, which allow GPS receivers to determine their current location, the time, and their velocity. Its official name is NAVSTAR GPS. Although NAVSTAR is not an acronym, a few backronyms have been created for it.

Since it became fully operational on April 27, 1995, GPS has become a widely used aid to navigation worldwide, and a useful tool for map-making, land surveying, commerce, scientific uses, tracking and surveillance, and hobbies such as geocaching. Also, the precise time reference is used in many applications including the scientific study of earthquakes and as a required time synchronization method for cellular network protocols such as the IS-95 standard for CDMA.

History

The first satellite navigation system, Transit, used by the United States Navy, was first successfully tested in 1960. Using a constellation of five satellites, it could provide a navigational fix approximately once per hour. In 1967, the U.S. Navy developed the Timation satellite which proved the ability to place accurate clocks in space, a technology that GPS relies upon. In the 1970s, the ground-based Omega Navigation System, based on signal phase comparison, became the first worldwide radio navigation system.

The design of GPS is based partly on similar ground-based radio navigation systems, such as LORAN and the Decca Navigator developed in the early 1940s, and used during World War II. Additional inspiration for the GPS came when the Soviet Union launched the first man-made satellite, Sputnik in 1957. A team of U.S. scientists led by Dr. Richard B. Kershner were monitoring Sputnik's radio transmissions. They discovered that, because of the Doppler effect, the frequency of the signal being transmitted by Sputnik was higher as the satellite approached, and lower as it continued away from them. They realized that since they knew their exact location on the globe, they could pinpoint where the satellite was along its orbit by measuring the Doppler distortion.

After Korean Air Lines Flight 007 was shot down in 1983 after straying into the USSR's prohibited airspace, President Ronald Reagan issued a directive making GPS freely available for civilian use as a common good. The satellites were launched between 1989 and 1993.

Initially the highest quality signal was reserved for military use, while the signal available for civilian use was intentionally degraded ("Selective Availability", SA). Selective Availability was ended in 2000, improving the precision of civilian GPS from about 100m to about 20m.

Of crucial importance for the function of GPS is the placement of atomic clocks in the satellites, first proposed by Friedwardt Winterberg in 1955. Only then can the required position accuracy be reached.

Basic Concept of GPS

A GPS receiver calculates its position by precisely timing the signals sent by the GPS satellites high above the Earth. Each satellite continually transmits messages containing the time the message was sent, precise orbital information (the ephemeris), and the general system health and rough orbits of all GPS satellites (the almanac). The receiver measures the transit time of each message and computes the distance to each satellite. Geometric trilateration is used to combine these distances with the location of the satellites to determine the receiver's location. The position is displayed, perhaps with a moving map display or latitude and longitude; elevation information may be included. Many GPS units also show derived information such as direction and speed, calculated from position changes.

It might seem three satellites are enough to solve for position, since space has three dimensions. However, even a very small clock error multiplied by the very large speed of light—the speed at which satellite signals propagate—results in a large positional error. Therefore receivers use four or more satellites to solve for x, y, z, and t, which is used to correct the receiver's clock. While most GPS applications use the computed location only and effectively hide the very accurately computed time, it is used in a few specialized GPS applications such as time transfer, traffic signal timing, and synchronization of cell phone base stations.

Although four satellites are required for normal operation, fewer apply in special cases. If one variable is already known (for example, a ship or plane may have known elevation), a receiver can determine its position using only three satellites. Some GPS receivers may use additional clues or assumptions (such as reusing the last known altitude, dead reckoning, inertial navigation, or including information from the vehicle computer) to give a degraded position when fewer than four satellites are visible.

Position Calculation Introduction

To provide an introductory description of how a GPS receiver works, measurement errors will be ignored in this section. Using messages received from a minimum of four visible satellites, a GPS receiver is able to determine the satellite positions and time sent. The x, y, and z components of position and the time sent are designated as where the subscript *i* is the satellite number and has the value 1, 2, 3, or 4. Knowing the indicated time the message was received, the GPS receiver can compute the indicated transit time,. of the message. Assuming the message traveled at the speed of light, c, the distance traveled, can be computed as.

Knowing the distance from GPS receiver to a satellite and the position of a satellite implies that the GPS receiver is on the surface of a sphere centered at the position of a satellite. Thus we know that the indicated position of the GPS receiver is at or near the intersection of the surfaces of four spheres. In the ideal case of no errors, the GPS receiver will be at an intersection of the surfaces of four spheres. The surfaces of two spheres, if they intersect in more than one point, intersect in a circle.

A circle and sphere surface in most cases of practical interest intersect at two points, although it is conceivable that they could intersect at zero points, one point, or in the very special case in which the centers of the three spheres are colinear (i.e. all three on the same straight line) the sphere surface could intersect the entire circumference of the circle. The two intersections are marked with dots. Again trilateration clearly shows this mathematically. The correct position of the GPS receiver is the intersection that is closest to the surface of the earth for automobiles and other near-Earth vehicles.

The correct position of the GPS receiver is also the intersection which is closest to the surface of the sphere corresponding to the fourth satellite. (The two intersections are symmetrical with respect to the plane containing the three satellites. If the three satellites are not in the same orbital plane, the plane containing the three satellites will not be a vertical plane passing through the center of the Earth. In this case one of the intersections will be closer to the earth than the other. The near-Earth intersection will be the correct position for the case of a near-Earth vehicle. The intersection which is farthest from Earth may be the correct position for space vehicles.)

Correcting a GPS Receiver's Clock

The method of calculating position for the case of no errors has been explained. One of the most significant error sources is the GPS receiver's clock. Because of the very large value of the speed of light, *c*, the estimated distances from the GPS receiver to the satellites, the pseudoranges, are very sensitive to errors in the GPS receiver clock. This suggests that an extremely accurate and expensive clock is required for the GPS receiver to work. On the other hand, manufacturers prefer to build inexpensive GPS receivers for mass markets. The solution for this dilemma is based on the way sphere surfaces intersect in the GPS problem.

It is likely that the surfaces of the three spheres intersect, since the circle of intersection of the first two spheres is normally quite large, and thus the third sphere surface is likely to intersect this large circle. It is very unlikely that the surface of the sphere corresponding to the fourth satellite will intersect either of the two points of intersection of the first three, since any clock error could cause it to miss intersecting a point. However, the distance from the valid estimate of GPS receiver position to the surface of the sphere corresponding to the fourth satellite can be used to compute a clock correction.

Let denote the distance from the valid estimate of GPS receiver position to the fourth satellite and let denote the pseudorange of the fourth satellite. Let. Note that is the distance from the computed GPS receiver position to the surface of the sphere corresponding to the fourth satellite. Thus the quotient,, provides an estimate of (correct time)-(time indicated by the receiver's on-board clock), and the GPS receiver clock can be advanced if is positive or delayed if is negative.

System Detail

System Segmentation: The current GPS consists of three major segments. These are the space segment (SS), a control segment (CS), and a user segment (US).

Space Segment: The space segment (SS) comprises the orbiting GPS satellites, or Space Vehicles (SV) in GPS parlance. The GPS design originally called for 24 SVs, eight each in three circular orbital planes, but this was modified to six planes with four satellites each. The orbital planes are centered on the Earth, not rotating with respect to the distant stars. The six planes have approximately 55° inclination (tilt relative to Earth's equator) and are separated by 60° right ascension of the ascending node (angle along the equator from a reference point to the orbit's intersection). The orbits are arranged so that at least six satellites are always within line of sight from almost everywhere on Earth's surface.

Orbiting at an altitude of approximately 20,200 kilometers about 10 satellites are visible within line of sight (12,900 miles or 10,900 nautical miles; orbital radius of 26,600 km (16,500 mi or 14,400 NM)), each SV makes two complete orbits each sidereal day. The ground track of each satellite therefore repeats each (sidereal) day. This was very helpful during development, since even with just four satellites, correct alignment means all four are visible from one spot for a few hours each day. For military operations, the ground track repeat can be used to ensure good coverage in combat zones.

As of March 2008, there are 31 actively broadcasting satellites in the GPS constellation, and two older, retired from active service satellites kept in the constellation as orbital spares. The additional satellites improve the precision of GPS receiver calculations by providing redundant measurements. With the increased number of satellites, the constellation was changed to a nonuniform arrangement. Such an arrangement was shown to improve reliability and availability of the system, relative to a uniform system, when multiple satellites fail.

Control Segment

The flight paths of the satellites are tracked by US Air Force monitoring stations in Hawaii, Kwajalein, Ascension Island, Diego Garcia, and Colorado Springs, Colorado, along with monitor stations operated by the National Geospatial-Intelligence Agency (NGA).

The tracking information is sent to the Air Force Space Command's master control station at Schriever Air Force Base in Colorado Springs, which is operated by the 2nd Space Operations Squadron (2 SOPS) of the United States Air Force (USAF). Then 2 SOPS contacts each GPS satellite regularly with a navigational update (using the ground antennas at Ascension Island, Diego Garcia, Kwajalein, and Colorado Springs). These updates synchronize the atomic clocks on board the satellites to within a few nanoseconds of each other, and adjust the ephemeris of each satellite's internal orbital model. The updates are created by a Kalman filter which uses inputs from the ground monitoring stations, space weather information, and various other inputs.

Satellite maneuvers are not precise by GPS standards. So to change the orbit of a satellite, the satellite must be marked 'unhealthy', so receivers will not use it in their calculation. Then the maneuver can be carried out, and the resulting orbit tracked from the ground. Then the new ephemeris is uploaded and the satellite marked healthy again.

User Segment

The user's GPS receiver is the user segment (US) of the GPS. In general, GPS receivers are composed of an antenna, tuned to the frequencies transmitted by the satellites, receiver-processors, and a highly-stable clock (often a crystal oscillator). They may also include a display for providing location and speed information to the user. A receiver is often described by its number of channels: this signifies how many satellites it can monitor simultaneously. Originally limited to four or five, this has progressively increased over the years so that, as of 2007, receivers typically have between 12 and 20 channels.

GPS receivers may include an input for differential corrections, using the RTCM SC-104 format. This is typically in the form of a RS-232 port at 4,800 bit/s speed. Data is actually sent at a much lower rate, which limits the accuracy of the signal sent using RTCM. Receivers with internal DGPS receivers can outperform those using external RTCM data. As of 2006, even low-cost units commonly include Wide Area Augmentation System (WAAS) receivers.

Many GPS receivers can relay position data to a PC or other device using the NMEA 0183 protocol, or the newer and less widely used NMEA 2000. Although these protocols are officially defined by the NMEA, references to these protocols have been compiled from public records, allowing open source tools like gpsd to read the protocol without violating intellectual property laws. Other proprietary protocols exist as well, such as the SiRF and MTK protocols. Receivers can interface with other devices using methods including a serial connection, USB or Bluetooth.

Navigation Signals

Each GPS satellite continuously broadcasts a Navigation Message at 50 bit/s giving the time-of-week, GPS week number and satellite health information (all transmitted in the first part of the message), an *ephemeris* (transmitted in the second part of the message) and an *almanac* (later part of the message). The messages are sent in frames, each taking 30 seconds to transmit 1500 bits.

Transmission of each 30 second frame begins precisely on the minute and half minute as indicated by the satellite's atomic clock according to Satellite message format. Each frame contains 5 subframes of length 6 seconds and with 300 bits. Each subframe contains 10 words of 30 bits with length 0.6 seconds each.

Words 1 and 2 of every subframe have the same type of data. The first word is the telemetry word which indicates the beginning of a subframe and is used by the receiver to synch with the navigation message. The second word is the HOW or handover word and it contains timing information which enables the receiver to identify the subframe and provides the time the next subframe was sent.

Words 3 through 10 of subframe 1 contain data describing the satellite clock and its relationship to GPS time. Words 3 through 10 of subframes 2 and 3, contain the ephemeris data, giving the satellite's own precise orbit. The ephemeris is updated every 2 hours and is generally valid for 4 hours, with provisions for updates every 6 hours or longer in non-nominal conditions. The time needed to acquire the ephemeris is becoming a significant element of the delay to first position fix, because, as the hardware becomes more capable, the time to lock onto the satellite signals shrinks, but the ephemeris data requires 30 seconds (worst case) before it is received, due to the low data transmission rate.

The almanac consists of coarse orbit and status information for each satellite in the constellation, an ionospheric model, and information to relate GPS derived time to Coordinated Universal Time (UTC). Words 3 through 10 of subframes 4 and 5 contain a new part of the almanac. Each frame contains 1/25th of the almanac, so 12.5 minutes are required to receive the entire almanac from a single satellite. The almanac serves several purposes. The first is to assist in the acquisition of satellites at power-up by allowing the receiver to generate a list of visible satellites based on stored position and time, while an ephemeris from each satellite is needed to compute position fixes using that satellite. In older hardware, lack of an almanac in a new receiver would cause long delays before providing a valid position, because the search for each satellite was a slow process. Advances in hardware have made the acquisition process much faster, so not having an almanac is no longer an issue. The second purpose is for relating time derived from the GPS (called GPS time) to the international time standard of UTC. Finally, the almanac allows a single-frequency receiver to correct for ionospheric error by using a global ionospheric model. The corrections are not as accurate as augmentation systems like WAAS or dual-frequency receivers. However, it is often better than no correction, since ionospheric error is the largest error source for a single-frequency GPS receiver. An important thing to note about navigation data is that each satellite transmits not only its own *ephemeris*, but transmits an *almanac* for all satellites.

All satellites broadcast at the same two frequencies, 1.57542 GHz (L1 signal) and 1.2276 GHz (L2 signal). The receiver can distinguish the signals from different satellites because GPS uses a code division multiple access (CDMA) spread-spectrum technique where the low-bitrate message data is encoded with a high-rate pseudo-random (PRN) sequence that is different for each satellite. The receiver knows the PRN codes for each satellite and can use this to reconstruct the actual message data. The message data is transmitted at 50 bits per second. Two distinct CDMA encodings are used: the coarse/acquisition (C/A) code (a so-called Gold code) at 1.023 million chips per second, and the precise (P) code at 10.23 million chips per second. The L1 carrier is modulated by both the C/A and P codes, while the L2 carrier is only modulated by the P code. The C/A code is public and used by civilian GPS receivers, while the P code can be encrypted as a so-called P(Y) code which is only available to military equipment with a proper decryption key. Both the C/A and P(Y) codes impart the precise time-of-day to the user.

Satellite Frequencies

- L1 (1575.42 MHz): Mix of Navigation Message, coarse-acquisition (C/A) code and encrypted precision P(Y) code, plus the new L1C on future Block III satellites.

- L2 (1227.60 MHz): P(Y) code, plus the new L2C code on the Block IIR-M and newer satellites.
- L3 (1381.05 MHz): Used by the Nuclear Detonation (NUDET) Detection System Payload (NDS) to signal detection of nuclear detonations and other high-energy infrared events. Used to enforce nuclear test ban treaties.
- L4 (1379.913 MHz): Being studied for additional ionospheric correction.
- L5 (1176.45 MHz): Proposed for use as a civilian safety-of-life (SoL) signal (see GPS modernization). This frequency falls into an internationally protected range for aeronautical navigation, promising little or no interference under all circumstances. The first Block IIF satellite that would provide this signal is set to be launched in 2009.

C/A Code

Demodulation and Decoding: Since all of the satellite signals are modulated onto the same L1 carrier frequency, there is a need to separate the signals after demodulation. This is done by assigning each satellite a unique pseudorandom sequence known as a Gold code, and the signals are decoded, after demodulation, using modulo 2 addition of the Gold codes corresponding to satellites n_1 through n_k, where k is the number of channels in the GPS receiver and n_1 through n_k are the pseudorandom numbers associated with the satellites. The results of these modulo 2 additions are the 50 bit/s navigation messages from satellites n_1 through n_k. The Gold codes used in GPS are a sequence of 1023 bits with a period of one millisecond. These Gold codes are highly mutually orthogonal, so that it is unlikely that one satellite signal will be misinterpreted as another. As well, the Gold codes have good auto-correlation properties.

There are 1025 different Gold codes of length 1023 bits, but only 32 are used. These Gold codes are quite often referred to as pseudo random noise since they contain no data and are said to look like random sequences. However, this may be misleading since they are actually deterministic sequences.

If the almanac information has previously been acquired, the receiver picks which satellites to listen for by their PRNs. If the almanac information is not in memory, the receiver enters a search mode and cycles through the PRN numbers until a lock is obtained on one of the satellites. To obtain a lock, it is necessary that there be an unobstructed line of sight from the receiver to the satellite. The receiver can then acquire the almanac and determine the satellites it should listen for. As it detects each satellite's signal, it identifies it by its distinct C/A code pattern.

The receiver uses the C/A Gold code with the same PRN number as the satellite to compute an offset, O, that generates the best correlation. The offset, O, is computed in a trial and error manner. The 1023 bits of the satellite PRN signal are compared with the receiver PRN signal. If correlation is not achieved, the 1023 bits of the receiver's internally generated PRN code are shifted by one bit relative to the satellite's PRN code and the signals are again compared. This process is repeated until correlation is achieved or all 1023 possible cases have been tried (see "How a GPS Receiver Gets a Lock"). If all 1023 cases have been tried without achieving correlation, the frequency oscillator is offset to the next value and the process is repeated.

Since the carrier frequency received can vary due to Doppler shift, the points where received PRN sequences begin may not differ from O by an exact integral number of milliseconds. Because of this, carrier frequency tracking along with PRN code tracking are used to determine when the received satellite's PRN code begins (see "How a GPS Receiver Gets a Lock"). Unlike the earlier computation of offset in which trials of all 1023 offsets could potentially be required, the tracking to maintain lock usually requires shifting of half a pulse width or less. To perform this tracking, the receiver observes two quantities, phase error and received frequency offset. The correlation of the received PRN code with respect to the receiver generated PRN code is computed to determine if the bits of the two signals are misaligned. Comparisons with correlation computed with receiver generated PRN code shifted half a pulse width early and half a pulse width late (see section 1.4.2.4 of) are used to estimate adjustment required. The amount of adjustment required for maximum correlation is used in estimating phase error. Received frequency offset from the frequency generated by the receiver provides an estimate of phase rate error. The command for the frequency generator and any further PRN code shifting required are computed as a function of the phase error and the phase rate error in accordance with the control law used. The Doppler velocity is computed as a function of the frequency offset from the carrier nominal frequency. The Doppler velocity is the velocity component along the line of sight of the receiver relative to the satellite.

As the receiver continues to read successive PRN sequences, it will encounter a sudden change in the phase of the 1023 bit received PRN signal. This indicates the beginning of a data bit of the navigation message (see section 1.4.2.5 of). This enables the receiver to begin reading the 20 millisecond bits of the navigation message. Each subframe of the navigation frame begins with a Telemetry Word which enables the receiver to detect the beginning of a subframe and determine the receiver clock time at which the navigation subframe begins. Also each subframe of the navigation frame is identified by bits in the handover word (HOW) thereby enabling the receiver to determine which subframe (see section 1.4.2.6 of and section 2.5.4 of "Essentials of Satellite Navigation Compendium"). There can be a delay of up to 30 seconds before the first estimate of position because of the need to read the ephemeris data before computing the intersections of sphere surfaces.

After a subframe has been read and interpreted, the time the next subframe was sent can be calculated through the use of the clock correction data and the HOW. The receiver knows the receiver clock time of when the beginning of the next subframe was received from detection of the Telemetry Word thereby enabling computation of the transit time and thus the pseudorange. The receiver is potentially capable of getting a new pseudorange measurement at the beginning of each subframe or every 6 seconds.

Then the orbital position data, or ephemeris, from the navigation message is used to calculate precisely where the satellite was at the start of the message. A more sensitive receiver will potentially acquire the ephemeris data more quickly than a less sensitive receiver, especially in a noisy environment.

This process is repeated for each satellite to which the receiver is listening.

Data Mining (DM)

Data mining is the process of extracting hidden patterns from data. As more data is gathered, with the amount of data doubling every three years, data mining is becoming an increasingly important tool to transform this data into information. It is commonly used in a wide range of profiling practices, such as marketing, surveillance, fraud detection and scientific discovery.

While data mining can be used to uncover patterns in data samples, it is important to be aware that the use of non-representative samples of data may produce results that are not indicative of the domain. Similarly, data mining will not find patterns that may be present in the domain, if those patterns are not present in the sample being "mined". There is a tendency for insufficiently knowledgeable "consumers" of the results to attribute "magical abilities" to data mining, treating the technique as a sort of all-seeing crystal ball. Like any other tool, it only functions in conjunction with the appropriate raw material: in this case, indicative and representative data that the user must first collect. Further, the discovery of a particular pattern in a particular set of data does not necessarily mean that pattern is representative of the whole population from which that data was drawn. Hence, an important part of the process is the verification and validation of patterns on other samples of data.

The term data mining has also been used in a related but negative sense, to mean the deliberate searching for apparent but not necessarily representative patterns in large amounts of data. To avoid confusion with the other sense, the terms *data dredging* and *data snooping* are often used. Note, however, that dredging and snooping can be (and sometimes are) used as exploratory tools when developing and clarifying hypotheses.

Background

Humans have been "manually" extracting information from data for centuries, but the increasing volume of data in modern times has called for more automatic approaches. As data sets and the information extracted from them has grown in size and complexity, direct hands-on data analysis has increasingly been supplemented and augmented with indirect, automatic data processing using more complex and sophisticated tools, methods and models. The proliferation, ubiquity and increasing power of computer technology has aided data collection, processing, management and storage. However, the captured data needs to be converted into information and knowledge to become useful. Data mining is the process of using computing power to apply methodologies, including new techniques for knowledge discovery, to data.

Data mining identifies trends within data that go beyond simple data analysis. Through the use of sophisticated algorithms, non-statistician users have the opportunity to identify key attributes of processes and target opportunities. However, abdicating control and understanding of processes from statisticians to poorly informed or uninformed users can result in false-positives, no useful results, and worst of all, results that are misleading and/or misinterpreted.

Although data mining is a relatively new term, the technology is not. For many years, businesses and governments have used increasingly powerful computers to sift through volumes of data such as airline passenger trip records, census data and supermarket scanner data to produce market research reports. (Note, however, that reporting is not always considered to be data mining). Continuous innovations in computer processing power, disk storage, data capture technology, algorithms, methodologies and analysis software have dramatically increased the accuracy and usefulness of the extracted information.

The term data mining is often used to apply to the two separate processes of knowledge discovery and prediction. Knowledge discovery provides explicit information about the characteristics of the collected data, using a number of techniques (e.g., association rule mining). Forecasting and predictive modeling provide predictions of future events, and the processes may range from the transparent (e.g., rule-based approaches) through to the opaque (e.g., neural networks).

Metadata, (data about the characteristics of a data set), are often expressed in a condensed data-minable format, or one that facilitates the practice of data mining. Common examples include executive summaries and scientific abstracts.

A primary reason for using data mining is to assist in the analysis of collections of observations of behaviour. Such data are vulnerable to collinearity because of unknown interrelations. An unavoidable fact of data mining is that the (sub-)set(s) of data being analysed may not be representative of the whole domain, and therefore may not contain examples of certain critical relationships and behaviours that exist across other parts of the domain. To address this sort of issue, the analysis may be augmented using experiment-based and other approaches, such as Choice Modelling for human-generated data. In these situations, inherent correlations can be either controlled for, or removed altogether, during the construction of the experimental design.

There have been some efforts to define standards for data mining, for example the 1999 European Cross Industry Standard Process for Data Mining (CRISP-DM 1.0) and the 2004 Java Data Mining standard (JDM 1.0). These are evolving standards; later versions of these standards are under development. Independent of these standardization efforts, freely available open-source software systems like RapidMiner, Weka, KNIME, and the R Project have become an informal standard for defining data-mining processes. Most of these systems are able to import and export models in PMML (Predictive Model Markup Language) which provides a standard way to represent data mining models so that these can be shared between different statistical applications. PMML is an XML-based language developed by the Data Mining Group (DMG), an independent group composed of many data mining companies. PMML version 3.2 was approved in May 2007, and was most recently updated in December 2008. Work on the next version of PMML, version 4.0, has begun.

Research and Evolution

In addition to industry driven demand for standards and interoperability, professional and academic activity have also made considerable contributions to the evolution and rigour of the methods and models; an article published in a 2008 issue of the *International Journal of Information Technology and Decision Making* summarises the results of a literature survey which traces and analyses this evolution.

The premier professional body in the field is the Association for Computing Machinery's Special Interest Group on Knowledge Discovery and Data Mining (SIGKDD). Since 1989 they have hosted an annual international conference and published its proceedings, and since 1999 have published a biannual academic journal titled "SIGKDD Explorations". Other Computer Science conferences on data mining include:

- DMIN-International Conference on Data Mining;
- DMKD-Research Issues on Data Mining and Knowledge Discovery;
- ECML-PKDD-European Conference on Machine Learning and Principles and Practice of Knowledge Discovery in Databases;
- ICDM-IEEE International Conference on Data Mining;
- MLDM-Machine Learning and Data Mining in Pattern Recognition;
- SDM-SIAM International Conference on Data Mining

Process

Knowledge Discovery in Databases (KDD) is the name coined by Gregory Piatetsky-Shapiro in 1989 to describe the process of finding interesting, interpreted, useful and novel data. There are many nuances to this process, but roughly the steps are to preprocess raw data, mine the data, and interpret the results.

Pre-processing

Once the objective for the KDD process is known, a target data set must be assembled. As data mining can only uncover patterns already present in the data, the target dataset must be large enough to contain these patterns while remaining concise enough to be mined in an acceptable timeframe. A common source for data is a datamart or data warehouse.

The target set is then cleaned. Cleaning removes the observations with noise and missing data.

The clean data is reduced into feature vectors, one vector per observation. A feature vector is a summarized version of the raw data observation. For example, a black and white image of a face which is 100px by 100px would contain 10,000 bits of raw data. This might be turned into a feature vector by locating the eyes and mouth in the image. Doing so would reduce the data for each vector from 10,000 bits to three codes for the locations, dramatically reducing the size of the dataset to be mined, and hence reducing the processing effort. The feature(s) selected will depend on what the objective(s) is/are; obviously, selecting the "right" feature(s) is fundamental to successful data mining.

The feature vectors are divided into two sets, the "training set" and the "test set". The training set is used to "train" the data mining algorithm(s), while the test set is used to verify the accuracy of any patterns found.

Data Mining

Data mining commonly involves four classes of task:

- Classification-Arranges the data into predefined groups. For example an email programme might attempt to classify an email as legitimate or spam. Common algorithms include Nearest neighbour, Naive Bayes classifier and Neural network.

- Clustering-Is like classification but the groups are not predefined, so the algorithm will try to group similar items together.
- Regression-Attempts to find a function which models the data with the least error. A common method is to use Genetic Programming.
- Association rule learning-Searches for relationships between variables. For example a supermarket might gather data of what each customer buys. Using association rule learning, the supermarket can work out what products are frequently bought together, which is useful for marketing purposes. This is sometimes referred to as "market basket analysis".

Results Validation

The final step of knowledge discovery from data is to verify the patterns produced by the datamining algorithms occur in the wider data set. Not all patterns found by the datamining algorithms are necessarily valid. It is common for the datamining algorithms to find patterns in the training set which are not present in the general data set, this is called overfitting. To overcome this, the evaluation uses a test set of data which the datamining algorithm was not trained on. The learnt patterns are applied to this test set and the resulting output is compared to the desired output.

For example, a datamining algorithm trying to distinguish spam from legitimate emails would be trained on a training set of sample emails. Once trained, the learnt patterns would be applied to the test set of emails which it had not been trained on, the accuracy of these patterns can then be measured from how many emails they correctly classify. A number of statistical methods may be used to evaluate the algorithm such as ROC curves.

If the learnt patterns do not meet the desired standards, then it is necessary to reevaluate and change the preprocessing and datamining. If the learnt patterns do meet the desired standards then the final step is to interpret the learnt patterns and turn them into knowledge.

Global Telecommunication System (GTS)

The Global Telecommunication System (GTS) is defined as: *"The co-ordinated global system of telecommunication facilities and arrangements for the rapid collection, exchange and distribution of observations and processed information within the framework of the World Weather Watch."*-WMO No 49 Technical Regulations WMO's Global Telecommunication System (GTS) is the communications and data management component that allows the World Weather Watch (WWW) to operate through the collection and distribution of information critical to its processes. It is implemented and operated by National Meteorological Services of WMO Members and International Organizations, such as ECMWF and EUMETSAT. As decided by Congress and the Executive Council the GTS also provides telecommunication support to other WMO programmes, facilitating the flow of data and processed products to meet requirements in a timely, reliable and cost-effective way, ensuring that all Members have access to all meteorological and related data, forecasts and alerts. This secured communication network enables real-time exchange of information, critical for forecasting and warnings of hydrometeorological hazards in accordance with approved procedures.

The GTS has a hierarchical structure on three levels:

The Main Telecommunication Network (MTN), linking together three World Meteorological Centres (WMCs) (Melbourne, Moscow and Washington) and 15 Regional Telecommunication Hubs (RTHs) (Algiers, Beijing, Bracknell, Brasilia, Buenos Aires, Cairo, Dakar, Jeddah, Nairobi, New Delhi, Offenbach, Toulouse, Prague, Sofia and Tokyo). This core network has the function of providing an efficient, rapid and reliable communication service between the Meteorological Telecommunication Centres (MTCs).

The Regional Meteorological Telecommunication Networks (RMTNs) is an integrated network of circuits covering the six WMO regions-Africa, Asia, South America, North America, Central America & the Caribbean, South-West Pacific, Europe and Antarctic-and interconnecting the MTCs thus ensuring the collection of observational data and regional selective distribution of meteorological and other related information to Members. Until the integrated network is completed, HF-radio-broadcasts may be used in order to meet the requirements of the WWW for the dissemination of meteorological information.

The National Meteorological Telecommunication Networks (NMTNs) enable the National Meteorological Centres (NMCs) to collect observational data and receive and distribute meteorological information on a national level.

Satellite-based data collection and/or data distribution systems are also integrated in the GTS as an essential element of the global, regional and national levels of the GTS. Data collection systems operated via geostationary or near-polar orbiting meteorological/environmental satellites, including ARGOS, are widely used for the collection of observational data from *Data Collection Platforms*. Marine data are also collected through the International Maritime Mobile Service and through INMARSAT. International data distribution systems operated either via meteorological satellites such as the Meteorological Data Distribution (MDD) of METEOSAT, or via telecommunication satellites, such as RETIM or FAX-E via EUTELSAT are efficiently complementing the point-to-point GTS circuits. Several Countries, including Argentina, Canada, China, France, India, Indonesia, Mexico, Saudi Arabia, Thailand and the USA, have implemented satellite-based multi-point telecommunication systems for their national Meteorological Telecommunication Network.

The MTCs function is to accommodate the volume of meteorological information and its transmission within the required time limits for global and interregional exchange of observational data, processed information and any other data required by its Members. Regional Telecommunication Hubs (RTHs) on the MTN perform an interface function between the RMTNs and the MTN.

The GTS is an integrated network of surface-based and satellite-based telecommunication links of point-to-point circuits, and multi-point circuits (see table), interconnecting meteorological telecommunication centres operated by countries for round-the-clock reliable and near-real-time collection and distribution of all meteorological and related data, forecasts and alerts. This secured communication network enables real-time exchange of information, critical for forecasting and warning of hydrometeorological hazards.

WMO Regions	Point-to-Point	Point-to-Multipoint
Africa	Point-to-Point	Point-to-Multipoint
Asia	Point-to-Point	Point-to-Multipoint
South America	Point-to-Point	Point-to-Multipoint
North America, Central America & the Caribbean	Point-to-Point	Point-to-Multipoint
South-West Pacific	Point-to-Point	Point-to-Multipoint
Europe	Point-to-Point	
Antarctic	Point-to-Point	

Circuits

WMO GTS is the backbone system for global exchange of data and information in support of multi-hazard, multipurpose early warning systems, including all meteorological and related data; weather, water and climate analyses and forecasts; tsunami related information and warnings, and seismic parametric data. WMO is building on its GTS to achieve an overarching WMO Information System (WIS), enabling systematic access, retrieval, and dissemination and exchange of data and information of all WMO and related international Programmes.

Disaster Analyzer and Tracking Environment (DATE)

A. Specific Aims

The Disaster Analyzer & Tracking Environment (DATE) Framework, a new software framework designed using the principles of the Software Stability Model (SSM) that provides a timeless and an open architecture for catastrophic disasters, such as epidemics of infectious diseases, earthquakes, terrorism, wildlife fires, contamination of resources such as water and food supplies, floods, etc. DATE is a core frameworks with bases for three sub-frameworks: (1) Content Integration & Interoperability (CII) (2) Unified Disaster Detection management (UDDM); and (3) Trace-Back Spatiotemporal

System (TBSS). The CII makes heavy use of the XML family of technologies in order to provide a user friendly and intuitive programming environment for the development of large-scale software systems. The framework, developed using a layered approach, allows for the development of many different types of integration software including applications that perform contents distribution, transformation, integration and automatic content generation to/from databases. The UDDM utilizes data mining techniques and new detection algorithms that are application specific.

For example, epidemic detection algorithms are based on data mining techniques to detect known and unknown epidemics or infectious diseases. This project outlines an agenda and proposes an innovative approach to develop a system that allows for reusability and expandability of content integration and epidemic detection algorithms based on data mining techniques to detect known and unknown epidemic illnesses that are caused by infectious diseases. The research for this grant proposal focuses on the following aims and challenges:

Specific Aim 1: Develop a large-scale distributed framework. The core framework and its bases form an environment called "DATE."

Specific Aim 2: Content Integration and Interoperability (CII) Framework that consists of content transformation, integration, presentation, and routing or distribution. Content Integration, as we vision it, is the ability to integrate, manage, standardize and make the available data interoperable.

Specific Aim 3: Unified Disaster Detection Management (UDDM) Framework is a major and critical component of DATE. It provides the structure and tools for easy integration of multiple applications and legacy components of data mining and disaster detection algorithms.

Specific Aim 4: Trace-Back Spatiotemporal System (TBSS). The spatiotemporal system can be used to organize disaster contents based on two different extents: a spatial extent which is a set of points in space "locations" of a given disaster and a temporal extent which a set of time instances when the disaster instances exist. Each spatiotemporal data model represents both spatial and temporal extents of each disaster where an instance of any disaster can be traced continuously over time by allowing periodic functions of time in the spatial attributes and periodic intervals in the temporal attributes.

Specific Aim 5: Collect and document all the core knowledge patterns. We will collect, analyze, and document all the stable core knowledge patterns of the entire framework based on software stability (Example is provided in Section D: Research Design and Methods). We will also collect, analyze, and document any disaster pattern for future reference. These patterns will help us to deal with any known or unknown disasters. The goal of this five-year project is to develop a timeless, stable, and open architecture framework where both stable classes (aspects) and application classes are designed separately from each other. Their composition is formally supported to ensure correctness. This separation of concerns allows for reusability and enables the building of software systems for content integration and disaster detection that are stable, adaptable and extendable.

Information Communication System (ICS)

Enhanced communications continue to be of vital importance for effective response to disasters. Lack of communications directly contributes to low levels of situational awareness for both high-level commanders and emergency responders in the field. When all lines of contact are down, effective response to disaster is greatly diminished. Establishing and maintaining lines of direct contact between decision makers, formal and informal responders, government officials, and the public is a primary objective in any emergency planning or response scenario. A continuing reexamination of providing emergency communications is critical for lessening the impacts of future disasters. Utilizing advances in technology that allow for higher degrees of mobility for communications systems introduces a new level of flexibility for operational command structures.

Bibliography

Abbott, P.: *Natural Disasters*, Dubuque: Brown & Co., 1996.

Adams, John: *Managing Water Supply and Sanitation in Emergencies.* Oxfam, Oxford, 1999.

Allen, L., and Santrock, J.W.: *Psychology: The Contexts of Behavior*, Madison: Brown and Benchmark, 1993.

Artz, S.: *Sex, Power, & the Violent School Girl*, Toronto, Trifolium Books, 1999.

Assar, M.: *Guide to Sanitation in Natural Disasters,* WHO, Geneva, 1971.

Auf der Heide, E.: *Disaster Response: Principles of Preparedness and Coordination,* St. Louis: CV Mosby Co., 1989.

Bemak, F.: *Violent and Aggressive Youth : Intervention and Prevention Strategies for Changing Times*, Thousand Oaks, CA: Corwin Press, 2000.

Besag, V.: *Bullies and Victims in Schools : A Guide to Understanding and Management*, Philadelphia: Open University Press, 1989.

Capozzili, Thomas: *Kids Killing Kids: Managing Violence and Gangs in School*, Boca Raton, St. Lucie Press, 2000.

Coch, N.K.: *Geohazards Natural and Human*, New Jersey, Prentice Hall, 1995.

Cole, Leonard: A. *The Anthrax Letters: A Medical Detective Story*. Washington, Joseph Henry Press, 2003.

David, L. & David, I.: *Violence in Our Schools*, Published: New York, Public Affairs Pamphlets, 1980.

Dignan, M.B. and Carr, P.A. : *Program Planning for Health Education and Promotion*, Philadelphia, Lea and Febiger, 1992.

Dixon. N.: *The Organisational Learning Cycle*, McGraw Hill, Maidenhead, UK, 1994.

Dolcemascolo, Glenn: *Environmental Degradation and Disaster Risk*, Asian Disaster Preparedness Centre, Sweden, 2004.

Frumkin, Howard: *Safe and Healthy School Environments*, New York, N.Y.: Oxford University Press, 2006.

Garratt, B.: *The Learning Organisation*, Harper Collins Publishers, London, 1987.

Grey, Michael R. and Kenneth R. Spaeth. *The Bioterrorism Sourcebook*. New York, N.Y.: McGraw-Hill Medical, 2006.

Hawes, H.W.R.: *Child to Child: Another Path to Learning*, Hamburg, Unesco Institute for *Education*, 1988.

Hays, J.N.: *Epidemics and Pandemics: Their Impacts on Human History*, Santa Barbara, Calif.: ABC-CLIO, 2005.

Inglis, S.: *Making the Most of Action Learning*, Gower, Aldershot, 1994.

Kim, H. H.: *Youth Violence*, San Diego, CA: Greenhaven Press, 1998.

Kiple, K.F.: *Cambridge World History of Human Disease*, Cambridge University Press, 1993.

Kozubska, J.: *Role of the Set Adviser*, Action Learning Resource, MCB University Press, 1989.

Kreiner, Anna: *Everything You Need to Know About School Violence*. New York, N.Y.: Rosen, 2000.

Lawler. A.: *Productivity Improvement Manual*, Gower, Aldershot, 1985.

Lessem, R.: *Business as a Learning Community-Applying Global Concepts to Organisational Learning*, McGraw Hill Book Company, Berkshire, 1993.

McCann, J. T.: *Threats in Schools : A Practical Guide for Managing Violence*, New York: Haworth Press, 2002.

McCann, Joseph T.: *Threats in Schools: A Practical Guide for Managing Violence*. New York, N.Y.: Haworth Press, 2002.

McGill, I. and Beaty, L.: *Action Learning: A Practitioner's Guide*, Kogan Page, London, 1992.

Meredith, C.: *Proving Public Fire Protection Works*, Arlington, TriData Corporation. 1990.

Mills, M.: *Challenging Violence in Schools : An Issue of Masculinities*, Philadelphia: Open University Press, 2001.

Mumford, A.: *How Managers can Develop Managers*, Gower, Aldershot, 1993.

Nairne, J.S.: *Psychology: The Adaptive Mind*, Pacific Grove, Brooks/Cole Publishing Co., 1997.

Patton, M.Q.: *Qualitative Evaluation and Research Methods*, Newbury Park: Sage Publications, 1990.

People in Aid: *Code of Good Practices in the Management and Support of Aid Personnel;* People in Aid, London, 2003.

Revans, R. W.: *ABC of Action Learning*, Chartwell Bratt, Bromley, 1983.

Revans, R.W.: *The Origins and Growth of Action Learning*, Chartwell Bratt Ltd, Bromley, 1982.

Sullivan, K.: *The Anti-bullying Handbook*, New York, Oxford University Press, 2000.

Turk, W. L.: *When Juvenile Crime Comes to School*, Lewiston, E. Mellen Press, 1999.

Weinstein, K.: *Action Learning*, Harper Collins, London, 1995.

Wells, Jo: *Protecting and Assisting Older People in Emergencies: Network Paper*; London; Humanitarian Practice Network; 2005.

Whitman, N.A.: *There is No Gene for Good Teaching: A Handbook on Lecturing for Medical Teachers,* Salt Lake City, University of Utah, 1982.

Wills, G.,: *Your Enterprise School of Management*, MCB University Press, 1993.

Zemke, R. and Zemke, S. "30 Things We Know for Sure About Adult Learning." *Training*, 1988.

Zuber Skerrit, O.: *Professional Development in Higher Education: A Theoretical Framework for Action Research*, Kogan Page, London, 1993.

Index

E

F

G

H

I

L

M

N

□□□